Professional and Practice-based Learning

Volume 3

For further volumes:
http://www.springer.com/series/8383

Series Editors:

Stephen Billett, Griffith University, Australia
Christian Harteis, University of Regensburg, Germany
Hans Gruber, University of Regensburg, Germany

Professional and practice-based learning brings together international research on the individual development of professionals and the organisation of professional life and educational experiences. It complements the Springer journal *Vocations and Learning: Studies in vocational and professional education.*

Professional learning, and the practice-based processes that often support it, are the subject of increased interest and attention in the fields of educational, psychological, sociological, and business management research, and also by governments, employer organisations and unions. This professional learning goes beyond, what is often termed professional education, as it includes learning processes and experiences outside of educational institutions in both the initial and ongoing learning for the professional practice. Changes in these workplaces requirements usually manifest themselves in the everyday work tasks, professional development provisions in educational institution decrease in their salience, and learning and development during professional activities increase in their salience.

There are a range of scientific challenges and important focuses within the field of professional learning. These include:

- understanding and making explicit the complex and massive knowledge that is required for professional practice and identifying ways in which this knowledge can best be initially learnt and developed further throughout professional life.

- analytical explications of those processes that support learning at an individual and an organisational level.

- understanding how learning experiences and educational processes might best be aligned or integrated to support professional learning.

The series integrates research from different disciplines: education, sociology, psychology, amongst others. The series is comprehensive in scope as it not only focusses on professional learning of teachers and those in schools, colleges and universities, but all professional development within organisations.

Anne Edwards

Being an Expert Professional Practitioner

The Relational Turn in Expertise

Prof. Anne Edwards
University of Oxford
Dept. Education
Norham Gardens 15
OX2 6PY Oxford
United Kingdom
anne.edwards@education.ox.ac.uk

ISBN 978-90-481-3968-2   e-ISBN 978-90-481-3969-9
DOI 10.1007/978-90-481-3969-9
Springer Dordrecht Heidelberg London New York

Library of Congress Control Number: 2010931508

© Springer Science+Business Media B.V. 2010
No part of this work may be reproduced, stored in a retrieval system, or transmitted in any form or by any means, electronic, mechanical, photocopying, microfilming, recording or otherwise, without written permission from the Publisher, with the exception of any material supplied specifically for the purpose of being entered and executed on a computer system, for exclusive use by the purchaser of the work.

Printed on acid-free paper

Springer is part of Springer Science+Business Media (www.springer.com)

Series Editors' Foreword

This aptly titled book discusses and elaborates contemporary professionals as needing to be highly agentic worker-learners: resourceful practitioners. The complexity of the work they engage in, its dynamic qualities, the increasing need to negotiate activities and interactions across disciplinary and other divides demands they are able to make appropriate decisions about their and others practice, and often quite independently. No amount of initial preparation can develop the kinds of capacities that will equip practitioners for lifetimes' of effective practice. So, the capacity to learn independently both during and after their initial preparation is essential for contemporary professional practitioners. Indeed, much, if not most of those capacities will need to be developed through forms of self-directed albeit socially engaged activities, including monitoring what have been learnt and what is being learnt.

Anne Edwards captures this requirement within this volume through positioning these practitioners as needing to be resourceful learners who need to direct their learning through practice including engagement with other professionals, and from other professions and those whom their profession serves (e.g. clients, patients, students). Central here is the concept of relational expertise with her idea of relational agency – a capacity that arises when professionals bring their specialist expertise to bear in their joint action. Having been working with the concept of relational agency for several years, this volume explains how it is brought into play in practice. Central here is the claim that common knowledge – shared understandings of what matters for each participant – needs to be built in order to be a resource for relational collaborations. In this book, she explains how common knowledge is created at the sites where practices intersect. In these ways, and based upon research that informs this claim, she proposes that these qualities are those required for a 'new professionalism'. This professionalism includes being respectful and mindful of the institutions whose purposes are both in advancing the interests of and developing professional expertise, yet also professionals being able to exercise both agency and interdependence in enacting their practice. So, rather than professional autonomy, the emphasis is on thoughtful practice that includes reflexivity and intentionality in similar measures.

These ideas are developed across the chapters of this volume and are auspiced by theoretical preferences that emphasise social forms and engagements, and yet that also afford key roles for personal capacities, intentionality and agency. This emphasis is most apt because it accommodates and contributes to the growing interest in explaining human action and development as arising through negotiations between the personal and social worlds, and in ways that are relational, rather than fixed or irreducible in the quality, potency and strength of their contributions. Indeed, Edwards adopts the term 'relational expertise' to capture the proposition that rather than expertise being taken as an objective and circumstantially enmeshed concept, it is something constructed and enacted through relations between the practice (and practice setting) and the practitioner. This concept is advanced across the volume as a key explanatory principle for what informs and engages practitioners in their work and learning for and through it. Consistent with its key premises, consideration is given to co-participative practices that comprise the relational turn and emphasise the relations between the personal and the social in thinking, acting, learning and remaking societally directed imperative, such as the on-going remaking of those practices as practitioners engage with specific tasks, at part points in time. A salient element of this remaking is captured in considerations about engagement in inter-professional practices that comprise increasingly what many professional do, and the need to negotiate across disciplinary boundaries. These negotiations illustrate the erosion of professional practice as being unassailable and autonomous and even tests the boundaries that traditionally have done much to make these disciplines irreducible. Now, the case made here argues for disciplinary potency to be premised on reducibility and permeability.

In all, this volume proposes a reworking of what constitutes professional practice, professionalism, and seeks to refresh considerations about learning for and through practice. In this way, it makes a valuable contribution to a book series focussed on professional and practice-based learning.

(March 2010)

Stephen Billett
Hans Gruber
Christian Harteis

Acknowledgements

Even single-authored books are produced relationally. I would therefore like to thank all the practitioners who have put up with my presence and questions over the last 15 years and from whom I have learnt so much. Also, for the same reason, thanks to the colleagues I have worked with in the five projects which are at the centre of this book. Particular gratitude is due to colleagues and research students in the OSAT research centre at Oxford, which is co-convened with Viv Ellis and Geoff Hayward, though special thanks go to Russell Francis, Ioanna Kinti, Natalie Lundsteen and Sheena Wagstaff, whose work I draw on in the book.

There are of course colleagues, in the United Kingdom and elsewhere, who work within or at the edges of the broad CHAT, cultural historical and socio-cultural fields and with whom I have tested these ideas. Their interest and criticism have been invigorating and their own work has been influential on the ideas as they have developed. In particular, I would like to thank Stephen Billett, Gill Boag-Munroe, Seth Chaiklin, Harry Daniels, Jan Derry, Ritva Engeström, Yrjö Engeström, Viv Ellis, Marilyn Fleer, Jan Georgeson, David Guile, John Hardcastle, David Hartley, Geoff Hayward, Mariane Hedegaard, Karen Jensen, Jane Leadbetter, Sten Ludvigsen, Åsa Mäkitalo, Neil Mercer, David Middleton, Monika Nerland, Joce Nuttall, Roger Säljö and Wim Wardekker. Also thanks to Judy Sebba and Mark Rickinson for encouraging the use of these ideas in the work we have been doing together on relationships between research and policy.

Finally, thanks to Gill Boag-Munroe for her thoughtful work on the manuscript, to Phil Richards for his unstinting secretarial support, and to my family for being so forgiving of my absences. As ever, all errors and infelicities are mine.

Contents

1 Introducing the Resourceful Practitioner 1
   1.1 What This Book Is About 1
   1.2 Being a Professional 2
   1.3 What Are Practices? 5
   1.4 Mediation and Knowledge in Practices 7
   1.5 Professional Identity 10
   1.6 Relational Expertise 13
   1.7 The Evidence Base 16
   References 18

2 Expertise: The Relational Turn 21
   2.1 Expertise in Task Accomplishment 21
   2.2 Psychological Accounts of Expertise and Environment 21
   2.3 Starting with the Cultural 24
   2.4 Distributed Expertise 26
   2.5 Networking Without Knowledge 32
   2.6 Collective Competence and Collaborative Intentions 34
   2.7 Expertise as Purposeful Engagement in Practices 36
   References 37

3 Knowledge Work at Practice Boundaries 41
   3.1 Boundaries: Where Practices Intersect 41
   3.2 Boundary Work 43
   3.3 What Happens in the New Boundary Spaces 45
   3.4 Alternative Envisioning at the Boundaries 48
   3.5 Constructing Sites for Sustained Boundary Work 50
   3.6 Knowledge Talk at the Boundaries 53
   References 58

4 Relational Agency: Working with Other Practitioners 61
   4.1 Relational Agency 61
   4.2 Agency and Mutuality 62
   4.3 Relational Agency and Cultural Historical Activity Theory ... 64
   4.4 Motives and Relational Agency 68

	4.5	Relational Agency and Demands on Practitioners	69
	4.6	Systemic Responses to the Demands of Relational Agency	71
	4.7	Relational Agency in Practice	73
	References		77
5	**Working Relationally with Clients**		81
	5.1	Personal Responsibility	81
	5.2	Participation	83
	5.3	Joint Work as Co-configuration	85
	5.4	Externalisation Co-configuration and Relational Agency	89
	5.5	Working with the Expertise of Those Who Use Services	95
	References		96
6	**Being a Professional**		99
	6.1	Working in Relation	99
	6.2	Knowledge and Commitment in Professional Work	100
	6.3	Expert Knowledge and Relational Agency	104
	6.4	Knowledge in Practices	109
	References		113
7	**Working Upstream**		117
	7.1	Systemic Learning from Operational Practices	117
	7.2	Distinctly Different Practices in Organisational Hierarchies	119
	7.3	Differences in Engagement with Knowledge Between Hierarchical Practices	122
	7.4	Differences in Temporalities	124
	7.5	Representations that Work Across Boundaries	125
	7.6	Upstream Learning and Resistance to Change in Organisations	126
	7.7	Mediation and Relevance	129
	7.8	Knowledge Flows from Research to Policy	132
	References		135
8	**Researching the Relational in Practices**		137
	8.1	Finding the Object of Enquiry	137
	8.2	Background and Foreground in Research Design	142
	8.3	Discursive Approaches to Researching Relational Aspects of Professional Practices	144
	8.4	Narratives and Personal Trajectories	146
	8.5	Interventionist Research	150
	8.6	The Challenges of Researching the Relational Turn	152
	References		153
Appendix A: Activity Theory			157
	A.1	What Is Activity Theory?	157
	A.2	Engeström and Activity Theory	158
	A.3	Developmental Work Research	160
	A.4	Inside the DWR Sessions	162

A.5	Analysing the Data from the DWR Sessions	163
	References	163

**An Analytic Protocol for the Building
of Common Knowledge: The D-Analysis** 165

    Reference 166

Index 167

Chapter 1
Introducing the Resourceful Practitioner

1.1 What This Book Is About

This book explores what it is to be a decision-making practitioner who works responsively with clients and other practitioners. It is about how relational work can strengthen practitioners' actions on complex problems by making accessible a wider range of resources in these actions. It draws on my own research carried out over 15 years in education and the welfare professions more broadly, and on studies carried out by colleagues and research students who have tackled the same problems among other professions such as accountancy, software engineering and e-science.

Lying in the background to the book is a shift from seeing professionals as the sole guardians of exclusive sets of knowledge, operating within established practices which are imbued with late nineteenth century Liberal values of personal trust and the care of others. The shift arose initially, as we shall see, from the bureaucratisation of the professions that are the focus of the book, and has been accelerated by a climate which has emphasised their accountability.

But these themes are just in the background, whereas the intention is to look forward. The argument will be made that as professionals work increasingly across professional boundaries on complex problems with other practitioners and with clients, they operate outside the safety net of their organisations' bureaucratic procedures. Consequently, rather than following established institutional practices, they have to rely on their specialist knowledge and their expertise in working with others while they negotiate the accomplishment of complex tasks. This kind of relational practice means that practitioners need to be able to label their own expertise; recognise, draw on and contribute to the funds of expertise available; and demonstrate a strong sense of their own identities as practitioners whose actions can make a difference in the world.

My research programme has convinced me that inter-professional work and more responsive work with clients can give rise to a new and enhanced form of professionalism. Engagement with the knowledge offered by others marks this new form of professional practice as different from the exclusivity and disinterest of that 100 years ago. Yet some of the same priorities are shaping professional action, including a concern with the wellbeing of vulnerable clients, professional values and expertise. These are broad topics which are given different weight across the professions.

Practitioners who bring their professional resources to complex problems, whether the social exclusion of vulnerable children or the development of radiography equipment, are finding themselves taking a stand, revealing what matters for them as they negotiate tasks and trying to discern what matters for others. These stands are bound up with their identities, but also with moral positions, with what Taylor calls 'the commitments and identifications which provide the frame or horizon within which I can try to determine from case to case what is good, or valuable, or what ought to be done, or what I endorse or oppose.' (1989: 7). These standpoints are developed and sustained relationally, as Benhabib (1992: 10) explains: we cannot ethically take a stand without knowing how to reason from 'the standpoint of the concrete other'.

My central argument is that offering one's professional resources to collaborating practitioners and to clients, and working with what they offer, involves an expertise which includes recognising and responding to the standpoints of others and is in addition to the specialist knowledge at the core of each distinct professional practice. It is this additional layer of expertise which is the focus of the book.

Professional expertise is no longer assumed by dint of social position: it has to be negotiated while problems are worked on. In order for these negotiations to happen, what matters most for the exercise of expertise in each profession needs to be made visible to others. This visibility needs to be achieved without reducing the central importance of the precision and depth of knowledge that characterise expert practices.

Therefore, as well as demanding that hitherto hidden aspects of expertise, such as what 'care' means for different caring professions, are made public, the additional layer of expertise includes the capacity to negotiate what matters with others. Exercising this additional form of expertise is not simply a question of collaboration, but is itself a complex phenomenon. Rather, this additional capacity involves recognising how others interpret and react to problems and aligning one's own interpretations and responses to theirs, to produce enriched understandings and practices.

I have called this capacity 'relational agency' (Edwards & Mackenzie, 2005; Edwards, 2005, 2009) and will elaborate it in Section 1.6, and in Chapter 4 and the chapters that follow. In the present chapter I outline some of the features of the landscape in which resourceful practitioners are working and learning, and how practices might be conceptualised as advance organisers for the themes that are developed in later chapters.

1.2 Being a Professional

This chapter is about practitioners, in part because what is a *professional* has been debated for at least the past 50 years (Evetts, 2003; Wilensky, 1964), and in part because, in some areas of care and elsewhere, responsibilities previously assumed by accredited professionals are carried out by untrained staff (Edwards, Lunt, &

1.2 Being a Professional

Stamou, 2010; Gunter, 2007; Kubiak, 2010). Conceptualisations of professionalism can be unclear. For that reason this book is focusing on expertise in practices that have some claim to being considered professional by virtue of their need to do more than simply follow routine procedures or tackle prescribed tasks. As Wilensky observed, the criteria for professionalism have been shifting. In an attempt to seek some stability, his view was that:

> ... the degree of professionalization is measured not just by the degree of success in the claim to exclusive technical competence, but also by the degree of adherence to the service ideal and its supporting norms of professional conduct. (Wilensky, 1964: 141)

He was concerned about the contemporary impact of bureaucracies on both the service ideal and the professionals' claims to be independent decision-makers: '... where comfortable organizational routines take command, the salaried professional ... may lose sight of client needs more quickly than his solo brother' (p. 148).

The bureaucratisation of professional practices provided institutional safety nets for practitioners who made potentially risky decisions during their work with clients, but it downplayed what used to be called professional autonomy in client-centred work. Instead, professional knowledge was embedded in routines, and practice, in turn, became shaped by these routines.

The 1980s and 1990s development of new public management (NPM) systems in the public sector (Hood & Peters, 2004; Hood, 1991), with their emphases on accountability, standards, performance management and outputs, may have disrupted the cosy picture painted by Wilensky. But in so emphatically shifting attention from procedures and processes to targets and outcomes, NPM was guilty of paying too little attention to practices and their development.

The problem was accountability, which, as Ranson has argued, limited the idea of service delivery to tightly specified purposes and tasks (Ranson, 2003). Services may have become more client-centred in their concern with outcomes, but there has been little space for negotiated and responsive practices, despite moves toward the tailored packages of support that might be characterised by personalisation (Leadbeater, 2004). The clear assignment of responsibility to managers who have been placed within hierarchies which are driven by top-down targets has meant that welfare organisations can be impervious to how they might respond to the changing needs of clients. All this has been made worse by a preoccupation with targets which can all too easily limit service delivery to being a response to the easily identifiable with the easily available.

Nowhere in this book will you find a plea for individual professional autonomy: that is not the way forward. But if practices are to be responsive to clients' needs, histories and intentions, they cannot be led by the needs, histories and intentions of organisations whether their *raisons d'être* are the stability and routine of bureaucracy or the accountability and targets of NPM. In Chapter 6, I argue that we need a refreshed version of being a professional in the public sector which sustains the service ideal, emphasises knowledge as a practitioner resource, and which offers some protection to practitioners who themselves may be vulnerable as they work responsively with clients and across professional boundaries; and in Chapter 7, I outline the challenges posed when attempting to promote 'upstream learning' from innovative practices, in order to inform organisational strategy.

Complex problems are not exclusive to the public sector. It is therefore worth turning to one of the newer service sectors where specialist expertise is brought into task-focused relationships to solve problems presented by others. Software engineering is certainly a young profession and is responsive to new resources such as the introduction of Java and to demands being made on it by clients in the public, private and voluntary sectors who need software that supports their needs. Expertise is being developed rapidly as software engineers work on new problems, refine tools and share information across networked systems of knowledge exchange, which enhance their sense of being part of a wider professional community (Nerland, 2008). These networks are crucial to being a professional software engineer:

> ... while certainly providing information about advancements in the field, these kinds of networks also offer developers professional identities that are grounded in certain technologies and which exceed the local work settings. The learning professional is constructed as a member of a technological community who is encouraged to commit himself/herself to certain technologies and invited to contribute to the collective knowledge of the community. Moreover the networks incorporate means for encouraging reciprocity and social commitment... (Nerland, 2008: 58)

But more than lifting their heads to see beyond local practices, these professionals, who were studied in the University of Oslo ProLearn project, were devising their own professional standards by making relevant knowledge explicit. The motive was to keep abreast of changing technologies without compromising the quality of their work, Nerland explains,

> Thus the accumulation of knowledge in this professional domain, for instance through practices of developing and reprocessing programming codes, is closely linked to the development and distribution of standards that have a formal character. In contrast to many other arenas of everyday life, where individuals constantly engage with standards without paying any attention because they are so taken for granted in their social practices, computer engineers are dealing with standards in a very explicit manner. This is to a large extent what their work is about: Knowing the technological standards that are in play, knowing how they may work or not work together, and knowing how to perform different tasks within the different technological regimes. The commercial ways of advancing the knowledge domain by launching new versions of technologies serve to reinforce the importance of knowing and understanding the relevant standards. (Nerland, 2008: 59)

In the Norwegian study it is striking that these workers, and the nurses and auditors with whom they were compared, saw their practices as shaped by the knowledge needed to do their jobs. For the auditors the knowledge embedded in spreadsheet templates was a resource for action, while for the software engineers and nurses the standards to which they were working were professionally driven to reflect their changing practices. Engagement with knowledge in changing systems characterises being a professional in these three cases and is as marked among the nurses, and particularly those who have undertaken research-based enquiries, as among the software engineers (Jensen & Lahn, 2005).

How far have we come from Wilensky's definition of a professional? Professional knowledge may be based on a 'claim to exclusive technical competence', but it is a competence that needs to respond to changing conditions, resources and problems and to be found in practices that can absorb new knowledge and ways of working. The service ideal does remain strong in those professions where there is sufficient freedom of movement for responsive engagement with clients; but here the origins of the 'norms of professional conduct' appear to be crucial. The ability of both the professionals and the settings in which they work to learn, adapt and develop their practice would seem to be essential. Let us therefore examine in more detail what is meant by resourceful practice in this book.

1.3 What Are Practices?

Most of the examples of practice to be discussed in the chapters that follow have come from studies which have been framed by one of the legacies of Vygotsky's writings on learning in Russia in the 1920s and 1930s (Cole, 1996; Daniels, Cole, & Wertsch, 2007). However, although the theory is useful, the terminology can be confusing, particularly as it is used differently by different writers. So here is some initial ground clearing. Practices, I suggest following Hedegaard (2009), occur in institutional settings such as social service departments, auditors' companies or families. The discussion is expanded in Chapter 6 (Section 6.4) where we see that practices are knowledge-laden, imbued with cultural values and emotionally freighted by the motives of those who already act in them.

Within these broad institutional practices people operate in different settings where they engage in activities such as finding a safe place for a homeless family to stay, ensuring that a company has dealt appropriately with financial risk, or that a sick relative is looked after. People are driven forward in these activities by what they see as the purposes of finding a safe place and so on. These purposes are usually derived from the knowledge and values that are embedded in their institutional practices. For example, a safe place is needed for the whole family because the wellbeing of children is paramount in that particular social services department.

Readers familiar with the activity theory aspects of Vygotsky's legacy will now be wondering what has happened to the activity system. However, my primary concern in this book is not with the system and how it changes, which is the focus of activity theory (Engeström, 1999): rather, it is with practices, how they are navigated and negotiated, questioned and developed; and with the expertise that is evident as people act in practices. Nonetheless, the systems in which practices arise and change need to be part of the picture and this is one reason for using Cultural Historical Activity Theory (CHAT) (Cole, 1996) as a dominant framework in the discussions that follow. The other reason is that Engeström's (1987) development of the idea of the 'object of activity' as a problem space to be worked in and transformed is, I think, a helpful one. Appendix A gives an outline of how the term 'object' is used, and in Chapter 4 (Section 4.3) I outline the development of CHAT as it connects with my focus on relational work.

To illustrate how the object of activity is to be used in these discussions, let us return to the idea that the purposes of activities are shaped by the practices in which they are set. If the activity is helping a family to find a safe place to live and the purpose is to prevent the child in the family from becoming socially excluded, unable to attend school etc., the problem space for the social workers is the child's vulnerability to social exclusion. The child's vulnerability is the long-term problem they are working on and trying to change when they are looking for somewhere for the family: it is the object of their activity. These ideas will be elaborated in Chapter 2 (Section 2.4) and I now move on from this brief ground clearing to focus on knowledge and value-laden practices.

One danger with the account of practices that I have just outlined is that it can be read to mean that practices are always pre-determined and that actors merely inhabit them. That would not do justice to Vygotsky's work on learning. There are two important points here. Firstly, he intended to offer an alternative to the behaviourism that dominated Russian psychology in the early 1920s by offering a cognitive account of learning. Secondly, he argued that learning involves both internalisation and externalisation.

His aim was to generate an account of learning in which mind is actively making sense and externalising understandings by acting on the world using the tools available to change it for the better. These tools may be material or conceptual, and indeed the resources we use in actions usually combine the material and the conceptual. His argument was that as we engage over time with the world and come to understand it better than we did, we act on it in more informed ways and in turn change it. It follows that when our engagement is through unreflective following of routines, externalisation is likely to make little difference to practices. But when we act thoughtfully on problems of practice, we bring to bear understandings that may override routines and we may come to recognise unanticipated aspects of the problems. I shall argue throughout this book that when the resources of several practitioners are brought to bear on a complex problem, their effect is enhanced.

CHAT accounts of practice have a great deal in common with Bourdieu's seminal analyses of practice: his focus on the interplay between habitus (what Bourdieu described as the organising principle of people's actions) and field; and the importance of 'interest' to practice (Bourdieu, 1977). The dynamic of habitus and field underpins his account of practices and indicates how habitus gives shape to or mediates interpretations of situations. Accordingly, we are not merely individuals whose decision-making in practices is unconnected with the practices, how they have arisen and what they mean for us and others.

> It is necessary to abandon all theories which explicitly or implicitly treat practice as a mechanical reaction, directly determined by the antecedent conditions and entirely reducible to the mechanical functioning of pre-established assemblies, "models" or "roles" ... But the rejection of mechanistic theories in no way implies that ... we should bestow on some creative free will the free and willful power to constitute, on the instant, the meaning of the situation ... and that we should reduce the objective intentions and constituted significations of actions and works to the conscious and deliberate intentions of their authors. (Bourdieu, 1977: 73)

This interconnection between historical practices and agency will be a recurring theme throughout the chapters that follow, where I shall tackle them using Vygotsky's conceptual legacy rather than that offered by Bourdieu.

Nonetheless, there are considerable overlaps between the preoccupations of Bourdieu and of Vygotskian theorists. For example, the importance of interest to action connects with accounts of motives and practices which are part of the Vygotsky legacy. Focusing on the primacy of interaction between habitus and field, Bourdieu argued that that actions and meanings are shaped by what he described as a 'socially constituted system of cognitive and motivating structures and the socially structured situation in which the agents' *interests* are defined, and with them the objective functions and subjective motivations of their practices.' (1977: 76). This attention to interests is in sympathy with CHAT analyses, as interests in both analytic frameworks arise within the practices. The CHAT line is based on Leont'ev's (1978) focus on the 'object motive' that calls forth our responses to problems of practice.

Leont'ev, a colleague of Vygotsky's, explained object motive in the following way.

> The main thing which distinguishes one activity from another, however, is the difference of their objects. It is exactly the object of an activity that gives it a determined direction. According to the terminology I have proposed, the object of the activity is its true motive. (Leont'ev, 1978: 62)

This line of reasoning suggests that, for example, a teacher and a social worker are likely to interpret the developmental trajectory of a vulnerable child in slightly different ways because they are located within different practices where the motives for engagement with objects of activity are also different.

In both CHAT and Bourdieu's framework, therefore, interests (or motives) arise in practices and give direction to actions. Also within both approaches, rules or routines are more likely to replace thoughtful responses when interest is lacking. The motives or interests that are embedded in and give shape and direction to practices can, if made visible, therefore operate as the glue that holds together relational work between the different practices of teachers and social workers. I examine this point in more depth in Chapters 3 and 4.

Bourdieu's idea of habitus is, however, different from the idea of person as decision-making agent, which will be pursued throughout this book. Rather habitus is 'the universalizing mediation', which ensures that an agent's practices seem "sensible" and "reasonable" (P. 79), within the socially constituted system of motivating structures. Let us therefore turn to the topic of mediation which is so central to Vygotskian accounts of practice and see what mediation means there.

1.4 Mediation and Knowledge in Practices

Vygotskian's work on practices is often concerned with how institutionally held knowledge and values are mediated, as mediation was a central concept in Vygotsky's work. The premise is that all action is mediated by the conceptual resources that are available to us in our cultures: unmediated action is consequently an impossibility for humans as cultural beings. In formal education settings curricula are mediated though text books, classroom tasks and teachers' interactions with learners. However, mediation also occurs in informal settings such as family meals and work-oriented meetings where the opportunities for learning are less contrived. Therefore, mediation is essential to understanding how the knowledge and values that are embedded in practices become passed on.

Wertsch has helpfully distinguished between explicit and implicit mediation in Vygotsky's writing (Wertsch, 2007). In particular, he offers insights into how institutional talk and, by extension, material genres, such as auditors' spreadsheets or social workers assessment forms, mediate accepted understandings in workplace settings. Explicit mediation, Wertsch suggests, involves the intentional introduction of what is to be learnt into a learning activity, which is managed by someone who is designated as 'teacher', and therefore reflects what is common in formal education settings. Implicit mediation, on the other hand, involves knowledge being carried in the natural, that is, the historically constructed, language of the situation.

Wertsch's idea of implicit mediation helps us to see a connection between talk and knowledge in practices, because the categories that we use to interpret the world as we engage in practices are evident in how we talk about the world and practices in everyday settings. Implicit mediation, therefore, usefully leads us to being alert to how meaning is shared in talk in activities in practices. The detailed analyses of discourse in workplaces carried out by Mäkitalo and Säljö (Mäkitalo, 2003, 2006; Mäkitalo & Säljö, 2002) similarly reveal how work-related categorisations shape actions, and, as we shall see in Chapter 8 (Sections 8.2 and 8.3), how these categorisations simultaneously sustain institutional practices.

Here is an example of categorisations being revealed in talk from one of our studies (Edwards & Kinti, 2009). The setting is a conversation between a teacher and an educational psychologist about how children's wellbeing can be promoted. There are others, including social workers and housing specialists, in the meeting who are listening. In this extract, the categorisations used by the psychologist, 'effects', 'target', 'boundary', 'underachievement' are being mediated into the discourse of the meeting, while at the same time he is being sympathetic to the standpoint of the school.

> There is a sense in which although the child is the same child outside and inside we sort of feel we can almost draw a boundary around the school and say when you are in here you can leave it at the gates or we can minimize the effects yeah . . . . I think we set ourselves a target which is almost unachievable, unattainable in the sense. And perhaps the way in which schools with others need to be bridging that boundary differently. It resonated with (name of nearby city) where the teachers' feeling was although a lot of the cause of underachievement and so on lie . . . are outside the school, it's their responsibility to do something about it. (Edwards & Kinti, 2009: 132)

These meanings do not 'readily become the object of conscious reflection', which is a sign that implicit rather than explicit mediation is occurring (Wertsch, 2007: 185); but they do begin to populate the conversation. Later in the meeting, one of the teachers started to use some of the language of the psychologist as a resource while she suggested what needed to be done to improve how they all worked with children.

With the idea of implicit mediation Wertsch, like Mäkitalo and Säljö (2002), provides a much needed link between the institutional priorities that are revealed in talk and the development of professional reasoning and action (see Section 8.3). In the present example, the psychologist employed his professional categories as resources to shape the practices associated with promoting children's wellbeing. As well as building some common ground between the school and the psychology service, he was, implicitly at least, making claims to the importance of his professional categories and inviting others to use them. Whose knowledge has the greatest influence in practices is a crucial question, whether working with other practitioners or with clients (Mehan, 1993) (See Chapter 8, Section 8.3).

The mediation of historically formed knowledge into practices, which are dealing with unpredictable and complex problems, may, however, be insufficient for the development of professions. I have argued that the practices in which expertise is enacted are the kinds of practices where problems and responses to them are not routine. They therefore need to involve practitioners in overt engagement with knowledge.

Knorr Cetina (2001: 175), when discussing research scientists, describes such engagement as forms of 'engrossment and excitement'. If expert knowledge-bases cannot be seen as static, because new problems arise with different clients, and policies require changing responses with new configurations of resources, Knorr Cetina's notion of 'engrossment' with knowledge is, I suggest, an important part of those professional practices which are not merely rule-following. Engagement with knowledge or epistemic objects will be taken up in Chapter 6 where we consider what is involved in being a professional.

There I shall argue (Section 6.2) that Knorr Cetina's analyses of 'the machineries of knowledge construction' (1999: 3) usefully direct attention from simply what experts know to how they know and how they build knowledge in knowledge-driven 'epistemic cultures'. Her work therefore adds to notions of practice by emphasising knowledge-building relationships. In her study of two groups of scientists at work (Knorr Cetina, 1999), she focused on their knowledge-in-action, including how knowledge was mobilised in technical gossip and passed along 'confidence pathways' between professionals, which were based on mutual trust. Technical gossip, rather like Wertsch's implicit mediation, revealed people's professional standpoints and their positions in relation to the 'organizational philosophies' (1999: 203) of potential collaborators.

These 'philosophies' were evaluated and appeared to operate as 'ritual displays of what she saw as the habitus of collaborations' (1999: 204). Knorr Cetina suggested that the displays operated as codes which informed decisions about future inter-personal collaborations and new configurations of practices. Knowledge-in-action was therefore bound up with evaluations of others, which were shaped by what was seen to matter in practices: for example, when people's ways of working were judged as 'slapdash' or 'too easy going' (1999: 207) they were not welcomed as colleagues. These were personal opinions which were related to standards of professional action about what was seen to be of consequence. Personal opinions and compelling interests, it seems, are important aspects of practices: motives in practices are, as we shall see in the chapters that follow, therefore not entirely historically pre-determined.

1.5 Professional Identity

The idea of identity pursued in this book is in sympathy with Roth et al. (2004) explanation that identity is not a stable characteristic, but is dialogical, negotiated and accomplished within activities. Identity is therefore seen as a way of describing how people participate in activities, which are in turn located in practices. But I suggest that it is also more than that. One's identity is also an organising principle for action: we approach and tackle what we think we are able to change and make changes in line with what matters to us: our interests. These interests are culturally mediated, but nonetheless experienced personally in terms of our commitments, standpoints and the resources available to us.

Holland, Skinner, Lachicotte and Cain describe identities in a similar way. For them, 'Identities are a key means through which people care about and care for what is going on around them' (1998: 5). Here the kind of social identity suggested by Roth et al. is being invested with the agency of the morally engaged self (Taylor, 1989), which we will return to in Chapter 4 (Section 4.2) and Chapter 8 (Section 8.2). Like Taylor's this agency is tempered by a connectedness to the social which, anticipating Wertsch's (2007) analyses of implicit mediation outlined in Section 1.4, Holland et al. suggested was mediated semiotically:

> These tools of agency are highly social in several senses: the symbols of mediation are collectively produced, learned in practice, and remain distributed over others for a long period of time. (Holland et al., 1998: 38)

When professional activities are new and are being negotiated, as was the case in our studies of inter-professional practices for the prevention of social exclusion, it follows that professional identities are sharply under negotiation and new mediational means may need to be created.

In the account of the Learning in and for Interagency Working (LIW) study (Edwards, Daniels, Gallagher, Leadbetter, & Warmington, 2009), we identified some of the newly formed mediational means employed by practitioners as conceptual tools as they learnt to work together for children's wellbeing (2009: 66). These are listed in Section 3.2, and included recognising the importance of making professional values explicit and of clarifying the purposes of work. Being able to use these new conceptual resources as a form of common knowledge from which they could negotiate activities and identities in order to work agentically with others was, as we shall see in Chapters 3 and 4, central to the formation of practitioners' new professional identities as people who could collaborate across professional boundaries to operate with the resources that others offered.

1.5 Professional Identity

These collaborations are not without their problems. Negotiations across professional boundaries with other practitioners or with clients may result in evaluations such as 'slapdash', which preclude collaboration, or they may give rise to changes in professional identity, through taking on board and working with the priorities of another profession. The resulting shifts in what professionals 'care about' may, therefore, be at odds with the practices which initially shaped their identities. Where there is some shared valuing of the purposes of practice, such as a child's wellbeing, it is unlikely that negotiations produce identities which present practitioners with strong personally felt conflicts. But where core practices, and the institutions that safeguard them, have not kept pace with the changes in work orientation that arise as practitioners work relationally with others, conflicts may occur. These will be personally experienced and will have institutional implications.

As Holland and Lave (2001) have pointed out in their discussion of institutions, self-hood and conflict, 'history in institutional structures and history in person are never simple equivalents'. Institutional histories may be reflected in professional identities, but the relationship is never predictable and is unlikely to be so when activities change in response to alterations in local circumstances and expectations. They suggest that as a result 'local practice always has the unfinished quality of an experiment for the future of these structures' (2001: 5). In other words, practices and the identities they sustain should be seen as always 'in the making'.

Practices are made and remade by the people who work in them as they operate both with and against structural histories; and so are the identities of those who inhabit them. In their 2001 collection of papers, Holland and Lave examined the social production of identity which arose when people were working against institutional structures in local conflicts such as strip searching in Northern Ireland or community responses to a new transport project in New York. These were struggles against powerful societal institutions undertaken by people with disproportionately less power. As well acting on institutional structures, these conflicts were also experienced personally by some participants as a reforming of a sense of who they were. Aretxaga in her discussion of strip searching explained.

> For the ex-prisoners I spoke to, being a woman took on a politicized dimension that it did not have before. What became problematized by this politicization was what being a woman meant. (Aretxaga, 2001: 57)

The 2001 collection of papers captured amplifications of the dialogical construction of self in purposeful actions: these were struggles rather than negotiations. But across our studies of inter-professional work aimed at preventing social exclusion, we found practitioners who struggled to develop a sense of responsible and informed decision-making in systems shaped by NPM. As we shall see in Chapter 4 (Section 4.5), personal conflicts between what matters and what is possible can be experienced quite painfully.

If, as I've suggested, identity is what connects practitioners to what they care about, it is central to non-routine responses to problems of practice. It is therefore not simply acquired through processes of acculturation in institutional practices where there is no engagement with the knowledge and values in the practices. Rather it is nurtured where knowledge and values are made visible, contested and developed, and where the interplay of structures and practices is an ongoing 'experiment' mediated by changing conceptions of what matters. Identity is therefore both social and personal, involves both internalisation and externalisation as we operate in the world, and gives direction to how we navigate practices, negotiate priorities and employ resources.

This summary returns us to Knorr Cetina's interest in the epistemic or knowledge-oriented practices that engross practitioners (1997, 1999) (and Section 6.2). Arguing for seeing knowledge as open and unfolding, she presents the idea of structures of wanting (Knorr Cetina, 1997) as prerequisites to an engagement with knowledge. These structures are characterised by an openness to searches to know more and understand better. The idea therefore offers a view of expertise as more than the rational exercise of cognition: instead the person-in-engaged-action is central. She explains.

> The conduct of expertise has long harbored and nourished an experiential *mentalité*, if 'experience' is defined, as I think it should be, as an arousal of the processing capabilities and sensitivities of the person in some combination. Apart from the possibility of a deep emotional investment in objects of knowledge which the notion of a structure of wanting entails, it should be seen as an open dynamic ... (1997: 14)

Structures of wanting, Knorr Cetina suggests, correspond with a sense of lack that pulls one forward to know more, to engage more fully with knowing, while being aware that one's knowledge will never be complete. Jensen and Lahn's (2005) exemplification of the 'binding power of knowledge' in forming the professional identities of nurses, who can no longer locate their sense of who they are in the situated practices of specific workplaces, draws on Knorr Cetina's analyses of lack and wanting. It offers a potentially fruitful way of conceptualising new professional identities where knowledge is a crucial resource as they act in practices. Jensen and Lahn explain what was happening with the nurses.

> Guided by the need to renew and revitalise itself, the profession has established closer links to science and has itself begun to participate more actively in the production of scientific knowledge. As a result, they have produced theories which in theme and genre engage the students, and which transform the professional community into a mediated and extended arena for mutual identification and reconstruction. Our data—although quite explorative in nature—suggest that these new communities distinguish themselves in important ways from the concrete, immediate and practice-based communities depicted in the literature on professionalization in several regards, but also have a binding function. (Jensen & Lahn, 2005: 318)

The arguments presented so far suggest quite strongly that professional identity as an informed decision-maker is intertwined with engagement in knowledge practices to which one contributes. Expertise as a practitioner in a world of potentially changing practices demands, I suggest, stronger ties with knowledge, ways of knowing, and knowledge production than was probably the case 100 years ago. In the chapters that follow I shall return to that suggestion to evaluate developments where the importance of expert knowledge has been underplayed. But now I turn to how expertise is conceptualised in the present discussion of expert practices.

1.6 Relational Expertise

This book is primarily about the relational turn in expertise as professionals work in and between work settings and interact with other practitioners and clients to negotiate interpretations of tasks and ways of accomplishing them. The central argument is that the resources that others bring to problems can enhance understandings and can enrich responses (Edwards, 2005). However, working in this way makes demands on practitioners. At the very least, it calls for an additional form of expertise which makes it possible to work with others to expand understandings of the work problem as an object of joint activity, and the ability to attune one's responses to the enhanced interpretation to those being made by other professionals.

This extra expertise is therefore based on confident engagement with the knowledge that underpins one's practice as a social worker or nurse, as well as a capacity to recognise and respond to what others might offer. The themes to be pursued in the chapters that follow centre on the offering and taking up of the resources offered by others, as expertise is exercised relationally in and across workplace practices. A prerequisite for this focus on the relational exercise of expertise is to recognise that expert knowledge is distributed across systems, a topic that is discussed in Chapter 2 (Section 2.4).

The expertise I shall examine may be supported by work practices which are knowledge and value-laden. Yet, it is also likely to raise questions about existing practices when old practices fail to connect with current purposes and intentions. The fluidity of response that the relational turn in expertise requires may over-ride, or at least destabilise, established pathways of collaboration. For example, it is likely to call for an engagement with priorities that are foreign to one's core work: such as when teachers need to downplay curricular demands in order to accommodate how a social worker is supporting a family. The relational turn in expertise therefore brings with it demands for new configurations of practices which require organisations to focus more on revealing the complexity of problems and on supporting and developing the expertise of practitioners, than on offering either the comfort of routines or the tight prescriptions of targets.

However, the intention is to get below the conditions that structure possibilities for the exercise of expertise, in order to examine the interactions in which knowledge is shared and generated. Østerland and Carlile (2005) have summarised the work still to be done at this level after analysing three research programmes which have been based on the Lave and Wenger (1991) notion of 'communities of practice'.

> We find that the relational thinking embedded in the three seminal works often gets distorted when adopted by other scholars or practitioners. Specific knowledge-sharing practices tend to become regarded as properties of a community and not rooted in fluid social relations. (Østerland & Carlile, 2005: 105)

The discussion of the relational turn in expertise is therefore an attempt to bring to the fore the relational aspects of engagement with others on work tasks. The idea that is at the centre of this book is 'relational agency' (Edwards & Mackenzie, 2005;

2008; Edwards, 2005; 2009). It is examined in detail in Chapter 4, where I draw on studies of inter-professional collaborations to explain its origins in CHAT and its implications for professions. In brief, it involves a capacity for working with others to strengthen purposeful responses to complex problems. It is helpful to see it arising from a two-stage process within a constant dynamic which consists of:

(i) working with others to expand the 'object of activity' or task being working on by recognising the motives and the resources that others bring to bear as they, too, interpret it; and
(ii) aligning one's own responses to the newly enhanced interpretations with the responses being made by the other professionals while acting on the expanded object.

A capacity for relational agency can be learnt and, because it involves working alongside others toward mutually agreed outcomes, is relevant to the work of practitioners who may feel vulnerable when acting responsively and alone without the protection of established procedures.

Its starting point in my work on the prevention of social exclusion was that the practitioners need to recognise the complexity of a child's trajectory before responses can be considered as the views of one professional acting alone are likely to miss aspects of vulnerability that also need addressing (Edwards et al., 2009). The framework for understanding collaboration offered by relational agency is therefore quite different from versions of networked support, which are based on the interpretations of a single professional who then asks others for the resources that she considers most appropriate for her interpretation (Nardi, Whittaker, & Schwarz, 2002).

The question of whose knowledge dominates in these relationships is, as I have already indicated, important. We came to similar conclusions to Mehan (1993) about the relative power of psychologists in conversations in educational settings, in the extract from an educational psychologist's contribution to an inter-professional conversation, which we discussed in Section 1.4 (Edwards & Kinti, 2009). An emphasis on the inter-professional can also inadvertently downplay the relational aspects of work with clients and the weaving of their knowledge into solutions to problems of practice.

If so it would undermine some important developments in social work which foreground the co-production of problems and solutions with clients (Folgheraiter, 2004; Hunter & Ritchie, 2007). Hunter and Ritchie summarise the current position in much social work practice:

> For most of the people most of the time, being able to discuss, define and shape their own interactions with the services they use is central to their sense of autonomy, dignity and agency. (Hunter & Ritchie, 2007: 10)

Folgheraiter is more ambitious, as he challenges social workers to share both interpretations of the problem and responsibility for solutions with clients in what he calls relational social work.

1.6 Relational Expertise

Relational practice with clients is, however, not without its tensions, demanding a great deal of practitioners who may not always be confident in their own professional knowledge-base (Edwards & Apostolov, 2007). Across the studies of social inclusion I have undertaken since 2003, we have found a reluctance among many practitioners to include parents and carers as resourceful and responsible partners in the reconfiguring of their children's life-trajectories. There may therefore be a danger that relational inter-professional work could lead to an exclusivity that could undo attempts at increasing the participation of service users in the co-production of solutions to problems, a point I return to in Chapter 5.

There are also other implications arising from weaving the private knowledge of clients into professional decision-making. Nowotny has pointed to how the current ease of access to information, together with policy emphases on choice and individual decision-making, makes it possible for 'everyone to become an expert in something of concern to him or herself' (2000: 12). She notes that this 'diffused' expertise has yet to replace public expertise, which is underpinned by standards and science; yet knowledge production is now more socially distributed and not simply the province of bounded expert groups.

The heterogeneity of the knowledge that arises raises questions for Nowotny about 'quality control' as there can no longer be claims to 'a monopolistic control of scientific authority' (2000: 19). Her solution is an expert system that develops a pluri-disciplinary knowledge-base and involves specialists and lay members (Nowotny, 2000; 2003). Although a macro-level analysis, Nowotny's arguments connect strongly with the relational turn in expertise to be discussed in the present book. She explains the implications of her analyses for expert practice:

> Experts must now extend their knowledge, not simply to be an extension of what they know in their specialist field, but to consist of building links and trying to integrate what they know with what others want to, or should know and do. Bringing together the many different knowledge dimensions involved constitutes specific mixes with other kinds of knowledge, experience and expertise. (Nowotny, 2003: 155)

I am not proposing a dilution of personal specialist expertise as a result of incorporating the motives and conceptual resources of other groups into specialist practice, quite the reverse. My argument is based on the importance of core expertise for the professions. However, recognising and working with the motives of others may lead to an expanded understanding of the problems being tackled.

To avoid the idea that specialist knowledge is to be downplayed in relational work, we need to distinguish between the ability to recognise and work with what matters for others and being able to do what they do. Collins makes this point very clearly in his discussion of what he calls 'interactional expertise' (Collins & Evans, 2007; Collins, 2004; Collins, Evans, Ribeiro, & Hall, 2006). Collins asked a question that is as relevant to relational expert practice as it is to the sociology of science in which he specialises: 'How much scientific knowledge do you need to have in order to do the sociology of a scientific domain?' (2004: 127). His response has been to differentiate between a specialist understanding, which is evidenced in the ability to both use the relevant professional language and to do the job, and the ability to use the language in conversations with others. One can learn to speak the language through what he describes as 'by being immersed in the community', without being able to carry out work tasks. Speaking the language so that one can communicate meanings is 'interactional expertise' which is different from what Collins calls 'contributory expertise' or the ability to act competently in the culture.

I am not suggesting that relational work calls for the kind of interactional expertise that comes from immersion in a culture, as Collins explains with masterly understatement that it is 'hard to attain' (2004: 129) and not gained by many. But his view that it can be acquired and its acquisition observed in a progression as a researcher of practice that moves from 'interview' to 'discussion' to 'conversation' as the science is increasingly understood (Collins & Evans, 2007) will be kept in mind when we consider how common knowledge is created and used as a basis of inter-professional negotiations in Chapters 3 and 4.

The processes of interpretation and negotiation are crucial to working with distributed expertise in the exercise of relational agency. The development of relational agency as an organising concept has been an attempt to get beyond analyses of role and expert knowledge in shifting work systems, to focus instead on the decision-making, acting and orchestration of work on complex problems which change as they are worked on. Barley and Kunda (2001) point to the need for this kind of approach to understanding work and its conditions:

> In everyday life roles are dynamic and behavioural; not only are their components negotiated and renegotiated in the flow of activity, but over time old roles disappear and new ones emerge .... What is required is a conceptualisation of role that emphasises action and interaction and that also articulates with an image of organisational structure in an empirically specifiable manner. (Barley & Kunda, 2001: 89)

The task is not an easy one: it calls for linking the agency of the practitioner with the motives of the practice while considering the implications for the institutions in which these practices are located. However, notions of relational agency and relational expertise encourage practitioners to assume an outward looking stance while working on complex problems, in doing so the raison d'être of activities is not to sustain routines or simply meet pre-determined targets, but to engage with others on complex tasks using the best resources available. In Chapter 7 I examine what this means for organisations.

1.7 The Evidence Base

In the chapters that follow I draw mainly on five studies[1] which I have undertaken with colleagues in the past 10 years. These studies have, among other things, examined how practitioners, in what are loosely termed the caring professions, have responded to policy demands that they work more relationally across professional boundaries and with service users to prevent the social exclusion of vulnerable children, young people and adults. The ideas of relational agency and the distribution of expertise have been refined in these studies, but they originated in my earlier

1.7 The Evidence Base

research on teacher development in schools and informal learning in the community. All of these studies have in some way been framed by the work of Vygotsky and those who have developed his legacy in an attempt to capture the interplay between individual learning and the repositioning in practices that can occur as a result and the sensitivity of institutions to changes in practices arising from the repositioning of practitioners. I shall not outline the studies as they have been discussed elsewhere, and I shall reference them when I draw on them.

These ideas have also been tested in doctoral studies at the Oxford Centre for Socio-cultural and Activity Theory Research (OSAT), which have included examining the negotiations that occur in on-line affinity groups, work-based learning, interdisciplinary collaborations based in e-science and supervisory relationships in higher education. I shall also draw, as I have already, on the ProLearn[2] study at the University of Oslo, which compared the professional learning of auditors, computer engineers, nurses and teachers (Jensen, Lahn and Nerland, in press). This study was framed by Knorr Cetina's work on epistemic cultures, knowledge machineries, knowledge ties and knowledge objects. Its attention to how practitioners are positioned in relation to knowledge and the forms of production of knowledge within their practices usefully augments my Vygotsky-based examination of expertise and expert action.

The systemic and cultural analyses afforded by Vygotsky's intellectual legacy will therefore be an important background to the discussions of practices, activities and action that are to be fore-grounded. I shall not assume a reader's broad knowledge of this legacy, but will explain it in the discussions where necessary. While focusing on practices and expertise, I shall claim that relational agency is a useful addition to the analytic tool-box that is being developed by Vygotskian researchers, as well as having implications for professional development and the structuring of practices at an institutional level. In particular, by focusing on object-oriented interpersonal negotiations in and across practices, I shall suggest that it tackles a much neglected element in CHAT, which has perhaps underplayed the more micro-interactional aspects of systemic change.

Notes

1. The five studies were:

    (i) Part of a study of family learning funded by the Joseph Rowntree Charitable Trust, with L. Mackenzie, S. Ranson and H. Rutledge – referred to in the book as the Drop in Centre Study;
    (ii) a DfES-funded National Evaluation of the Children's Fund with M. Barnes, K. Morris and I. Plewis – referred t o as NECF;
    (iii) an ESRC-TLRP Phase III study 'Learning in and for Interagency Working' ESRC RES-139-25-01 with H. Daniels, J. Leadbetter, D. Martin, D. Middleton, P. Warmington, A Apostolov, A Popova and S. Brown – referred to as LIW;
    (iv) an ESRC funded study RES-000-22-2305 – Expanding Understandings of Inclusion: implications of preventing social exclusion for practices in schools with I. Lunt referred to as PSE; and

(v) a DCSF-funded study of the Early Learning Partnerships Project with M. Evangelou, K, Sylva and T. Smith – referred to as ELPP.

2. The ProLearn study was funded by Norwegian National Council for Research, based at the University of Oslo and led by K. Jensen, L. Lahn and M. Nerland.

References

Aretxaga, B. (2001). Engendering violence: Strip-searching of women in Northern Ireland. In D. Holland & J. Lave (Eds.), *History in person* (pp. 37–61). Oxford: James Currey.
Barley, S., & Kunda, G. (2001). Bringing work back in. *Organization Science, 12*(1), 77–95.
Benhabib., S. (1992). *Situating the self*. New York, NY: Routledge.
Bourdieu, P. (1977). *Outline of a theory of practice*. Cambridge: Cambridge University Press.
Cole, M. (1996). *Cultural psychology: A once and future discipline*. Cambridge, MA: Harvard University Press.
Collins, H. (2004). Interactional expertise as a third kind of knowledge. *Phenomenology and the Cognitive Sciences, 3*, 125–143.
Collins, H., & Evans, R. (2007). *Rethinking expertise*. Chicago, IL: University of Chicago Press.
Collins, H., Evans, R., Ribeiro, R., & Hall, M. (2006). Experiments with interactional expertise. *Studies in History of Philosophy of Science, 37*, 656–674.
Daniels, H., Cole, M., & Wertsch J. V. (Eds.) (2007). *The Cambridge companion to Vygotsky*. Cambridge: Cambridge University Press.
Edwards, A. (2005). Relational agency: Learning to be a resourceful practitioner. *International Journal of Educational Research, 43*(3), 168–182.
Edwards, A. (2009). Relational agency in collaborations for the wellbeing of children and young people. *Journal of Children's Services, 4*(1), 33–43.
Edwards, A., & Apostolov, A. (2007). A cultural-historical interpretation of resilience: The implications for practice. *Outlines: Critical Social Studies, 9*(1), 70–84.
Edwards, A., Daniels, H., Gallagher, T., Leadbetter, J., & Warmington, P. (2009). *Improving inter-professional collaborations: Multi-agency working for children's wellbeing*. London: Routledge.
Edwards, A., & Kinti, I. (2009). Working relationally at organisational boundaries: Negotiating expertise and identity. In H. Daniels, A. Edwards, Y. Engeström & S. Ludvigsen (Eds.), *Activity theory in practice: Promoting learning across boundaries and agencies* (pp. 126–139). London: Routledge.
Edwards, A., Lunt, I., & Stamou, E. (2010). Inter-professional work and expertise: New roles at the boundaries of schools. *British Educational Research Journal, 36*(1), 27–45.
Edwards, A., & Mackenzie, L. (2005). Steps towards participation: The social support of learning trajectories. *International Journal of Lifelong Education, 24*(4), 287–302.
Edwards, A., & Mackenzie, L. (2008). Identity shifts in informal learning trajectories. In B. van Oers, E. Elbers, R. van der Veer, & W. Wardekker (Eds.), *The transformation of learning: Advances in cultural-historical activity theory* (pp. 163–181). Cambridge: Cambridge University Press.
Engeström, Y. (1987). *Learning by expanding: An activity-theoretical approach to developmental research*. Helsinki: Orienta-Konsultit.
Engeström, Y. (1999). Activity theory and individual and social transformation. In Y. Engeström, R. Miettinen, & R.-L. Punamäki (Eds.), Perspectives on Activity Theory (pp. 19–38). Cambridge: Cambridge University Press.
Evetts, J. (2003). The sociological analysis of professionalism. *International Sociology, 18*(3), 395–415.
Folgheraiter, F. (2004). *Relational social work: Toward networking in societal practices*. London: Jessica Kingsley.

References

Gunter, H. (2007). Remodelling the school workforce in England: A study in tyranny. *Journal for Critical Education Policy Studies*, 5(1), 1–11.

Hakkarainen, K., Palonen, T., Paavola, S., & Lehtinen, E. (2004). *Communities of networked expertise: Professional and educational perspectives*. Amsterdam: Elsevier.

Hedegaard, M. (2009). A cultural-historical theory of children's development. In M. Hedegaard & M. Fleer (Eds.), *Studying children: A cultural-historical approach* (pp. 10–29). Buckingham: Open University Press.

Holland, D., Lachicotte, W., Skinner, D., & Cain, C. (1998). *Identity and agency in cultural worlds*. Cambridge, MA: Harvard University Press.

Holland, D., & Lave, J. (Eds.) (2001). *History in person*. Oxford: James Currey.

Hood, C. (1991). A public management for all seasons. *Public Administration*, 69(Spring), 3–19.

Hood, C., & Peters, G. (2004). The middle aging of New Public Management: Into the age of paradox?. *Journal of Public Administration Research and Theory*, 4(3), 267–282.

Hunter, S., & Ritchie, P. (Eds.) (2007). *Co-production and personalisation in social care*. London: Jessica Kingsley.

Jensen, K., & Lahn, L. (2005). The binding role of knowledge: An analysis of nursing students' knowledge ties. *Journal of Education and Work*, 18(3), 305–320.

Jensen, K., Lahn, L., & Nerland, M. (Eds.) (in press). *Professional learning in the knowledge society*. Rotterdam: Sense.

Knorr Cetina, K. (1997). Sociality with objects: Social relations in post-social knowledge societies. *Theory Culture Society*, 14(1), 1–29.

Knorr Cetina, K. (1999). *Epistemic cultures: How sciences make knowledge*. Cambridge, MA: Harvard University Press.

Knorr Cetina, K. (2001). Objectual practice. In T. Schatzki, K. Knorr Cetina, & E. von Savigny (Eds.), *The Practice turn in contemporary theory* (pp. 175–188). London: Routledge.

Kubiak, C. (2010). Paraprofessional development in the UK. In T. Seddon, L. Henriksson, & B. Niemeyer (Eds.), *Learning and work and the politics of working life* (pp. 123–141). London: Routledge.

Lave, J., & Wenger, E. (1991). *Situated learning: Legitimate peripheral participation*. Cambridge: Cambridge University Press.

Leadbeater, C. (2004). *Personalisation through participation*. London: DEMOS.

Leont'ev, A. N. (1978). *Activity, consciousness and personality*. Upper Saddle River, NJ: Prentice Hall.

Mäkitalo, Å. (2003). Accounting practices as situated knowing: Dilemmas and dynamics in institutional categorization. *Discourse Studies*, 5(4), 465–519.

Mäkitalo, Å. (2006). Effort on display: Unemployment and interactional management of moral accountability. *Symbolic Interaction*, 29(4), 531–556.

Makitälo, Å., & Säljö, R. (2002). Invisible people: Institutional reasoning and reflexivity in the production of services and 'social facts' in public employment agencies. *Mind, Culture, and Activity*, 9(3), 160–178.

Mehan, H. (1993). Beneath the skin and between the ears: Case study in the politics of representation. In S. Chaiklin & J. Lave (Eds.), *Understanding practice: Perspectives on activity and context* (pp. 241–268). Cambridge: Cambridge University Press.

Nardi, B., Whittaker, S., & Schwarz, H. (2002). NetWORKers and their activity in intensional networks. *Computer Supported Cooperative Work*, 11(1–2), 205–242.

Nerland, M. (2008). Knowledge cultures and the shaping of work-based learning: The case of computer engineering. *Vocations and Learning: Studies in Vocational and Professional Education*, 1, 49–69.

Nowotny, H. (2000). Transgressive competence: The narrative of expertise. *European Journal of Social Theory*, 3(1), 5–21.

Nowotny, H. (2003). Dilemma of expertise. *Science and Public Policy*, 30(3), 151–156.

Østerland, C., & Carlile, P. (2005). Relations in practice: Sorting through practice theories on knowledge sharing in complex organizations. *The Information Society*, 21, 91–107.

Ranson, S. (2003). Public accountability in the age of neo-liberal governance. *Journal of Education Policy, 18*(5), 459–480.

Roth, M., Tobin., K., Elemsky, R., Carambo, C., McKnight, Y.-M., & Beers, J. (2004). Re/making identities in the praxis of urban schooling: A cultural historical perspective. *Mind, Culture, and Activity, 1*(11), 48–69.

Taylor, C. (1989). *Sources of the self: The making of modern identity*. Cambridge: Cambridge University Press.

Wertsch, J. V. (2007). Mediation. In H. Daniels, M. Cole, & J. V. Wertsch (Eds.), *The Cambridge companion to Vygotsky* (pp. 178–192). New York, NY: Cambridge University Press.

Wilensky, H. (1964). The professionalization of everyone?. *The American Journal of Sociology, 70*(2), 137–158.

Chapter 2
Expertise: The Relational Turn

2.1 Expertise in Task Accomplishment

This chapter is about one aspect of expertise: working resourcefully with others. In Chapter 1 (Section 1.6), I suggested that this expertise involves being able to make what matters for you as a professional visible, and being able to negotiate interpretations and responses to complex problems that incorporate what others can offer. It is a task-oriented expertise that involves a sensitivity to the standpoints and values of those you are working with.

The starting point for my attempts to unpack the relational aspects of expertise was the 1996 account of expertise offered by Engeström and Middleton. They described it as the 'collaborative and discursive construction of tasks, solutions, visions, breakdowns and innovations' within and across systems rather than individual mastery of specific areas of relatively stable activity (Engeström & Middleton, 1996: 4). It was presented there, in line with Engeström's focus on systemic change, as a collective attribute which is spread across systems and which is drawn upon to accomplish tasks. It therefore lies in both the system and in individuals' abilities to recognise and negotiate its use.

My main focus, based on an interest in how practitioners work, is not the system, but the middle layer of relational action that lies analytically between the system and the individual and which is connected to both. As I discuss views of expertise in this chapter, I will move between the relational aspects of activities and the practices that comprise the systemic in order to understand how relational task accomplishment is achieved. This shifting focus will also pick up two concerns from the previous chapter (Section 1.6): the need to see relational activity in terms of the 'fluid social relations' identified as important by Østerland and Carlile (2005: 105) and Barley and Kunda's concern for articulating changes in roles and relationships 'with an image of organisational structure' (2001: 89).

2.2 Psychological Accounts of Expertise and Environment

While my attention to action in activities in practices may appear to be different from standard psychological accounts of individual expertise, that assumption would not do justice to some well-developed themes in psychological research on expertise. Feltovich, Prietula, and Ericsson (2006), for example, indicate a strong sensitivity to contextual affordances in recent research on expert performance:

> Experts certainly know more, but they also know differently. Expertise is appropriately viewed not as simple (and often short-term) matter of fact or skill acquisition, but rather as a complex *construct* of adaptations of mind and body, which include substantial self-monitoring and control mechanisms, to task environments in service of representative task goals and activities ... the nature of adaptations reflects differential demands of the task environment and mediates the performance evidenced by highly skilled individuals. Adaptation matters . . . .. (Feltovich et al., 2006: 57)

This view reflects a distancing, in the study of personal expertise, from the focus on rational decision-making in Artificial Intelligence, which dominated research on expertise for so much of the latter part of the past century. Here, instead, the psychological 'subject' is described in interactions with the environment, which are mediated by their expertise. Expertise is evident in the capacity to read the environment and to respond so that intentional action can be achieved. While this account of expertise does not go as far as to acknowledge the intertwining of mind, action and practice over time that is central to the Vygotskian view of human development, attention to adaptation brings this theme closer to relational concerns than studies which have focused on rational choice.

Research on expert teams similarly connects at times with many of the points about relational work outlined in the previous chapter. Salas, Rosen, Burke, Goodwin, and Fiore (2006: 440) listed the current state of knowledge about expert teams broadly as follows:

- team members need to be able to combine their individual technical expertise and co-ordinate their actions to achieve a common goal in such a way that their actions seem fluid;
- they need to possess routine expertise to be able to solve problems quickly and understand them in terms of principles and concepts;
- members must be able to flexibly apply existing knowledge structures, so that when faced with a novel situation they can make predictions and invent new procedures;
- expert teams seem to hold shared mental models of the task, the situation, their team members and the equipment which produce 'implicit' co-ordination; and
- they must possess 'adaptive expertise', i.e. the ability to invent new procedures based on knowledge: the key to adaptive expertise is a deep understanding of the domain.

The ideas of relational expertise and relational agency outlined in Section 1.6 are, however, not limited to teamwork: joint responses to complex problems need not necessarily involve people in being team members. Practitioners may instead be elements in a networked or even loosely linked system of expertise where participants, at different times, are focused on the same problem space. Nonetheless, the importance to expert teamwork of common goals, understandings of others, 'adaptive expertise' and deep knowledge of the core domain suggest that, from a psychological standpoint, the study of relational expertise as an additional form of expertise to be developed alongside core expertise may be worthwhile.

Another relevant theme in psychological work on expertise is Sternberg's 'prototype' view of expertise. Arguing that success in task accomplishment is determined by one's analytic, creative and practical abilities, which improve with practice and experience (Cianciolo, Matthew, Sternberg, & Wagner, 2006), Sternberg has suggested that experts differ from novices in three ways. In his influential paper on teacher expertise he outlined the differences as follows:

> The first difference pertains to domain knowledge. Experts bring knowledge to bear more effectively on problems within their domains of expertise than do novices. The second difference pertains to efficiency of problem solving. Experts do more in less time (in their domain of expertise) than do novices. The third difference pertains to insight. Experts are more likely to arrive at novel and appropriate solutions to problems (again, within their domains) than are novices. Together, these three differences between experts and novices comprise our current best guess about the features, or constellations of features, upon which a prototype of the expert teacher should be founded. (Sternberg & Horvath, 1995: 10)

The prototype view of expertise was presented in the paper as a way of recognising teachers' expertise in terms of 'family resemblance' or a 'summary representation' of the qualities of experts, which Sternberg and Horvath regarded as 'generative' rather than closing down a view of what teacher expertise is. It emphasized the ability to use knowledge to act on problems and how knowledge and experience can produce insight. It was not assumed that all teachers would become expert by following a simple staged pathway from novice to expert, but that judgments could be made about a profile of expertise by looking across the three broad areas they outlined.

Importantly, expertise is seen by Sternberg and his colleagues as domain-specific and likely to be developed in response to environmental conditions, i.e. 'expertise and its requisite knowledge skills and abilities are defined quite differently, depending on the environment in which people develop and express their expertise' (Cianciolo et al., 2006: 614). These ideas were refined in Sternberg and Wagner's (1992) work on practical intelligence and tacit knowledge, but also resonate strongly with Vygotsky's view that our consciousness, how we make sense of the world in order to act in and on it, is shaped by the activities in which we take part. Managing actions, therefore, involves managing the systems in which minds are formed. I shall return to how expertise is developed throughout this chapter.

Expertise, according to the psychological accounts offered in this section, involves interpreting, assessing and responding. But these accounts also recognize that actions do not usually occur through a process of systematic rational decision-making where facts are marshalled and alternatives are weighed: most of the activities where expertise is required are too complex. Intuition therefore plays a part in the adaptations that people make in order to accomplish tasks.

Dreyfus and Dreyfus (1986, 2005; Dreyfus H., 2006) have long argued, from a phenomenological standpoint, against simplistic rule-based analyses of expertise and expert systems promoted in much Artificial Intelligence research, and for recognising the importance of intuition. For example, in a 1991 paper they brought the affective aspects of decision-making into a description of expert ethical action by proposing that even when experts meet novel problems they do not produce strong decisions if they depend only on abstract principles. The decisions people make are 'crude' because 'they have not been refined by the experience of the results of a variety of intuitive responses to emotion-laden situations and the experience that comes from subsequent satisfaction and regret' (1991: 241). They were describing an engaged expertise taken forward by 'what matters', and 'what matters' has arisen in practices that are laden with knowledge, values and emotions.

Recognising the expertise that lies in relational task accomplishment is therefore not at odds with the lines taken in this brief overview of some themes and associated debates in recent psychological work on expertise. Two aspects of the overview particularly resonate with the discussion of notions of expertise within the literature that is based on Vygotsky's work and which I shall turn to next. The first is attention to the purposeful and agentic decision-maker. The second is the recognition that these decisions are mediated by expectations of what matters and what might be possible, which are both personal and cultural. The expectations lead, in turn, to adaptations as task accomplishment is negotiated.

2.3 Starting with the Cultural

While some of the psychological accounts of expertise have moved towards context-sensitive explanations, some anthropological accounts have gone a deal further by recognising that individuals can work agentically with, and indeed take control over, the social practices in which they develop expertise. Holland's analyses of the figured worlds in which identities are formed (Holland & Lachicotte, 2007; Holland, Lachicotte, Skinner, & Cain, 1998) have been particularly influential, taking us some of the way towards Barley and Kunda's concern with connecting understandings of fluid role relationships with an image of organisational structure discussed in Section 1.6. Holland and her colleagues explain:

> By "figured world" then, we mean a socially and culturally constructed realm of interpretation in which particular characters and actors are recognized, significance is assigned to certain acts, and particular outcomes are valued over others. Each is a simplified world populated by a set of agents ... who engage in a limited range of meaningful acts ... these collective 'as if' worlds are sociohistoric, contrived imaginations that mediate behavior and so ... inform participants' outlooks. (Holland et al., 1998: 52)

Figured worlds are sites made up of social practices where expertise is acquired, developed and exercised. In Holland's work these sites have included the practices that sustain the romantic lives of college students and attempts by non-drinking alcoholics to establish and sustain figured worlds, in which it is difficult for them to revert to drinking. The interplay between the figured worlds of practices and people's actions within in them is central to an explanation of how people become expert

2.3 Starting with the Cultural

within these worlds. Holland's account of becoming expert draws primarily on her study of how women students in a college in the south east of the United States develop and employ expertise in the world of romance. The analysis is, however, relevant to how specialist identities are formed and come to mediate the development of expertise in the workplace.

Drawing on the Dreyfus and Dreyfus (1986) ladder of developing expertise, which runs in stages from novice through advanced beginner, competency and proficiency to expertise, Holland and her colleagues (1998) note that in the final three stages there is a qualitative change in the relationship between individual and system. This change is marked by people moving on from mainly following rules to being able to devise their own moves. This change, Holland et al. suggest, means that individuals begin to understand themselves in terms of the activity as it occurs in the cultural world, or in the terms of the present book, in an activity in a practice. This shift means that people can manipulate the practices to take forward their intentional actions.

'Identification' with the figured world is the term preferred by Holland et al. This they see as 'the formation of a concept of self as an actor in a culturally devised system' (1998: 120). Identification, they suggest, is evident when 'the figured world in which one has been acting according to the directions of others becomes a world that one uses to understand and organize aspects of one's self and at least some of one's own feelings and thoughts' (p. 121). In other words, expertise is evident in how one employs the resources of the figured world to carry out culturally appropriate and intentional actions. It is also more than that, as actions are given direction by the culturally valued motives which people appropriate as individuals.

Motivations and their cultural origins are therefore also important. Lave (1988: 181) explains the cultural origins of motives in ways which connect with the present analytic focus on activities in practices: 'priority, perspective and value are continuously and inescapably generated in activity'. Personal engagement or identification with the motives embedded in activities in practices does appear to be an important aspect of expert work. For example, as a social worker becomes expert in the activities in which he/she participates, he/she becomes less of a rule follower and more identified with social work practice and its deeper and longer-term purposes. Motivation is, therefore, neither simply internal nor only in the practices: it arises in people's activities in practices. Dreyfus, S. has outlined the importance of emotional engagement in activities as a sign of expertise:

> As the competent performer becomes more and more emotionally involved in a task, it becomes increasingly difficult for him or her to draw back and adopt the detached, rule-following stance of the beginner. If the detached stance of the novice and advanced beginner is replaced by involvement, and the learner accepts the anxiety of choice, he or she is set for further skill advancement. Then, the resulting positive and negative emotional experiences will strengthen successful perspectives and inhibit unsuccessful ones, and the performer's theory of the skill, as represented by rules and principles, will gradually be replaced by situational discriminations. (Dreyfus, 2004: 179)

Situational discrimination appears to be quite central to cultural accounts of expertise. However, although Holland and Lave (2001) offer poignant examples of the historicity of personal identity as people move into new-to-them practices, the accounts of culturally based figured worlds discussed so far have not tackled what happens when people enter unfamiliar figured worlds in order to work with others on complex problems.

There are individually oriented explanations of how people make sense of unfamiliar practices and how transitions into new practices may be eased by ensuring that the differences between the old and the new are not too great (Greeno, 1997, 2006; Lave, 1988). There are also analyses which suggest convincingly that what are important in transitions into new practices are the 'consequences' – for their sense of who they are and want to be – of the adaptations that people make in order to function in the new practices (Beach, 1999).

However, there are few accounts of what moving out of the safety of what Sennett (1999: 21) has called 'institutional supports' for action, means for practitioners who need to negotiate task accomplishment with others in activities where their expertise is not shored up by a historically accumulated set of practices which they can expertly navigate and manipulate. Rather, the cultural account of expertise presents quite starkly how difficult it can be to be expert when working relationally with others outside the practices with which one has become identified.

The cultural arguments pursued in this book offer two, compatible, ways forward. The first is to extend the line offered by Lave and look to the 'constitutive order ' or 'structuring resources' (1988: 189) to be found in practices and to recognise, as Lave does, that transformations of activities can be seen as open-ended and in interaction with the practices in which they are located. For example, as practitioners find themselves working together in fluid, responsive and family-oriented activities one might expect that the practices which are shaping the activities and the knowledge and values embedded in them will adjust to accommodate changes in professional activity. As we shall see, this is not always inevitable, particularly when practices have become routines set up to protect practitioners. The second possibility is, in line with the arguments offered in Chapter 1 (Section 1.6), that we recognise the need for an additional layer of relationally oriented expertise which enables this more fluid way of working.

2.4 Distributed Expertise

The Engeström and Middleton description of expertise as the 'collaborative and discursive construction of tasks, solutions, visions, breakdowns and innovations' within and across systems (1996: 4) set the scene for the analyses of distributed cognition and communication at work that comprised the papers in their 1996 edited collection. The contributions reflected developments in understanding cognition as distributed in activities and across settings that had been underway over the previous ten or so years. Lave had earlier outlined this new approach to understanding how action is directed and supported as follows:

> "Cognition" observed in everyday practice is distributed – stretched over, not divided among – mind, body, activity and culturally organized settings. (Lave, 1988: 1)

2.4 Distributed Expertise

These ideas were taken up quite broadly. Bruner, for example, has discussed the extended intelligence of research labs (Bruner, 1996). Hutchins' studies of the activity of bringing a large naval vessel into port and of operating in an aeroplane cockpit (Hutchins & Klausen, 1996; Hutchins, 1995) illustrated this new approach in detail. He took the system of distributed cognition in the work system as a unit of analysis, which allowed him to foreground different aspects of it. These aspects included the formation and violation of expectations, inter-subjectivity in communication between the officers, the off-loading of memory onto artefacts, and the representations of relevant knowledge offered by these artefacts. These different facets interacted to create what Hutchins and Klausen described as a 'complex cognitive system' (1996: 33).

Systemic analyses of human interactions with each other and with material artefacts, which are potentially loaded with knowledge, have also had an impact on the design of computer-mediated learning environments (Clark, 1997; Littleton & Light, 1999; Pea, 1993). This work has demonstrated that environments can be designed so that actors can draw easily on the intelligence located in artefacts. Pea's highly influential 1993 paper, for example, was an attempt to shift emphases from interactional or social approaches to the support of learning and instead to show how intelligent artefacts can support action. What Pea described as 'distributed intelligence' can be seen as a resource that is distributed across people and artefacts and which can be accessed by participants in the system.

There is now an interest, in studies of workplace learning, in how people draw on the expertise of others. In one example of using others as resources, Nardi, Whittaker and Schwarz (2002) examined the emergence of personal social or 'intensional' networks, describing them as the hidden underpinnings of organisational structures enabling work to be accomplished. Arguing that in new more fluid organisational systems 'It's not what you know, it's who you know', they traced the formation, maintenance and activation of networks in what they describe as netWORK, which benefited both individual workers and their organisations. Here networks were presented as resource-laden and requiring nurturing so that they could be accessed to accomplish the work identified by the netWORKER. However, networks that are centred on individual netWORKERs who define the task and then call upon the resources of others to help them to accomplish it are not illustrating the exercise of relational agency. Relational agency, as we saw in Chapter 1 (Section 1.6), emphasises working together to interpret the problem as well as collaborating to respond to it.

'Knotworking' (Engeström, 2008; Engeström, Engeström, & Vähäaho, 1999) comes closer to meeting the kind of challenge offered by collaboration on a complex problem where each specialist contributes to the diagnosis of the problem. By focusing on the bringing together of loosely connected people to work on complex tasks over relatively short periods, Knotworking certainly captures the ebb and flow of work as, for example, medical practitioners from different teams co-operate to save a life. However, while they may bring different expertise to bear, the work settings were rarely inter-professional, but were, for example, health-care workers, with a shared set of professional values working in a system which was in place to enable the bringing together. Engeström has started to tackle the more challenging aspects of inter-professional work in what he describes as 'fluid organizational fields' at the level of the system (Engeström, 2005, 2008), and I shall return to these developments later in Section 2.6 and in Chapter 4 (Section 4.1).

Gherardi and Nocolini (2002) have studied collaboration across more distinct boundaries between practices in their research on how engineers, site managers and contractors in a building co-operative negotiate an understanding of safety that meets their different criteria while working on a common building project. Using the metaphor of 'a constellation of interconnected practices', they suggested that learning to operate together can be seen as a form of 'brokering', which relates situated bodies of knowledge 'to the minimum extent necessary to "perform" the community'. There are certainly strong resonances here with the goal-oriented collaborations and the building of common knowledge as a prerequisite for the exercise of relational agency discussed in Chapters 3 and 4. However, the participants in this study were already connected through their membership of the co-operative; and their expertise, priorities and the timing of their contributions were easily recognizable and could be planned for.

The idea of distributed expertise also has much in common with the Hakkarainen, Palonen, Paavola, and Lehtinen (2004) analyses of communities of networked expertise. They cast their enquiry in terms of the 'skills and competencies needed for the knowledge society' (p. 8) and, in particular, the development of networked expertise. Their aim was to understand better the relations between the 'individual and collective competencies' (p. 9) that occur in networked environments. Their detailed and thoughtful micro level analyses of networked communities, though not at all contradicting the focus on working relationally as a professional in the present book, has slightly less emphasis on how relational work arises, and is negotiated across the boundaries of different institutional practices than is to be found here.

The distributed expertise that we observed while examining practices aimed at the prevention of social exclusion was emergent rather than existing in environments which were already usefully networked. It arose in response to policy demands and funding incentives, which required practitioners to look across a child's life in order to identify the accumulated risk that might make them vulnerable to long-term social exclusion. The professional task was to respond to the vulnerability that was the outcome of, for example, intertwined problems of housing, parental health and language difficulties. One practitioner who spoke to the National Evaluation of the Children's Fund (NECF) (Edwards, Barnes, Plewis, & Morris, 2006) explained the purposes of the new relationships which emerged and which were seen as laden with relevant expertise:

> What we very quickly realized ... is that we could not meet the all the needs of every child and family so what we had to be able to do was at least find access to people who could do that. Either provide the support or provide the service or provide the wherewithal for the children and family to get what it was that they needed.

The expertise observed in NECF was stretched across localities between loosely connected practitioners who had some responsibility for preventing the social

2.4 Distributed Expertise

exclusion of children and young people. Their shared, if sometimes differently interpreted, purpose was crucial to building the trust that made rapid responses possible.

We also encountered examples of long-established networks being used for the new activity of preventing social exclusion. These were signalled by statements like 'I know (name of locality) so I know where to go'. These networks were often driven by their original, and often defunct, purposes and were unable to adapt to the new demands of preventative work. Indeed, there were clear differences in the flexibility and responsiveness of services that were taken forward by the new emergent looser groupings and by the pre-existing networks. The key seemed to be that the old networks were not focused on prevention as a new goal, while the newer groupings shared the common purpose of trying to understand what was meant by the prevention of social exclusion and how they might tackle it. Castells has also pointed to the need to relate networks to purposes if social change is desired:

> ... my hypothesis is that there is little chance of social change within a given network, or network of networks. Understanding by social change, the transformation of the programme of the network, to assign to the network a new goal, following a different set of values and beliefs. (Castells, 2000: 22).

These emergent, flexible configurations of practices, as we shall see in Chapter 3 (Section 3.3), originated in, and were sustained by, meetings where purposes were thrashed out, resources made explicit and trails between services revealed. The configurations were, however, not uniform. In the Learning in and for Interagency Working (LIW) study (Edwards, Daniels, Gallagher, Leadbetter, & Warmington, 2009), we found different types of inter-professional groupings in the three case studies of local authorities at the core of the project: Castletown, Seaside and Wildside.

In Wildside, there was a loosely coupled team which was working with Children in Public Care (CiPC). It was in a local authority where there were exceptionally robust historically embedded inter-professional networks. The temptation to rely entirely on these networks was clearly strong for some practitioners. However, as the team became increasingly sure about the purpose of their preventative work, they became impatient with the lack of precision and engagement with the task that was offered by some of the people who were historically linked with the work of the team. For example, respondents explained that too many people attended team meetings, with the result that there was sometimes confusion about what expertise was actually available. Their response was to create an electronic assessment tool which could hold information about specific children and the responses underway and which could be available to all.

In Castletown, we studied an emergent loose grouping of distributed expertise around a secondary school. A recurrent theme throughout our meetings with participants in the study was the school's isolation from existing and developing systems of expertise in the local authority. At the same time practitioners who were based outside the school were struggling with both knowing what resources were available from other professionals and the thresholds at which other professionals could take action. The lack of clarity about the developing system increased the school practitioners' concerns about working more flexibly outside the tightly bounded practices of the school.

When Wildside and Castletown are compared, two important issues arise. Firstly, the Wildside team had a clear single focus in their work with CiPC, whereas the focus of the Castletown work outside the school was never clear. The idea of a child's trajectory gave coherence to discussions in Castletown, but participants constantly returned to differences in forms of assessment and thresholds for responses. The second difference between the two cases was that, although there was agreement about a focus on children's wellbeing in both sites, in Castletown discussions focused on the difficulties in working together, for example, on how the school's practices needed to prevail. That is, there was a concern with the instrumental aspects of working together. In Wildside, in contrast, the child's trajectory as an agreed object of activity was a reality. Participants could name specific children and, because of their focus on children's wellbeing, participants were able to think about how they might work together to develop alternative futures for them. The tools, both material and conceptual, that they developed in Wildside to enable them to work together reflected their professional values and helped to take forward children's trajectories. The Wildside grouping was oriented clearly towards work on children's long-term wellbeing.

In Seaside, the third case study, we worked with a multi-professional team. As in Wildside, ideas and artefacts which allowed a long-term view of a child's progress and the on-going roles of other professionals were an important part of the team's development. For this reason explaining professional values was crucial, as these shared values operated as a kind of 'glue' helping trust to develop and holding team members together as they looked forward and developed ways of working together.

Across all three cases, the inter-professional collaboration in these different configurations of distributed expertise was mediated by the capacity to 'know how to know who' (can help). Knowing how to know who was not an instrumental skill that could be acquired on a training programme. Rather it arose in discussions of object-oriented purposeful activities in which expertise and values were clarified and where 'know who' could be supported by tools, such as electronic assessment systems, which reflected the professional values that shaped the engagement of professionals with clients. The trust that developed was not the trust born of old well-established relationships, but of mutual respect as professionals oriented towards the same goals for children.

We were not alone in recognising the importance of 'know who'. Lundvall, working in the area of development economics, has long argued that 'know who' is an important aspect of knowledge at work alongside know what, how and why:

> Know-who involves information about who knows to do what. But especially it involves the social capability to establish relationships to specialized groups in order to draw on their expertise. (Lundvall, 1996: 7)

Lundvall argues that 'know who' is embedded and learnt in social practice, and cannot simply be codified into, for example, a register of names, though lists of

2.4 Distributed Expertise

names of local professionals are useful. What seems to matter is how and why the tools such as lists are used in task accomplishment in the activities to which the connected practitioners contribute.

I have so far avoided the term practice when discussing what these inter-professional configurations do, as earlier I described practices as arising in institutions and carrying strong socio-historical legacies, which give shape to the activities that occur within them. Networks and similar groupings are likely to be less stable and more open to change of purpose and configuration. Nonetheless, evidence from these studies does suggest that the networks were not ephemeral systems of information exchange, but instead exhibited features of practices: values, understandings and expectations. They were not, however, exhibiting routines: rather, people were working in-relation-to each other in fluid responses on complex problems and the knowledge they contributed was important to working on, and transforming, the object of activity which was, in each case, children's developmental trajectories.

The practitioners were bound together not only by common purposes but also by a reciprocal need for the knowledge that others could bring to bear. These were not the kinds of knowledge exchanges characterized by Hakkarainen et al. (2004) as 'weak' ties, which were 'context free and independently understandable' (2004: 75). They were nearer to what that team described as 'strong' ties, which dealt with complex knowledge and were context bound; but as I have already indicated in Section 1.6, they did not exhibit all the qualities of strong ties. People were not being drawn into the knowledge cultures of each participating expert: rather, they were learning how to access enough specialist knowledge to allow them to expand their interpretations of children's vulnerability and to align their responses.

These knowledge ties are different from the knowledge ties that hold together distinct professional groups, such as the nurses in the Jensen and Lahn study (2005) discussed in Chapter 1 (Section 1.5). It seems that practitioners in the NECF and LIW studies were learning a form of *networking*, which recognised that each contributed to and drew on the resources in local systems to accomplish complex tasks. The capacity for a type of the relational expertise outlined in Chapter 1 (Section 1.6) is clearly important to networking, if what one practitioner offers is to be recognised and ultimately aligned with responses that have arisen in other specialist practices. The distributed expertise revealed in the NECF and LIW studies was located in local systems, which could also involve face-to-face meetings, and was focused on solving problems that required different kinds of specialist knowledge. While not exactly connected through 'strong' knowledge ties in the Hakkarainen et al. sense, they were bound together by a broadly common purpose when they worked together.

These configurations of different professionals were, however, quite different from the kinds of on-line knowledge networks used by masters students at Oxford to sustain their academic and social identities who are discussed by Francis (2007, in press). They were also different from the computer engineers in the ProLearn study who developed expert knowledge through on-line communication with other computer engineers (Nerland, 2008) (see Section 1.2). In both of these studies, although participants both gave and received knowledge from other network participants, they were seeking knowledge to help them solve problems that they identified and were working on independently. These networks were therefore not similar to the purposeful task-oriented systems we studied in the local authorities. Indeed, in Francis' study, some of the networks were quite loosely organised affinity groups where the relative proportion of asking and giving might depend very much on the level of expertise of each participant. Indeed, these on-line networks demonstrated many of the characteristics of coherent communities of expert practice, if somewhat widely distributed, rather than sites where different types of expertise might be made visible to work on a jointly constructed problem.

2.5 Networking Without Knowledge

As much as working with locally distributed expertise can be seen as a way of combining skills to achieve the best outcomes for children, there is the danger that the knowledge available in networks may be used as resource to support the work of under-qualified staff. One of the studies on inter-professional work for the prevention of social exclusion mentioned in Chapter 1 (Edwards, Lunt, & Stamou, 2010) offers such an example. It is discussed in more detail in Chapter 6 (Section 6.3).

The preventing social exclusion (PSE) study set out to identify how secondary schools were adjusting to new policy demands that they work more collaboratively with other services for children in their localities. We had expected to see changes in the structures and practices of schools such as more open boundaries around the schools and a stronger focus on the child as an active participant in society and not simply as a pupil. However, the schools' response to these new demands was to take advantage of what the English government calls 'workforce remodelling' (Gunter, 2007) and to appoint unqualified teaching assistants (TA) to new roles, which we labelled welfare managers. These workers then took on responsibility for pupil wellbeing in and outside the schools.

The study revealed that, rather than provoking changes in the academic systems of the schools, the new demands for inter-professional working led to the development of new spaces of action at the boundaries of the schools. These spaces were distinctly different from the academic systems of the schools and were populated by, among others, welfare managers, community police, children and family workers, mental health specialists, and practitioners working with children in public care. Work in the new spaces centred on building new professional networks to support vulnerable children. This activity was seen as 'plugging a gap' and was in almost every case being driven forward by the welfare managers who needed to access the specialist advice of the professionals I have just listed.

They needed that advice because, although they were described by teachers as 'completely there for the children' as they were unconstrained by the rigid practices of schools, they had no professional knowledge-base. In order to do their jobs, they therefore relied heavily on their capacity for 'know who'.

The activities carried out by the welfare managers included many of the features to be expected of being a professional. They were propelled forward by long-term value-laden goals related to children's wellbeing, which gave shape to their

2.5 Networking Without Knowledge

actions and their negotiations (Engeström, 2005; Pickering, 1995); they negotiated these actions with children and other professionals (Nixon, Martin, McKeown, & Ranson, 1997); they made judgments about how to work with children (Glisson & Hemmelgarn, 1998); and they carved out new object-oriented practices rather than complying to standard sets of expectations (Edwards et al., 2009). However, they lacked a solid knowledge-base of the kind that has traditionally marked being a professional (Wilensky, 1964).

Their capacity to carry out their work depended almost entirely on their knowledge of locally distributed expertise. Their expertise was context-dependent. 'Know who' was all and they were consequently keen to learn as much as possible about the professional knowledge that was distributed locally. They described their expertise in terms of their building local support networks through attending 1-day courses where 'know who' was the main knowledge outcome. It seems that the welfare managers were inhabiting and shaping the affinity or solution spaces identified by Hartley (2007).

Hartley argued that these spaces, which intersect existing organisational structures, are necessary if public service provision is to cope with personalised support for its clients, but they also need to be recognised as associations rather than communities. At worst, they are 'calculative' (p. 699) networks rather than permanent or deep connections and, at best, they represent the looser and more widespread 'connections' (p. 699) of which are representative of what Bauman (2000) has referred to as 'liquid modernity'.

Hartley's argument is focused on the implications of these new 'inter' spaces for forms of governance and policy-making. However, they also represent new spaces of action where the knowledge and values that are embedded in existing professional practices need to be renegotiated. Practitioners who lack core professional knowledge are, I suggest, unable to contribute to the developing practices and take part in networks as users of the resources offered by others. Substituting networked support for core knowledge is a worrying development. Some element of exclusive knowledge which can be contributed to the joint interpretation and response of problems is important.

Nowotny's (2003) analysis that 'Experts must now extend their knowledge ... to building links and trying to integrate what they know with what others want to or should know and do' (p. 155) is worth reiterating, if only to remind us of the importance to others of what people know. Relational agency requires that practitioners are not only able to recognise and draw on the expertise that is distributed across local systems but also to contribute to it.

But this lack of attention to the knowledge-base of expert practice is not unique to the position of women in some of the areas of child and family work. Lundsteen's current DPhil (Lundsteen, in preparation) is set in an investment bank where she is studying how interns, in their summer vacation placements, navigate the practices of the bank and begin to shape their identities in line with its cultural practices. The data were collected 2 years before the bank was quite dramatically reshaped by the recession, which hit the industry in 2008. The over-reliance on 'know who' rather than core knowledge was alarming. One intern who was studying physics at university illustrates this reliance with his description of the trading floor on which he was working:

> The thing is I'm not sure yet whether people can just bypass ... certainly in physics you can't bypass, like, the foundations of the knowledge that you want to achieve, 'cause then the knowledge of what you have achieved is worthless and you can't adapt it ... It seems that it is possible to me that you can do that in finance. You can have knowledge that has no real underpinning, and you can still be a good trader. So I think maybe something you have to learn about having a professional job is that, like, you don't have time to understand like in academia, you just have to understand enough to be able to do your job.
>
> I didn't understand before at all that guys that are, say, real money investors, they don't have, like, perfect understanding of all the products. They just know vaguely what they do. Like with futures, they know kind of that these things give you exposure to interest rates, but they don't know the specifics because there's so much to learn in this world that, you know ... other people have to know that sort of stuff and they just need to be sold it by kind of having it roughly explained to them; like, this kind of works with interest rates so you can hedge interest rates with it. So I guess the limitations of people's knowledge is something I didn't really realise, you know, gave everyone a bit too much credit.

He was not alone in his misplaced expectations of the core knowledge of traders: his remarks are chillingly prescient of the problems that arose from lack of foundational knowledge that contributed to the 2008 crash.

2.6 Collective Competence and Collaborative Intentions

I am not suggesting that 'knowing how to know who' is unimportant, but that it needs to be connected with other core knowledge. One attempt to make that connection is Boreham's notion of 'collective competence' (Boreham, 2004a, b), which he sees as an attribute of groups, teams and communities. Describing the locally responsive self-managing teams which he studied, as part of the modernising of the workplace, he argued that these teams need to be seen as collectively competent if they are to be responsible for a whole product or service. The argument went that at the centre of this collective competence is the common knowledge-base of the team, which includes both specialist knowledge and a knowledge of work processes. Work process knowledge, he suggested, should not be seen simply as an organisational asset, but as a 'culture to be nurtured' (2004a: 2). Importantly, however, Boreham did not lose sight of the substantive knowledge-base of teams while also urging that team interdependency is nurtured.

Hakkarainen and his colleagues (2004) also use the term collective competence. They have presented a compelling picture of developing and mutually sustaining competence for organisations.

> Intelligent organizations have developed practices of knowledge management because they rely on the cognitive competencies of their employees, and capitalize on competencies emerging through a sustained problem-solving process, rather than found there to begin with. Within a community, people are able to reciprocally strengthen each other's competencies and expertise so that the amount of collective competence is larger than the total sum of individual participants. (Hakkarainen et al., 2004: 214)

2.6 Collective Competence and Collaborative Intentions

Developing this interdependency is, however, particularly demanding when Boreham's common knowledge-base of a 'team' or of Hakkarainen et al.'s 'community' of diverse expertise is absent. Interdependency and the conditions for sustaining it are different when knowledge is brought into play across organizational and professional boundaries which do not share histories, while following an object of activity which is itself always under development, as was the case in the prevention work we studied.

Engeström has been tackling the problem of working on changing objects of activity at the level of loosely connected systems by offering, quite tentatively, two new concepts which he presents as a response to seeing 'the shape and implications of spatio-temporally distributed work and expertise' as 'fragile and open, literally under construction' (Engeström, 2005: 324). His aim is to find a way of reflecting and supporting work under these new conditions. He describes the concepts he offers as 'immature', and presents them with the intention of opening up the field for further theoretical work (Edwards, 2009). They are therefore not a substitute for collective competence, but begin to reveal the challenges involved in expert work outside established practices.

Both of Engeström's new concepts operate at the level of the systemic or collective rather than the individual or the relational. The first is the idea of 'collaborative intentionality capital' as 'an emerging form of organisational assets'. Then, perhaps echoing Knorr Cetina's notion of 'engrossment' (2001: 175) discussed in Section 1.4, the second concept he suggests is the 'tentative concept of object-oriented interagency'. This he sees as a form of 'connecting and reciprocating' while 'circling around a complex object' and 'dwelling in' the object and maintaining a long-term relationship with it (p. 333).

The CHAT recognition that activities are object-oriented and that our interpretations of the problems, or objects of activity, that we are working on are shaped by the historical practices of the systems in which we are operating is central to both concepts. This recognition means that firstly, our interpretation of an object of activity is restricted by the system in which it is located; and secondly, an object may motivate us to act in particular ways by eliciting the responses from us that are permissible within a specific practice.

However, contradictions can arise between systems where a potentially shared object of activity is interpreted very differently. For example, the LIW study revealed large differences in some sites between the ways in which objects of activity, such as children's trajectories, are interpreted in teaching and social work. Engeström's two concepts are intended to help when the contradictions are between systems. He is therefore developing the tools of activity theory (Appendix A) to work on what Blackler and McDonald (2000) have called the 'fluctuating collaborative relations' of an increasing amount of work.

However, while these concepts might alert organisations to the need to orient towards the intention to collaborate, they do, as Engeström suggests, need elaboration. This is certainly the case if we are to understand what is involved in developing the collective competence, or common knowledge-base, and relational expertise needed for collaborative relations. My present contribution is to try to move below the collective level discussed by Engeström to examine how the relational aspects of distributed expertise connect with the knowledge-laden practices to create a propensity for the relational turn in expertise.

2.7 Expertise as Purposeful Engagement in Practices

In Section 2.3, I drew on Holland's work on identity and practices in 'figured worlds' in order to outline a cultural account of identity and its relationship with expertise. In brief, expertise within a set of practices is evident when people can use the practices to propel themselves forward: they manipulate the practices to shape their intentional actions. At the same time I emphasised that these intentional actions are given direction by the culturally valued motives to be found in the practices.

This account of identity formation presupposes the socio-historic development of the practices with which individual actors become identified. Identification with practices, the knowledge carried in them and the values and motives that direct them is important in inter-professional work. Social workers, for example, identify with 'heavy end' child protection work that only social workers can do, rather than with lower level prevention activities that could be carried out without social work qualifications (Jack, 2006), while participants in the LIW study were accused of 'going native' when they described the different priorities of other agencies to their specialist colleagues. We found that people therefore needed to demonstrate their expertise both inside the socio-historic practices which had shaped their professional identities and outside them in the new inter-professional activities where practices intersected and where they may even be in conflict.

The opening up of these intersecting practices, in order to deal responsively and fluidly with complex tasks, undercuts the stability that has been seen as central to the development of professional identities, which are bound up with a shared set of working practices. Sennett outlined the loss of stability as follows.

> The rigid large scale bureaucracies which developed at the end of the nineteenth century provided an institutional architecture in which dependence became honourable, to which the learner could become loyal. Static institutions provide, unfortunately, a framework of daily trust, a reality which has to be acknowledged in thinking about efforts in our own time to take these institutions apart. (Sennett, 1999, p. 19)

Sennett's argument is that we need to be aware of the implications of breaking down these institutional supports and should avoid the rampant individualism that might occur when they are gone. A similar point is made by Folgheraiter (2004) who was worried about whether autonomy and social responsibility in social work might find themselves in conflict.

One element of my response to these concerns is discussed in Chapter 4, where I outline how relational agency can strengthen the actions of practitioners who may, themselves, feel vulnerable while working outside the institutional supports of bureaucracies. The other element is to emphasise the purposes of the manipulation of practices in inter-professional work.

Manipulation is a loaded word. Howard Kirk, Malcolm Bradbury's fictional 'history man' was an expert manipulator of practices to serve his own personal ends, to the point where others were damaged. Inter-professional work may also degenerate into a form of self-serving where the purported object of activity is kept safely out of reach and performance becomes the purpose. However, if inter-professional work is to connect to and benefit society, its values and purposes need to be fore-grounded, made visible and discussed in relation to societal needs.

I am suggesting that the relational turn requires professionals to be both insiders and outsiders in relation to their core practices. Being an insider means maintaining a stake in the practices, knowledge and values that mark a discrete profession while also attempting to contribute to them to help reshape them towards, echoing Engeström (2005), an 'intentionality for collaboration'. Being an outsider means achieving a detached, though not disengaged, perception of the differences that one sees in practices and their purposes across professions. It also involves being able to note distinctions between these different approaches, so that approaches can be discussed, evaluated, refined and taken forward. The figured world of familiar practices is usually invisible to us and those of unfamiliar practices are not, and thoughtful scrutiny of these differences can illuminate the more familiar worlds, help to evaluate the familiar and to adapt actions in activities and ultimately the practices within which the activities are located.

What one foregrounds and how one evaluates are important. Motives are therefore central to inter-professional activities and the practices in which they are located, whether they are discrete or intersecting. The relational turn in expertise is not simply a low-cost way of maximizing competence by seeing others as resources to be drawn upon. Relational work calls for an enhanced form of professionalism, which includes the capacity to identify organisational goals, to question organisational purposes and practices as well as to contribute to and recognise the distributed expertise available to support actions on complex problems.

References

Barley, S., & Kunda, G. (2001). Bringing work back in. *Organization Science, 12*(1), 77–95.

Bauman, Z. (2000). Education policy and the 'inter'-regnum. *Journal of Education Policy, 22*(6), 695–708.

Beach, K. (1999). Consequential transitions: A sociocultural expedition beyond transfer in education. *Review of Research in Education, 24*, 101–139.

Blackler, F., & McDonald, S. (2000). Power, mastery and organisational learning. *Journal of Management Studies, 37*(6), 833–851.

Boreham, N. (2004a, September). *Collective competence and work process knowledge*. European conference on Educational Research, Crete

Boreham, N. (2004b). A theory of collective competence: Challenging the neo-liberal individualisation of performance at work. *British Journal of Educational Studies, 52*(1), 5–17.

Bruner, J. S. (1996). *The culture of education*. Cambridge, MA: Harvard University Press.

Castells, M. (2000). Materials for an exploratory theory of the network society. *British Journal of Sociology, 51*(1), 5–24.

Cianciolo, A., Matthew, C., Sternberg, R., & Wagner, R. (2006). Tacit knowledge, practical intelligence and expertise. In A. Ericsson; N. Charness; P. Feltovich, & R. Hoffman (Eds.),

The Cambridge handbook of expertise and expert performance (pp. 613–632). Cambridge: Cambridge University Press.

Clark, A. (1997). *Being there: Putting brain, body and world together again.* Cambridge, MA: MIT Press.

Dreyfus, S. (2004). The five stage model of adult skill acquisition. *Bulletin of Science, Technology and Society, 24*(3), 177–181.

Dreyfus, H. (2006). Overcoming the myth of the mental. *Topic, 25,* 43–49.

Dreyfus, H., & Dreyfus, S. (1986). *Mind over machine: The power of human intuition and expertise in the era of the computer.* New York, NY: Free Press.

Dreyfus, H., & Dreyfus, S. (1991). Towards a phenomenology of ethical expertise. *Human Studies, 14,* 229–250.

Dreyfus, H., & Dreyfus, S. (2005). Expertise in real world contexts. *Organization Studies, 26*(5), 779–792.

Edwards, A. (2009). Agency and activity theory: From the systemic to the relational. In A. Sannino, H. Daniels, & K. Guttierez (Eds.), *Learning and expanding with activity theory* (pp. 197–211). Cambridge: Cambridge University Press.

Edwards, A., Barnes, M., Plewis, I., & Morris, K. (2006). *Working to prevent the social exclusion of children and young people: Final lessons from the National Evaluation of the Children's Fund.* London: DfES. (Research Report 734).

Edwards, A., Daniels, H., Gallagher, T., Leadbetter, J., & Warmington, P. (2009). *Improving inter-professional collaborations: Multi-agency working for children's wellbeing.* London: Routledge.

Edwards, A., Lunt, I., & Stamou, E. (2010). Inter-professional work and expertise: New roles at the boundaries of schools. *British Educational Research Journal, 30*(1), 27–45.

Engeström, Y. (2005). Knotworking to create collaborative intentionality capital in fluid organizational fields. In M. M. Beyerlein, S. T. Beyerlein, & F. A. Kennedy (Eds.), *Collaborative capital: Creating intangible value* (pp. 307–336). Amsterdam: Elsevier.

Engeström, Y. (2008). *From teams to knots: Activity theoretical studies of collaboration and learning at work.* Cambridge: Cambridge University Press.

Engeström, Y., Engeström, R., & Vähäaho, T. (1999). When the center does not hold: The importance of knotworking. In S. Chaikin, M. Hedegaard, & U. J. Jensen (Eds.), *Activity theory and social practice: Cultural-historical approaches* (pp. 345–374). Aarhus: Aarhus University Press.

Engeström, Y., & Middleton, D. (Eds.), (1996). *Cognition and communication at work.* Cambridge: Cambridge University Press.

Feltovich, P., Prietula, M., & Ericsson, A. (2006). Studies of expertise from a psychological perspective. In A. Ericsson, N. Charness, P. Feltovich, & R. Hoffman (Eds.), *The Cambridge handbook of expertise and expert performance* (pp. 41–67). Cambridge: Cambridge University Press.

Folgheraiter, F. (2004). *Relational social work: Toward networking in societal practices.* London: Jessica Kingsley.

Francis, R. (2007). *The predicament of the learner in the new media age.* DPhil, University of Oxford. Available at http://ora.ouls.ox.ac.uk/objects/uuid:0cbd0185-c7ed-4306-b34e-993acd125e96

Francis, R. (in press). The decentring of the traditional university: The future of (self) education in virtually figured worlds. London: Routledge.

Gherardi, S., & Nocolini, D. (2002). Learning in a constellation of interconnected practices: Canon or dissonance? *Journal of Management Studies, 39,* 419–436.

Glisson, C., & Hemmelgarn, A. (1998). The effects of organizational climate and interorganizational coordination on the quality and outcomes of children's service systems. *Child Abuse and Neglect, 22*(5), 401–421.

Greeno, J. (1997). On claims that answer the wrong question. *Educational Researcher, 26*(1), 5–17.

References

Greeno, J. (2006). Authoritative, accountable positioning and connected general knowing: Progressive themes in understanding transfer. *The Journal of the Learning Sciences, 15*(4), 537–547.

Gunter, H. (2007). Remodelling the school workforce in England: A study in tyranny. *Journal for Critical Education Policy Studies, 5*(1), 1–11.

Hakkarainen, K., Palonen, T., Paavola, S., & Lehtinen, E. (2004). *Communities of networked expertise: Professional and educational perspectives.* Amsterdam: Elsevier.

Hartley, D. (2007). Education policy and the 'inter'-regnum. *Journal of Education Policy, 22*(6), 695–708.

Holland, D., & Lachicotte, W. (2007). Vygotsky, Mead and the new sociocultural studies of identity. In H. Daniels, M. Cole, & J. Wertsch (Eds.), *The Cambridge companion to Vygotsky.* Cambridge: Cambridge University Press.

Holland, D., Lachicotte, W., Skinner, D., & Cain, C. (1998). *Identity and agency in cultural world.* Cambridge, MA: Harvard University Press.

Holland, D., & Lave, J. (Eds.), (2001). *History in person.* Oxford: James Currey.

Hutchins, E. (1995). *Cognition in the wild.* Cambridge, MA: MIT Press.

Hutchins, E., & Klausen, T. (1996). Distributed cognition in an airline cockpit. In Y. Engeström and D. Middleton (Eds.), *Cognition and communication at work* (pp. 15–34). Cambridge: Cambridge University Press.

Jack, G. (2006). The area and community components of children's well-being. *Children and Society, 20*(5), 334–347.

Jensen, K., & Lahn, L. (2005). The binding role of knowledge: An analysis of nursing students. *Journal of Education and Work, 18*(3), 305–320.

Knorr Cetina, K. (2001). Objectual practice. In T. Schatzki, K. Knorr Cetina, & E. von Savigny (Eds.), *The practice turn in contemporary theory* (pp. 175–188). London: Routledge.

Lave, J. (1988). *Cognition in practice.* Cambridge: Cambridge University Press.

Littleton, K., & Light, P. (Eds.), (1999). *Learning with computers.* London: Routledge.

Lundsteen, N. (in progress) *Learning between university and the world of work.* DPhil study, Department of Education, University of Oxford.

Lundvall, B.-A. (1996). *The social dimension of the learning economy* (Druid working paper, 96-1). Accessed August 24th, 2008, from http://papers.ssrn.com/sol3/papers.cfm?abstract_id=66537

Nardi, B., Whittaker, S., & Schwarz, H. (2002). NetWORKers and their activity in intensional networks. *Computer Supported Cooperative Work, 11*(1–2), 205–242.

Nerland, M. (2008). Knowledge cultures and the shaping of work-based learning: The case of computer engineering. *Vocations and Learning: Studies in Vocational and Professional Education, 1*, 49–69.

Nixon, J., Martin, J., McKeown, P., & Ranson, S. (1997). Towards a learning profession: Changing codes of occupational practice within the new management of education. *British Journal of Sociology of Education, 18*(1), 5–28.

Nowotny, H. (2003). Dilemma of expertise. *Science and Public Policy, 30*(3), 151–156.

Østerland, C., & Carlile, P. (2005). Relations in practice: Sorting through practice theories on knowledge sharing in complex organizations. *The Information Society, 21*, 91–107.

Pea., R. (1993). Practices of distributed intelligence and designs for education. In G. Salomon (Ed.), *Distributed cognitions: Psychological and educational considerations.* Cambridge: Cambridge University Press.

Pickering, A. (1995). *The mangle of practice: Time, agency and science.* Chicago, IL: University of Chicago Press.

Salas, E., Rosen, M., Burke, S., Goodwin, G., & Fiore, S. (2006). The making of a dream team: When expert teams do best. In A. Ericsson, N. Charness, P. Feltovich, & R. Hoffman (Eds.), *The Cambridge handbook of expertise and expert performance* (pp. 439–453). Cambridge: Cambridge University Press.

Sennett, R. (1999). Growth and failure: The new political economy and culture. In M. Featherstone & S. Lash (Eds.), *Spaces of culture* (pp. 14–26). London: Sage.

Sternberg, R. J., & Horvath, J. A. (1995, Augutst–September). A prototype view of expert teaching. *Educational Researcher, 24*(6), 9–17.

Sternberg, R., & Wagner, R. (1992). Tacit knowledge: An unspoken key to managerial success. *Creativity and Innovation Management, 1*(1), 5–13.

Wilensky, H. (1964). The professionalization of everyone? *The American Journal of Sociology, 70*(2), 137–158.

Chapter 3
Knowledge Work at Practice Boundaries

3.1 Boundaries: Where Practices Intersect

In this chapter I shall not describe the differences that are marked by boundaries. Instead, I shall examine them as spaces where the resources from different practices are brought together to expand interpretations of multifaceted tasks, such as support for a child or the next phase in product design. The intersecting of practices while interpreting these tasks can lead to learning. However, as I explained in Chapter 1 (Section 1.6), the learning that occurs in these boundary sites is not a matter of learning how to do the work of others. Rather it involves gaining sufficient insight into purposes and practices of others to enable collaboration; and it will make demands on the practices that are brought together.

Despite the relational emphasis in the arguments to be presented, I do not entirely agree with the social worker who was quoted in a recent UK government report as saying, "relationships are crucial; it's not about structures, it's about making it work out there for children" (Laming 2009: 36). The relational turn in expertise is not about *depending on* relationships and is not about ignoring the importance of structures. It is about knowing how to engage in fluid working relations in activities where actions are co-ordinated to provide enriched responses to complex problems: these activities need structuring conditions which allow people to develop expertise in working with the resources that are available to them. These structuring conditions need to include the integration of the 'collaborative intentionality' suggested by Engeström (2005) (see Section 2.6) into practices in systems; but they also need to include attention to the spaces at the boundaries where the intersection of practices actually occurs.

Most of the examples of work at the boundaries that I will present will come from studies of inter-professional work, but these boundaries can also be between different sections within the same organisation which are working in parallel, rather than in an integrated manner, with each other. The boundaries I have been studying are social constructions (Midgley, 1992) which separate different communication systems, different meaning systems, different priorities, different time-scales and so on. Sometimes these historically developed differences may not appear to be huge. For example, an educational welfare officer and social worker may be able to work to similar time-scales on similar priorities, but there will nevertheless be differences in the backgrounds from which their actions spring (Taylor, 1995), which need to be understood and negotiated.

These differences in background will be evident when problems are discussed and responses planned, as a lack of shared background means that there is also likely to be a lack of common knowledge that might mediate negotiations. Edwards (Derek) and Mercer have written about the importance of developing common knowledge or shared understandings as the basis for successful classroom teaching. They argued the sociocultural line that 'we must now seek the essence of human thought in its cultural nature, its communicability, in our transactions with other people' (1987:165); and described its construction as: '(The expression of stance and counter-stance . . . a negotiative depiction of education, a rhetorical, argumentative meeting of minds . . .' (1987: 164).

The discursive meeting of minds that gives rise to the common knowledge, that Edwards and Mercer suggested was central to learning in classrooms was also identified by Middleton in his 1996 analyses of team working in medical settings. Common knowledge based on shared experiences within team practices can, as Middleton observed, offer resources for joint decision-making, a point echoed by Boreham (2004) in his discussion of collective competence outlined in Section 2.6. However, although Edwards and Mercer outlined how it can be constructed pedagogically in the bounded systems that are school classrooms, we know all too little about how common knowledge is built at the boundaries of systems or practices.

Carlile's (2004) work on managing knowledge across boundaries is useful here. He found that knowledge held in common was particularly helpful in linking sub-units within an organisation so that knowledge could be managed across boundaries to provoke innovation. He made an important distinction between what he termed transfer, translation and transformation when knowledge enters new practices, and linked this distinction to the ways in which knowledge was mediated across boundaries by drawing on the knowledge that was held in common.

The argument went that what matters for knowledge mobilisation is the 'capacity of the common knowledge to represent the differences and dependencies now of consequence and the ability of the actors involved to use it' (2004: 557). He suggested that when the difference between what is known and what is new increases, the demands on the knowledge held in common, and therefore the difficulty in working with the new knowledge also increases.

Accordingly, simple 'transfer' may be possible when new ideas are not too distant from existing specialist knowledge in a practice, such as when a paediatrician talks to a family doctor about a new treatment; but some translation may be needed when the doctor then talks about the treatment with the child's parents and discusses it in relation to the symptoms they are both familiar with. However, domain-specific knowledge may need to be 'transformed' if it is to take on radically new ways of thinking such as, in the examples we have been pursuing, a new focus on children's mental health in curriculum-oriented schools. This argument therefore suggests that building common knowledge, which enables quick transfer or makes translation easy, is an important pre-requisite to the quick and responsive relational work I am discussing in this book.

I am therefore suggesting that efforts to create common knowledge at the boundaries of practices are important. These 'inter' spaces (Hartley, 2007), which are a feature of innovation work in the welfare services, are frequently a response to some of the failures of the top-down approaches of NPM to deal with complex problems in the public services and, as Hartley has observed, have been set up as new solution spaces. I suggest that we need to know more about what happens in them. In the present chapter the focusing question is: what goes on in these spaces to build the common knowledge that can mediate quick knowledge transfer between practitioners who are working together on complex problems?

3.2 Boundary Work

The large body of work on boundaries (Midgley, 1992; Ulrich, 1983), building on the work of Churchman (Ulrich, 1988), points to boundaries as social constructions which define who is included and excluded from interactions and which knowledge or meaning system is considered relevant in those interactions. They are therefore important to organisations. Santos and Eisenhardt (2005) have argued that boundaries serve several purposes for organisations including:

- demarcating power in decision-making in specific fields of action, evident as either defensive or offensive strategies to ensure a sphere of influence;
- identifying the limits of an organization's resources to ensure that they are used to best advantage in a competitive market; and
- defining the organization's identity, its sense of 'who we are' in relation to other organisations.

Boundaries, according to this analysis, are constructed to sustain practices, though not necessarily to restrict their development. They are places where practices are alerted to changes which may affect their relative power, their existing resources and particular identities. Working relationally at organisational boundaries, therefore, involves the personal challenges of negotiating expertise in settings where one may not be able to manipulate practices, and where the practices that were being protected by the boundary may themselves be destabilised by your actions. As Kerosuo (2003) has observed organisational boundaries can be uncomfortable places to be. Boundaries nonetheless seem to be serving two purposes in relation to practices: stabilising the organisation and offering possibilities of organisational adaptation.

Kerosuo's analyses are interesting because they examine the negotiations that occur across practices at boundaries. She uses an Engeström activity theory framework and argues that boundaries, like the systems they protect, have historical layers which can be analysed. However, she notes that what was lacking in the boundary work in the medical settings that she observed (2003) were other aspects of an activity system, i.e. the tools, rules and redefinitions of responsibilities for care that might assist the negotiations and the work that arose from them. A cultural historical analysis of boundaries, drawing on the studies of expertise discussed in Chapter 2, comes to similar conclusions by recognising how difficult it can be to become expert at boundary work until one can manipulate the practices that matter there.

What are the boundary practices that matter if relational expertise is to be developed? In the LIW study (Edwards, Daniels, Gallagher, Leadbetter, & Warmington, 2009), we elicited what practitioners, such as social workers, teachers, educational psychologists and so on, who were learning to work together, found they needed to know and be able to do if they were to collaborate to support children's wellbeing. The following features of boundary practices seemed to form the basis of the common knowledge, both substantive and relational, that was mediating their collaboration at the boundaries.

- *Focusing on the whole child in the wider context.* This was crucial to (i) recognising vulnerability by building a picture of accumulated risk and (ii) orchestrating responses focused on children's wellbeing.
- *Clarifying the purpose of work and being open to alternatives.* Talking with other professionals about the purposes and implications, i.e. the 'why' and 'where to', of possible actions with children eroded inter-professional barriers by revealing common long-term values and purposes.
- *Understanding oneself and one's professional values.* Articulating their own expertise and values in order to negotiate practices with other professionals helped practitioners understand them better. Practices were enhanced by examining how values-driven practices might be reconfigured in relation to other professionals and their purposes.
- *Knowing how to know who.* Knowing the people and resources distributed across local networks was an important capacity but was not enough. Knowing how to access and contribute to systems of locally distributed expertise by informing interpretations and aligning responses with others was crucial.
- *Taking a pedagogic stance at work.* This involved: (i) making one's own professional expertise explicit and accessible and (ii) being professionally multi-lingual i.e. having a working knowledge of what mattered for other professions in order to 'press the right buttons' when working with them.
- *Being responsive to others: both professionals and clients.* Professionals demonstrated a growing awareness of the need to work relationally with each other and moved towards working more responsively with the strengths of their clients to build their resilience.
- *Rule-bending and risk-taking.* Practitioners described taking risks involving rule-bending to pursue the wellbeing of children. Rule-bending was a response to contradictions between emergent practices and the established systems of rules, protocols and lines of responsibility in their home organisations.
- *Creating and developing better tools for collaboration.* It was important for practitioners from all potentially collaborating services to be involved in developing

new assessment tools so that the purposes of their services could be included and the assessments could be seen to be of value across services.
- *Developing processes for knowledge sharing and pathways for practice.* Another important tool for collaboration was the opportunity to discuss cases and, in those discussions, reveal and learn about the expertise available locally. These discussions helped practitioners develop an outward-looking stance and openness to collaboration as well as learning about other expertise available.
- *Learning from practice.* Lack of organisational adjustment in response to changing practices was a major source of frustration for practitioners, leading some to identify the need to communicate with strategists in their organisations as a new skill to be learnt.

The substantive elements in the list are, of course, specific to the collaborations we studied, but there are aspects of an emergent and more generic boundary working practice which include being alert to the long-term purposes of practices, understanding oneself and one's professional values, knowing how to know who, being pedagogic and being responsive. I will return to how boundaries can be constructed to exclude those who may potentially inform the substantive elements of the common knowledge in play in Chapter 5, and in Chapter 7 to institutional responsiveness to changes in practices. At this point I shall simply outline some of the features of these boundary spaces.

3.3 What Happens in the New Boundary Spaces

In this chapter my focus is the boundaries between different professional groups who are involved in accomplishing tasks together. These are the vertical boundaries between workers who may make horizontal links at these boundaries in order to work together. There will of course be power differences between, for example, an educational psychologist and a social care assistant, which are revealed in talk and decision-making, but these differences are not built into a pre-structured hierarchy in the boundary space.

Typical spaces include local strategic partnerships in local authorities, set up to prepare a local strategy to allow access to national funding by bringing together public, private and voluntary sectors (Powell & Dowling, 2006). They may be the Partnership Boards, which bring together providers, local authority representatives and users to commission services once funding is gained (Edwards, Barnes, Plewis, & Morris, 2006). They may be the solution teams identified by Kinti in her study of innovation work at the interface of radiography and e-science (Kinti, 2008). They may be less formally constituted, such as the locality meetings run by local programme managers in the Children's Fund initiative, where practitioners met regularly to share ideas and discuss children (Edwards, in press). Or they may be meetings set up to solve immediate problems, but which nonetheless develop as sites for sharing understandings and revealing expertise, such as the multi-professional meetings that take place in secondary schools across the United Kingdom to deal with vulnerable children (Edwards, Lunt, & Stamou, 2010); or the meetings that take place between software developers and their clients (Mørch, Nygård, & Ludvigsen, 2009).

From the perspective of practitioners in the public sector, these spaces present a counterweight to the single-purpose, target-driven organisations, which are a feature of NPM, by recognising the complexity of the problems to be tackled. They also, in some cases, allow central government to control local strategies by channelling funds directly to local partnerships, which have been set up to take forward specific initiatives rather than passing them to local government. Their virtues for the public sector are therefore at least open to debate. These spaces for interagency work are also not easy to sustain.

Describing the centralizing processes of a 'whole of government' approach to public sector reform, Christensen and Lægreid (2007) outline some of the problems of working across the vertical boundaries between agencies. These include the time and other resources that are used when 'working horizontally', a tendency to be over ambitious, and unintended risks and uncontrolled consequences. Horizontal working across boundaries between organisations, they argue, also needs 'cooperative effort and cannot be easily imposed from the top down', so that 'the role of a successful reform agent is to operate more as a gardener than as an engineer or an architect' (Christensen & Laegreid, 2007: 1063). Evidence from our studies would suggest that this analysis is valid. We therefore need to examine in some detail how collaboration is nurtured in these spaces and their implications for changes in how professionals work together.

The Children's Fund initiative offered the opportunity to examine what was happening in a number of 'inter' spaces. The National Evaluation of the Children's Fund (NECF) worked with Partnerships Boards in 19 local authorities in England and examined both the Boards and the services they commissioned to prevent the social exclusion of vulnerable children. These services tended to be in the same localities, allowing the initiative to develop local systems of professional support for the children who were being targeted. In some of the more effective partnerships considerable effort was expended by locally based programme managers, who acted as reform agents, on creating and supporting locality-based meetings. These meetings functioned as 'boundary zones' (Konkola, 2001) between the different statutory and the voluntary sector services that were receiving funding. Importantly, the meetings needed constant organisation and support since, because they were working against the grain of NPM accountability, they did not arise spontaneously. Indeed, there were frequent attempts to reduce the administrative support for the meetings by senior staff in the participating services who, at best, failed to see the value of them and, at worst, felt threatened by them.

In operating as boundary zones, the Children's Fund locality meetings aimed at being neutral spaces where the values and professional priorities of each practitioner were respected, where information about resources could be shared and where trust could be built. They were places where local expertise could be made explicit so that it might be drawn on later. The spaces were inhabited by workers from different

3.3 What Happens in the New Boundary Spaces

practitioner backgrounds and projects, but who were all receiving short-term funding from the same source. They each wanted their project to succeed and recognised that collaboration would help with the complex problems with children and families that they were dealing with. While the meetings were underway they were not competing with each other for limited resources, rather they were able to draw on the resources that others could offer as these practitioners explained.

> We try to have meetings in different places so that allows us to go to different projects; and in that way we have learnt about other people's projects and maybe been able to get an understanding and see where we can learn... you know, gain knowledge about that project.
>
> It's about understanding at a deeper level. It's about connections. Maybe you are not sure about the child we are thinking about; but as we talk it through there may be a connection and if not for that child, maybe for another.

These spaces therefore operated as springboards for horizontal linkages between practitioners as they etched new trails across local landscapes to reconfigure the trajectories of the children they worked with. The sessions were problem-focused, but also began to open up discussions between participants about the purposes and principles of the new preventative activities. Here a practitioner outlines what she was gaining from Children's Fund locality meetings:

> I think the very first step is understanding about what the sort of issues are.... Professions have very, very different ideas about need, about discipline, about responsibility, about the impact of systems on families... So I think the first step is actually to get some shared understanding about effective practices and about understanding the reasons behind some of them. Understanding some of the reasons why we are seeing these sorts of issues in families.

These meetings demanded that practitioners looked outwards beyond their own services and kept open minds. The conversations there then helped practitioners to see the need to work against entrenched patterns of inter-professional mistrust.

> Social Services could be seen in a very negative way, but because we have had the same person come along every week people have got to know her. They understand the reasons why they don't do this and why they do that, so they are less likely to be negative about it (Practitioner talking to NECF).

Experience of collaboration could also lead practitioners to question those practices which were invoked by their own organisations to strengthen boundaries.

> One of the things that I think has dogged agencies is the cloak of secrecy. Now I think there is a difference between confidentiality and secrecy; a sort of jealously guarding their own territory (Practitioner talking to NECF).

Inter-professional meetings swallowed resources, but were quite clearly enriching inter-professional responses in the Children's Fund. What Hansen describes as 'regularly occurring contacts between groups of people' (1999: 83) appear to strengthen social ties, which in turn led to the sharing of knowledge and other resources. There is support for this in the management literature, for example, Brachos, Kostopoulos, Sonderquist, and Prastacos (2007), writing about innovation, have argued that social interaction helps the flow of what is seen as relevant knowledge, assists an orientation to learning but will depend on management support.

But setting up inter-professional social ties is not enough, the ties need to be oriented towards a reworking of practices to take forward the purposes of more fluid and flexible work. The expansive practice that began to emerge in some parts of the Children's Fund initiative consisted of generative negotiations of interpretations and responses, which were propelled forward by the core idea of preventing social exclusion. A crucial feature in the places where it occurred was the ability to move beyond the 'here and now' of finding immediate solutions and to, in addition, reveal alternative possibilities which reflected the professional ideals of participants.

3.4 Alternative Envisioning at the Boundaries

CHAT analyses of an ability to visualise alternative futures usually refer to Wartofsky's analyses of artefacts outlined by Cole (1996: 121). Cole explains that primary artefacts are those tools such as axes which are actually used in production; secondary artefacts are representations of primary artefacts and include recipes, beliefs and norms which preserve and transmit ways of acting and thinking; while tertiary artefacts, while still imbued by the human needs and intentions that shaped the other forms of artefact, present the possibility of an imagined world. Wartofsky described tertiary artefacts as follows.

> The upshot, however, is that the construction of alternative imaginative perceptual modes, freed from the direct representation of ongoing forms of action, and relatively autonomous in this sense, feeds back into actual praxis, as a representation of possibilities which go beyond present actualities. (Wartofsky, 1973: 209)

Most, but not all, Children's Fund locality meetings operated at the level of recipe exchange with a few examples of an emergent focus on prevention as an imagined artefact to be worked towards. However, the sessions run by the research team in the LIW study specifically encouraged participants to construct 'alternative imaginative' perceptions which might shape future action. Here we can see a practitioner from a multi-professional team in the LIW study moving towards an alternative envisioning:

> Because I think that in a sense there needs to be ... my concern is that at the moment we've got a lot of children who are being seen by more than one person. And when they're open cases or not open cases [the problem] is a long term one. But I think that there was still ... there ... unless we know ... unless you know that X is seeing that child why would you contact her to actually discuss it? We haven't got a system by which children ... we are making sure that children are being seen by more than one person and those people are connecting together.

Engeström (2007a), also drawing on Wartofsky, has described these new perceptions as 'where to tools' which, reflecting Wartofsky's concern with

3.4 Alternative Envisioning at the Boundaries

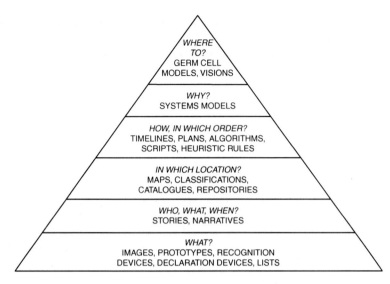

Fig. 3.1 Epistemic levels of mediational artefacts (Engeström, 2007a)

representing human needs and intentions, contain the germ cell of professional practice. Figure 3.1 shows Engeström's categorisation of tools and their use. The term 'germ cell' in Vygotskian theory refers to the key concepts in an area of knowledge, their relationships with each other and any tensions in those relationships. The germ cell is therefore always open to change as it is taken into use in the world. The practitioner just quoted is beginning to reveal the germ cell for inter-professional work and how her local system falls short, opening up the opportunity for developing new models of practice.

According to Engeström (2007a), the same tool or resource may be used in different ways depending on how the problem is being interpreted and how the expectations and social practices of an organization shape how a tool might be used. For example in the LIW study, we observed that an assessment of a child may be used as a 'how' tool to arrange support, as a 'why' tool which may involve questioning the value of each option for the needs of the child, or as a 'where to' tool where the child, carers and practitioners discuss what they want for the child in the longer term. 'Where to' conversations start to reveal values and intentions and open up possibilities for the exercise of relational forms of agency on the part of practitioners and families.

Therefore, the idea that professional knowledge can be pinned down and controlled by 'how' tools, such as bureaucratic procedures, is seriously challenged by the idea of 'why' and 'where to' tools outlined by Engeström. When practitioners meet together at the boundaries of their organisation to discuss a 'where to' that is informed by each profession, this can present a threat to both bureaucratic and NPM systems. These future representations, such as children's wellbeing, are not prescriptive, rather they are open-ended and sufficiently indeterminate to enable people to subscribe to them. Their purpose is to give shape to the small steps that comprise professional action.

Engeström argues for maintaining a close relationship between longer-term goals of systems and day-to-day actions. For him this is the key to engaging agentic, or purposeful, practitioners with the long-term goals of the systems in which they work and the implications for their professional agency are strong.

> Human agency gains unusual powers when future-oriented activity-level envisioning and consequential action-level decision-making, come together in close interplay. (Engeström, 2005: 313)

Pickering (1993, 1995) has also emphasised the importance of long-term goals for understanding how practices remain focused yet develop over time. His propositions have a great deal in common with Holland's analysis of agency arising in practices, which was discussed in Section 2.3. He therefore explains the relationship between immediate practices and distant purposes slightly differently from Engeström, by working with a more individual notion of human agency which he sees arising through practices which are connected with long-term goals.

> ... we should see the intentional nature of human agency as itself temporally emergent, albeit on a longer timescale than the details of practice. (Pickering, 1993: 598)

Both Engeström and Pickering are, however, seeing the temporal dimension of intentional action as central to their analyses and the longer-term goals as ways of stabilising activities so that they might connect over time.

Discussions with practitioners in the LIW study suggest that the distinction between immediate activities and longer-term intentions is helpful when moving into action. An activity, such as collaboration between a teacher and a social worker to reintegrate a child into a school after complex family breakdown, might be seen as part of the longer-term collaborative practice oriented towards ensuring her wellbeing. A sense of the longer-term purpose allows the social worker and teacher to orchestrate their responses with that long-term agreed intention in mind. In other words, the 'why' and 'where to' of collaboration gives shape to the 'how' as practitioners work on objects of activity which change as they are worked on.

3.5 Constructing Sites for Sustained Boundary Work

But what were the structuring conditions in the LIW meetings that gave rise to discussions of 'where to' and 'why' and led to the common understandings discussed in Section 3.2? The meetings were inter-professional sessions of 2 hours in length, which were convened by the research team in order to elicit the concepts being developed by practitioners such as psychologists, social workers and teachers, as they undertook new forms of inter-professional collaboration. The detail of the study and the analysis of talk in the sessions can be found in Edwards et al. (2009). The sessions were based on Engeström's Developmental Work Research (DWR)

3.5 Constructing Sites for Sustained Boundary Work

methodology (Engeström, 2007b) (see Section 8.5 and Appendix A), which in turn is based on Vygotsky's method of dual stimulation (Vygotsky, 1999).

Vygotsky developed the method of dual stimulation as a way of accessing how children understand the world: the concepts they were able to use when taking action in it. Children would be presented with problems and resources that might help them solve the problem. How they interpreted the problem and used resources, including language, revealed their thinking. DWR echoes that use of dual stimulation by providing people with a problem, such as a mismatch between intentions and procedures, which has been revealed in the data collected in their workplace and with analytic tools with which they might work on the mismatch.

In DWR, practitioners identify the problem together with the researchers who represent it during the 2 hours sessions. To do this, the researchers use the words of practitioners, pictures of the workplace or case studies of incidents as 'mirror data', which reflect aspects of their work situation back to the participants. The researchers then provide the tools of activity theory as resources for the practitioners to identify and work on the tensions and contradictions that are often evident in the mirror data. Researchers observe how participants interpret the work problem and use the tools to work with the evidence. Both their interpretations and their responses to the mirror data reveal the concepts being brought into play as they together accomplish accounts of practice and in doing so build common knowledge.

The DWR sessions are led by one of the research team who keeps the focus on the problem, or emerging new problems, and encourages the use of the analytic resources of activity theory. As a result, practitioners are helped to identify what matters for them and to reveal the motives embedded in their interpretations of the purposes of their practices, the professional values that these imply and the knowledge in use as they respond.

An additional strength of DWR, reflecting Engeström's focus on systems, is that these discussions bring to the surface contradictions in systems, for example, between the rules that govern practices and new interpretations of how the resources available might be used, or between the existing division of labour and the purposes of emergent practices.

DWR licenses question about purposes and principles and guides practitioners into asking quite fundamental questions about the 'why' and 'where to' of their practices, as they reveal the concepts they employ to do their work. In Engeström's work the focus is on revealing contradictions in and between activity systems and on working with these contradictions to bring about systemic change. In the LIW study, as we explain in Edwards et al. (2009), and out line in Section 8.5, our aim was to reveal concepts in use in emergent inter-professional practices.

Soft systems methodology (SSM) (Checkland & Scholes, 1990) is a close relation to Engeström's approach, and, like Engeström's work, aims at helping participants in interventions to model desirable future activity and also attempts at times to work across organizational boundaries. Gregory and Midgley (2000) outlined their intentions when using SSM with 19 agencies to plan a regional disaster counselling service as follows.

> ... any proposals that were developed without their participation would have failed to engender their commitment. Indeed this is a common problem in [operational research] and systems practice: the need to foster commitment through participation is one of the strongest arguments for the use of problem structuring methods sometimes called 'soft OR' or 'soft systems thinking'. (2000: 280)

Gregory and Midgley, as is also common in DWR, resisted the development of what could be restrictive definitions, which might 'prevent the design of a sufficiently flexible system' (p. 282), coped with some resistance to the challenges to identity and the scale of change needed that arose initially, and found that participants learnt a great deal from each other in the process. There is therefore a great deal in common between DWR and this example of SSM: indeed, Turner and Turner (2002) have described the methods as complementary. However, DWR, because of the attention Engeström pays to systemic disturbances and contradictions, is perhaps less focused on identifying and solving problems and more on surfacing problems and tackling the systemic contradictions they reveal as new understandings are generated.

Attention to the 'why' and 'where to' of practice can also be achieved by using some of the features of DWR, without either the LIW study's attention to concept formation and common knowledge or Engeström's focus on strong contradictions in order to provoke organisational transformation. In the PSE study of how secondary schools were adjusting to inter-professional work discussed in Chapter 2 (Section 2.5) (Edwards et al., 2010), we structured the one feedback session we gave in each participating school by using extracts from interviews which revealed contradictions as mirror data and by employing the terminology of activity theory.

In the practitioners' responses to the mirror data the 'why' of practice was inescapable, as this extract from a reflection on a contradiction in her school by a senior teacher at one feedback session shows:

> I kind of wonder where's the balance, you know, have we got the balance right for heads of year and the team. Not that I would want to lose any of this [pastoral support for pupils], but I think members of the senior team and heads of year, that level, do get incredibly enmeshed day-to-day with the individual children and their situations. And that does prevent you from working strategically to develop systems, processes for the whole school, you know, the grey majority who are just as entitled to tutor time as the vulnerable needy children.

The sessions run in the PSE study show that meetings set up to enable relational work can be quite informally structured, while still retaining the DWR principles of reflection on evidence and the surfacing of contradictions. The mirror data become an object of reflection which reveal the motives embedded in the practices that are brought together in the session.

Several years ago I was asked by workers in an inner-city 'drop in' centre for vulnerable adults to convene a staff development day. The workers were beginning to see tensions between how the new money advice unit in the centre and the older community-oriented team of practitioners were working with the same clients. A contradiction that had arisen in a conversation with one of the original team when talking about clients was 'we think of them as friends and they think of us as workers'. This statement provided enough mirror data for a 1-day conversation about motives, purposes and alignments of activities and responses to clients in the centre, which created mutual understanding and shifted practices in the organisation.

I have suggested elsewhere (Edwards & Kinti, 2009; Edwards, 2009) that meetings which give time to the purposes of practices are a prerequisite to relational work across boundaries within and between organisations. They serve three important functions in building the common knowledge which is likely to lead to flexible responsive work with others. These are:

- recognising similar long-term open goals, such as children's wellbeing, which give broad coherence to the specialist activities of practitioners;
- revealing categories, values and motives in the natural language of talk about problems of practice;
- recognising and engaging with the categories, values and motives of others in discussions of potential objects of activity.

Let us therefore turn to the matter of categorisations already pointed towards in Chapter 1 (Section 1.4).

3.6 Knowledge Talk at the Boundaries

Here my concern is with the way people reveal the ready meanings of their practices in their use of categorisations: needy parent, single-mother, working mum, poorly educated carer and so on. Their use gives insights into the practices in which they arise, and can assist other practitioners in developing the kind of professional multi-lingualism that will allow them to negotiate across boundaries, or 'press the right buttons' as one LIW practitioner put it.

Following Collins' distinctions (mentioned in Section 1.6) between the kinds of expertise needed to be able to hold a meaningful conversation with another specialist, rather than actually do the job (Collins & Evans, 2007; Collins, 2004; Collins, Evans, Ribeiro, & Hall, 2006), I have no expectation that the multi-lingualism I envisage will arise from a desire to have a 'full-blown immersion in a form of life' (Collins & Evans, 2007*f*: 20). My interest is in professional expertise and not in generalist hybridity. Recognition of how categories are used, therefore, does not imply access to the tacit knowledge held in practices, though it can open a window onto it. Engaging with the ready meanings of different discourse groups can, therefore, give us only limited access to what Taylor (1995: 69) describes as the background which 'makes certain experiences intelligible to us'. There will always be differences in how practices and purposes are understood by professionals working out of different practices, and I shall argue that these differences have the potential to be generative.

My focus on how language is used to construct meanings in boundary spaces is not a slide into the relativism of the more radical interpretations of constructivism nor is it seeing either the boundary space or connecting practices as mere linguistic constructions (Gergen, 1992). Rather the intention is to recognise meanings as representations of how institutions are shaped and shape themselves, and therefore of what matters within practices, to examine struggles to make new meanings at boundaries and to consider the implications for the practice of boundary work.

In doing so, it is impossible to disregard the politics of representation or what Mehan (1993: 264) has described as a 'ranking' of representations 'on a vertical plane' where, in his example, the categories of the psychologist have primacy over those of the teacher when discussing a child. Hjörne and Säljö (2004) undertook a similar analysis of multi-professional discussions of children with special needs and observed how bio-medical representations and the resources they brought in their wake were shaping discussions of children's vulnerability and potential treatment.

> At present, biomedical, psychiatric, and neuropsychological categories offering neuropsychiatric diagnoses play an important role in schools in many countries, including Sweden, where this line of research has been very active. Labels such as MBD (minimal brain dysfunction), DAMP (deficit in attention, motor control, and perception), ADHD (attention deficit hyperactivity disorder), Aspergers, Dyslexia, Dyscalculia, and so on, are used widely in schools as categories for classifying children, for organizing teaching and learning opportunities, and for the distribution of economic and other kinds of resources. This practice has resulted in a rapid increase in the number of children in Sweden who are categorized as in some sense handicapped. (Hjörne & Säljö, 2004: 2–3)

The meanings revealed and agreed among dominant groups may also lead to the exclusion of others from the boundary space. Midgley's analyses of how differences in values can give rise to differences in where boundaries are drawn and the marginalization of the less dominant group drew on Douglas (1966) for an anthropological account of what occurs at the margins. Midgley identified the 'gray areas in which marginal areas lie that are neither fully included in, nor excluded from, the system definition' (Midgley, 1992: 6).

These analyses have strong practical relevance. Midgley and his colleagues, for example, revealed how users of a housing service for elderly people were marginalized in the processes of service development (Midgley, Munlo, & Brown, 1998). Here the service users were given what Midgley et al. describe as a 'profane' status by service providers who wanted to exclude them from discussions about service improvement.

In both the LIW study and the PSE examination of secondary schools and prevention, it seemed that parents as potential partners in reconfiguring their children's trajectories were placed in a similar marginal position. This was perhaps unsurprising, as we shall see in Chapter 5, as practitioners needed to become comfortable with inter-professional negotiations before they could negotiate their positions vis à vis the expertise of parents.

Even when resources are not a concern, boundary talk is often far from neutral, despite the laudable aims of, for example, the Children's Fund locality meetings. Rather, there are strong emotional elements which reflect the vulnerability that can be experienced when professionals are removed from the practices that sustain their identities. We saw in Chapter 1 (Section 1.4) how an educational psychologist in a LIW DWR session started to populate the discussion with the categories, which mattered for him as he took forward the re-shaping of local services. This kind of

3.6 Knowledge Talk at the Boundaries

assertion of one's professional categories is tied up with the identity as a professional, and is not simply institutional power-play. As Sarangi and Roberts explain, institutional discourse is 'a central means of socialization into the professions – actively becoming a professional' (1999: 37). The use of the categories that are shaped in and by specialist practices are hard to discount, because they shape professional decision-making and the arguments used to account for decisions (Mäkitalo, 2003).

For this reason if for no other, for boundary spaces to be generative, they need some managing to produce the structuring conditions in which specialist knowledge can be brought into play and create new spaces for the knowledge work that can sustain changing professional identities. The need for a 'solution team' to orchestrate links between potentially collaborating work groups in Kinti's (2008) study of an e-science-radiography collaboration (see Section 4.7) illustrates this suggestion. Meetings that focus on finding solutions, I propose, need to be augmented by the meta-level aim of developing mutual recognition by revealing and discussing what matters in the intersecting practices. This is the role of Christensen and Lægreid's (2007) 'gardener'. It is this work that can be central to the development of common knowledge at the boundaries.

Evidence from the LIW study suggests that narrative accounts of past, present and future practices can reveal the conceptual resources embedded in intersecting practices and how values and intentions shape the use of the resources to be found there. As Bruner (2004) explains '*world making* is the principle function of mind' (2004: 691); and the narrative mode of world making allows participants to imbue concrete accounts of experience with meanings that can accommodate complexity and contradictions (Bruner, 2004). These meanings include, as Tsoukas observes, the motives that infuse the narratives, allowing them to operate as a 'device for framing motives' (2005: 251).

However, LIW evidence also suggests that narratives can have different functions within conversations. Past and present narrative accounts may operate in the same way as Wartofsky's (1973) secondary artefacts, as representations aiming at preserving the status quo of established practices; but future-oriented accounts of desired possibilities may reveal tertiary artefacts with 'why' and 'where to' qualities which take knowledge sharing beyond mere exchange of information to a shared ascription to longer-term goals. Contrast how the following account is used as a secondary artefact by a senior teacher in a school in the LIW study, with the more 'why' and 'where to' future-oriented account of the educational psychologist at the same school. First the teacher reveals the categories that allocate children to specific levels of need that reflect the historical practices of the school.

> I was just going to say, in the scheme of things this child [who was in a family with problems] will be low priority I have to say because, you know, they're doing well, they've got good friendship groups, ... and if you think about the volume of youngsters that come to us with categories of special need, categories of 'school action plus' that's failed in primary schools, categories of need with kids who haven't made any progress, they're not regarded as special needs kids, they're not statemented, and yet their literacy is an issue, which is very often connected with bad literacy in the family, or need in the family. So if you think about

the high risk categories of youngsters that transfer [from primary school], ... this child will not be in a target group they will just be a normal kid. So they would only be picked up, if I'm quite honest with you, if their attendance dropped or, or if they hit somebody or some, some crisis really would have to bring that child to the fore, really, in reality. Maybe that's not the right, what you want to hear, but that's the reality.

A few turns later the psychologist responds with a narrative of future intentions which attempts to disrupt existing categories and indicate future possibilities.

What we need to be doing is to be looking perhaps far more carefully at precisely what difficulties exist, why we think they exist and what support might actually be appropriate to help. And then recognise the paradigms that a whole range of professionals and voluntary sectors want to work from. There's you know, education has its particular paradigm, medicine has a particular paradigm and the voluntary social work. And those sort of paradigms inform how people operate and their expectations. So when you get people into a room ... there's a different expectation and different way of working. Accepting all of that, what we're attempting to do, and it is an attempt, is to begin to support schools in coordinating this performance out there. And what I'm particularly interested in is, because I've been seconded to that role, so we'll be actually taking on the, the coordination role. It's about opening schools up, making the boundaries more permeable and it's not just about you know people coming in and people going out. But I need clear purposes to what we're about, it has to be about making a difference for children and young people and their families.

Wertsch's notion of 'implicit mediation' (2007) outlined in Chapter 1 (Section 1.4) suggests that knowledge is often carried in the natural language of the situation and is therefore different from the explicit mediation that occurs in the more contrived mediational conversations of formal teaching. In boundary spaces the natural language of the situation might be seen, following the Mehan and the Hjörne and Säljö studies, to be the language of asserting particular representations at the expense of others. Indeed, the use of a tertiary artefact to respond to a secondary artefact in the LIW example may be seen in such a way. In order to understand a little better the meta-level task of the 'gardener', we need to turn to the relational element of the common knowledge that may mediate meaning-making at organisational boundaries.

Earlier in this chapter, in Section 3.2, I presented the features of boundary practices which seemed to form the basis of the 'common knowledge', both substantive and relational, that was mediating action at the boundaries in the LIW study. The interactional aspects included 'knowing how to know who', 'taking a pedagogic stance at work' and 'being responsive to others, both professionals and clients', indicating a relational aspect of expertise which includes being alert to the standpoints of others and being willing to work with them towards shared ethical goals (Benhabib, 1992; Taylor, 1989, 1991).

Benhabib elaborates her view of what she terms 'communicative ethics' as a 'form of ethical cognitivism' (p. 51). She explains how an ethically grounded discursive rationality is produced, and in the process may offer some ground-rules for the relational aspects of knowledge work at the sites of intersecting practices.

In conversation, I must know how to listen, I must know how to understand your point of view, I must learn to represent myself to the world and the other as you see them. If I cannot listen, if I cannot understand, and if I cannot represent, the conversation stops, develops into an argument, or maybe never gets started. (Benhabib, 1992: 52)

This is not simply a description of conversational reciprocity driven by moral concerns about visions of the good life. Her agenda is ambitious:

What I propose is a procedural reformulation of the universalizability principle along the model of a moral conversation in which the capacity to reverse perspectives, that is, the willingness to reason from the others' point of view, and the sensitivity to hear their voice is paramount. (Benhabib, 1992: 8)

The capacity to reverse perspectives does not imply the seeking of consensus, rather a willingness to 'seek understanding with the other and reach some reasonable agreement in an opened ended moral conversation' (Benhabib, 1992: 9). These practices of reaching 'reasonable agreement' are, I suggest, to be seen as the practices of generative boundary work in which 'open ended moral' conversations are the vehicle for the production of a value-laden common knowledge to which people can ascribe, contribute and argue against, and which in turn, *pace* Bourdieu (1977) (Section 1.3), mediates what is seen as reasonable.

These conversations cannot be dismissed as knowledge transfer or knowledge exchanges, they are predicated on never entirely knowing the 'background' (Taylor, 1995) on which the other draws with the result that the acknowledgement of differences can render them generative. The distinctions to be made in dialogues between practitioners with different cultural histories can, as we shall see in the next chapter, lead to their learning. They can also, as Tsoukas (2009) points out, create new knowledge.

In his analysis of knowledge-creating dialogues Tsoukas (2009) has usefully distinguished between what he describes as 'relational engagement' with the other, and 'calculated engagement'. These distinctions connect with the discussion earlier in this section of how narratives may be used as secondary and tertiary artefacts. In relational engagement, actors have favourable expectations of their dialogue partner which mean they put on one side any expectations that impede what Tsoukas terms productive dialogue; while in calculated engagement actors cooperate minimally to protect their interests and dialogues are not productive. It is important to note that relational engagement does not mean the ignoring of differences. Rather, it should, in the terms I have been using, create and be predicated on a form of common knowledge that represents the differences that matter between knowledge domains.

The discussion so far in this chapter suggests that these 'inter' spaces at the sites of intersecting practices can be seen as sites of a practice in their own right. This inter-practice can assert a history rooted in the contributing practices and a future direction which is the long-term goal; while at the same time it can acknowledge that participants will also inhabit other specialist practices. Relational engagement with the knowledge and motives of others can produce a form of common knowledge which comprises a partially shared understanding of what matters for other contributing experts and the know-how associated with revealing, accessing and working with the knowledge of others in a common, if perhaps slightly differently interpreted, endeavour. This analysis therefore returns us to the argument made in Chapters 1 and 2, that the relational turn in professional practice requires an additional layer of expertise which arises in the practices of these boundary spaces.

References

Benhabib., S. (1992). *Situating the self*. New York, NY: Routledge.
Boreham, N. (2004). A theory of collective competence: Challenging the neo-liberal individualisation of performance at work. *British Journal of Educational Studies, 52*(1), 5–17.
Bourdieu, P. (1977). *Outline of a theory of practice*. Cambridge: Cambridge University Press.
Brachos, D., Kostopoulos, K., Sonderquist, K. E., & Prastacos, G. (2007). Knowledge effectiveness, social context and innovation. *Journal of Knowledge Management, 11*(5), 31–44.
Bruner, J. S. (2004). Life as narrative. *Social Research, 71*(3), 691–710.
Carlile, P. (2004). Transferring, translating and transforming: An integrative framework for managing knowledge across boundaries. *Organization Science, 15*(5), 555–568.
Checkland, P., & Scholes, J. (1990). *Soft systems methodology in action*. Chichester: Wiley.
Christensen, T., & Laegreid, P. (2007, November/December). The whole of government approach to public service reform. *Public Administration Review, 67*, 1059–1066.
Cole, M. (1996). *Cultural psychology: A once and future discipline*. Cambridge, MA: Harvard University Press.
Collins, H. (2004). Interactional expertise as a third kind of knowledge. *Phenomenology and the Cognitive Sciences, 3*, 125–143.
Collins, H., & Evans, R. (2007). *Rethinking expertise*. Chicago, IL: University of Chicago Press.
Collins, H., Evans, R., Ribeiro, R., & Hall, M. (2006). Experiments with interactional expertise. *Studies in History of Philosophy of Science, 37*, 656–674.
Douglas, M. (1966). *Purity and danger: An analysis of the concepts of pollution and taboo*. London: Ark.
Edwards, A. (2009). Relational agency in collaborations for the wellbeing of children and young people. *Journal of Children's Services, 4*(1), 33–43.
Edwards, A., Barnes, M., Plewis, I., &Morris, K. (2006). *Working to prevent the social exclusion of children and young people: Final lessons from the National Evaluation of the Children's Fund*. London: DfES. (Research Report 734).
Edwards, A., Daniels, H., Gallagher, T., Leadbetter, J., & Warmington, P. (2009). *Improving inter-professional collaborations: Multi-agency working for children's wellbeing*. London: Routledge.
Edwards, A., & Kinti, I. (2009). Working relationally at organisational boundaries: Negotiating expertise and identity. In H. Daniels, A. Edwards, Y. Engeström, & S. Ludvigsen (Eds.), *Activity theory in practice: Promoting learning across boundaries and agencies* (pp. 126–139). London: Routledge.
Edwards, A., Lunt, I., & Stamou, E. (2010). Inter-professional work and expertise: New roles at the boundaries of schools. *British Educational Research Journal, 30*(1), 27–45.
Edwards, D., & Mercer, N. (1987). *Common knowledge: The development of understanding in the classroom*. London: Routledge.
Edwards, A. (in press). Learning how to know who: Professional learning for expansive practice between organisations. In S. Ludvigsen, A. Lund, & R. Saljo (Eds.), *Learning across sites*. London: Routledge.
Engeström, Y. (2005). Knotworking to create collaborative intentionality capital in fluid organizational fields. In M. M. Beyerlein, S. T. Beyerlein, & F. A. Kennedy (Eds.), *Collaborative capital: Creating intangible value* (pp. 307–336). Amsterdam: Elsevier.
Engeström, Y. (2007a). Enriching the theory of expansive learning: Lessons from journeys toward co-configuration. *Mind, Culture and Activity, 14*(1 and 2), 23–39.

References

Engeström, Y. (2007b). Putting activity theory to work: The change laboratory as an application of double stimulation. In H. Daniels, M. Cole, & J. V. Wertsch (Eds.), *The Cambridge companion to Vygotsky* (pp. 363–382). Cambridge: Cambridge University Press.

Gergen, K. (1992). Organization theory in the postmodern era. In M. Reed & M. Hughes (Eds.), *Rethinking organization; new directions in organization theory and analysis* (pp. 207–226). London: Sage.

Gregory, W. J., & Midgley, G. (2000). Planning for disaster: Developing a multi-agency counselling service. *The Journal of the Operational Research Society, 51*(3), 278–290.

Hansen, M. T. (1999). The search-transfer problem: The role of weak ties in sharing knowledge across organization subunits. *Administrative Science Quarterly, 44*, 82–111.

Hartley, D. (2007). Education policy and the 'inter'-regnum. *Journal of Education Policy, 22*(6), 695–708.

Hjörne, E., & Säljö, R. (2004). "There is something about Julia": Symptoms, categories, and the process of invoking attention deficit hyperactivity disorder in the Swedish school: A case study. *Journal of Language, Identity, and Education, 3*(1), 1–24.

Kerosuo, H. (2003). Boundaries in health care discussions: An activity theoretical approach to the analysis of boundaries. In N. Paulsen & T. Hernes (Eds.), *Managing boundaries in organizations: Multiple perspectives* (pp. 169–187). Basingstoke: Palgrave.

Kinti, I. (2008). *Balancing at the boundaries of organizations: Knowledge co-configuration between experts*. DPhil thesis, University of Oxford.

Konkola, R. (2001). Developmental process of internship at polytechnic and boundary-zone activity as a new model for activity. (in Finnish) cited in T. Tuomi-Gröhn, Y. Engeström, & M. Young (Eds.) (2003), *Between school and work: New perspectives on transfer and boundary crossing*. Oxford: Pergamon.

Laming (Lord). (2009). *The protection of children in England: A progress report*. London: The Stationery Office. Accessed September, 2009, from http://publications.everychildmatters.gov.uk/eOrderingDownload/HC-330.pdf.

Mäkitalo, Å. (2003). Accounting practices as situated knowing: Dilemmas and dynamics in institutional categorization. *Discourse Studies, 5*(4), 465–519.

Mehan, H. (1993). Beneath the skin and between the ears: Case study in the politics of representation. In S. Chaiklin & J. Lave (Eds.), *Understanding practice: Perspectives on activity and context* (pp. 241–268). Cambridge: Cambridge University Press.

Middleton, D. (1996). Talking work: Argument, common knowledge, and improvisation in teamwork. In Y. Engeström & D. Middleton (Eds.), *Cognition and communication at work* (pp. 233–256). Cambridge: Cambridge University Press.

Midgley, G. (1992). The sacred and profane in critical systems thinking. *Systems Practice, 5*(1), 5–16.

Midgley, G., Munlo, I., & Brown, M. (1998). The theory and practice of boundary critique: Developing housing services for older people. *Journal of the Operational Research Society, 49*(5), 467–478.

Mørch, I., Nygård, K., & Ludvigsen, S. (2009). Adaptation and generalisation in software product development. In H. Daniels, A. Edwards, Y. Engeström, T. Gallagher, & S. Ludvigsen (Eds.), *Activity theory in practice: Promoting learning across boundaries and agencies* (pp. 184–206). London: Routledge.

Pickering, A. (1993). The mangle of practice: Agency and emergence in the sociology of science. *American Journal of Sociology, 99*(3), 559–589.

Pickering, A. (1995). *The mangle of practice: Time, agency and science*. Chicago, IL: University of Chicago Press.

Powell, M., & Dowling, B. (2006). New labour's partnerships: Comparing conceptual models with existing forms. *Social Policy and Society, 5*(2), 305–314.

Santos, F., & Eisenhardt, K. (2005). Organizational boundaries and theories of organization. *Organization Science, 16*(5), 491–508.

Sarangi, S., & Roberts, C. (1999). Introduction: Discursive hybridity in medical work. In S. Sarangi & C. Roberts (Eds.), *Talk, work and institutional order: Discourse in medical, mediation and management settings*. Berlin: Mouton de Gruyter.

Taylor, C. (1989). Sources of the self: The making of modern identity. Cambridge, MA: Harvard University Press.

Taylor, C. (1991). *The ethics of authenticity*. Cambridge, MA: Harvard University Press.

Taylor, C. (1995). *Philosophical arguments*. Cambridge, MA: Cambridge University Press.

Tsoukas, H. (2005). *Complex knowledge*. Oxford: Oxford University Press.

Tsoukas, H. (2009). A dialogical approach to the creation of new knowledge in organizations. *Organization Science, 20*(6), 941–957.

Turner, P., & Turner, S. (2002). Surfacing issues using activity theory. *Journal of Applied Systems Science, 3*(1), 134–155.

Ulrich, W. (1983). *Critical heuristics of social planning: A new approach to practical philosophy*. Haupt: Berne.

Ulrich, W. (1988). C. West Churchman – 75 years. *Systems Practice and Action Research, 1*(4), 341–350.

Vygotsky, L. S. (1999). Tool and sign development in the child. In R. W. Rieber (Ed.), *The collected works of L.S. Vygotsky. Vol 6: Scientific legacy*. New York, NY: Plenum.

Wartofsky, M. (1973). *Models*. Dordrecht: Reidel.

Wertsch, J. V. (2007). Mediation. In H. Daniels, M. Cole, & J. V. Wertsch (Eds.), *The Cambridge companion to Vygotsky* (pp. 178–192). New York, NY: Cambridge University Press.

Chapter 4
Relational Agency: Working with Other Practitioners

4.1 Relational Agency

In this chapter I move to the person acting on tasks in practices, to examine what the relational turn means for how we think about self and agency in professional work. The main idea to be discussed is relational agency, which was outlined in Chapter 1 (Section 1.6), where it was described as working alongside others towards negotiated outcomes. Relational agency, as a joint and more powerful form of agency, will be presented as an alternative to the idea of professionals as heroic individuals who are given status through their ability to work autonomously. Instead, the argument will be made that the relational turn in professional practice offers the opportunity for an enhanced form of practice, which is potentially more beneficial to professionals than claims to individual autonomy might be.

Although relational agency involves being attuned to each other's purposes and ways of working, it is not the same as the kind of inter-subjectivity, where the more expert partner mediates what matters in a culture and supports a novice as she learns to participate as an agentic individual in that culture. It is therefore not a form of apprenticeship though, as we shall see, apprenticeships can incorporate aspects of relational expertise. Rather, it involves working together purposefully towards goals that reflect the motives that shape the specialist expertise of each participant, and using the resources that each specialism can bring to bear.

Learning does occur as people work together, but that is not the prime motive for working relationally. Instead, its purpose is more successful task accomplishment through working in relation to what each participant brings to the task. The distinction is therefore being made between relational work for apprenticeship and relational work in flexible and innovative practices where the focus is the task, whether it be changing a child's trajectory or developing a new piece of radiography equipment. In this chapter I shall discuss the flexible, responsive and purposeful interactions that characterise the latter in terms of collaborations in the heat of action.

I ended the previous chapter by suggesting that the boundary spaces and meetings discussed there can be seen as sites of practice in their own right with histories and a future direction. In the discussions I argued that working in these boundary sites involves sustaining a core expertise alongside the more relational demands of developing the common knowledge that will mediate inter-professional interactions in the heat of action. In this chapter I shall examine what happens when practitioners collaborate outside these meetings using the common knowledge generated in them.

I shall therefore make a distinction between the conversations that occur in boundary spaces and in which common knowledge is built, which were discussed in Chapter 3, and the more fluid and responsive joint actions that occur while practitioners work together on complex problems and draw on common knowledge to mediate their interpretations and responses. It is the latter collaborations that I characterise as imbued with relational agency.

Relational agency in the heat of action might be found in a series of events, which start with a teacher recognising that a child's poor behaviour arises from a set of interconnected difficulties with her family that put the child at immediate risk of being without a home over the next few weeks. Alerting other practitioners to the child's vulnerability so that they can add their interpretations and respond quickly according to their own specialist strengths is one aspect of relational agency in action, as is ensuring that teacher colleagues work sympathetically with the child focusing on her wellbeing and maintaining awareness of what other professionals are doing. This kind of rapid response may involve cutting through waiting lists, permissions and other procedures and ignoring institutional objectives, such as curriculum targets, in order to ensure a focus on a child's safety.

The example I have given has much in common which what Engeström (2008: 194) has described as 'negotiated knotworking', though perhaps lacks the drama of Engeström's description where he describes a 'knot' as:

> ... (a) rapidly pulsating, distributed, and partially improvised orchestration of collaborative performance between otherwise loosely connected actors and activity systems. Knotworking is characterized by a movement of tying, untying and retying together seemingly separate threads of activity. The tying and dissolution of a knot of collaborative work is not reducible to any specific individual or fixed organizational entity as the center of control. The center does not hold. (Engeström, 2008: 1994)

He explains that knotworking is not the same as working within a network, as relations lack the stability of a network and collaboration occurs without predetermined rules. The shared responsibility and the lack of rigidity in responses that characterise knotworking are certainly features of the work that have given rise to the idea of relational agency. However, relational agency is an attempt at understanding how purposeful action on the world with others is co-ordinated, however loosely, and what it means for those who are able to engage with others to exercise it.

4.2 Agency and Mutuality

I first observed what I began to conceptualise as relational agency in a study of a women's drop in centre, where practitioners from different professional backgrounds worked alongside the women who used the centre to strengthen their ability to, for example, deal with arrears in rent or domestic violence. What was striking in

4.2 Agency and Mutuality

that study (Edwards & Mackenzie, 2005; 2008) was that the women who used the centre, having experienced relational support for their own agentic actions, demonstrated an equivalent relational support for each other and in particular newcomers to the centre. We described what we saw in the following way.

> Relational agency involves a capacity to offer support and to ask for support from others ... One's ability to engage with the world is enhanced by doing so alongside others. What the (women's) centre was doing was creating an open enough system for a fluid form of relational agency to emerge. The fluidity of such relationships is important as it was clear that they were not encouraging dependency and were encouraging a capacity to both seek and give help when engaging with the world. (Edwards & Mackenzie, 2005: 294)

The idea of agency is central and distinguishes my focus from that of Engeström and his description of the processes of knotworking. Charles Taylor, some time ago, described individual agency as evident in the ability to identify the goals at which one is directing one's action and to evaluate whether one had been successful (Taylor, 1977). His emphasis on evaluation as well as intention is, I think, an important sign of agentic action. However, he subsequently became concerned with the problem of the overweening selves that are produced by modernity's focus on the individual, and the need for a stronger connection of individual selves with the common good. His (1991) critique of modernity's emphasis on individual action and the concomitant dependence on recognition from others for the development of identity, at the expense of responsibility to and for other others, meshes strongly with the focus on mutual responsibility in joint action that is so central to the exercise of relational agency. He summarises the thesis of *The Ethics of Authenticity* as follows:

> If authenticity is being true to ourselves, is recovering our own 'sentiment de l'existence', then perhaps we can only achieve it integrally if we recognize that this sentiment connects us to a wider whole. (Taylor, 1991: 91)

We can see similar moves towards the relational in psychology more generally. The year 2005 was 'The Year of Relationships' for the British Psychological Society, signalling that psychology is recognising some of the methodological challenges posed by the fluidity and flux that characterises late modernity. Goodwin (2005), echoing years of research on social capital (Field, 2002; Halpern, 2005), explained why, as a psychologist, he studies relationships: 'Everywhere, however, we found that close relationships acted as important 'social glue', helping people deal with the uncertainties of their changing world ...' (p. 615).

The breakdown of social certainties that are reflected in the new forms of professionalism outlined in Chapter 1 (Section 1.2) make the need for enhanced forms of agency all the more important. Seddon, Henriksson, and Niemeyer (2010) have made a similar point in their analyses of how occupations have been destabilised by concepts such as lifelong learning societies and knowledge economies, requiring workers to negotiate boundaries and seek 'cultural anchor points' (p. 3), and producing a tension between 'on the one hand, fragmentation and individual isolation and, on the other, new forms of collective agency' (p. 3).

Elsewhere I have argued along the same lines, focusing on the implications for personal identity (Edwards, 2005a). The argument went that it appears that the mobile and dislocated communities of late capitalism create paradoxical tensions for those who inhabit them and these put strain on a sense of self. For example, as Friedland and Boden (1994) have argued, individual lives are interconnected as never before, yet the old boundaries that sustained a sense of self as part of a specific community are increasingly difficult to maintain. At the same time, individuals are expected to exhibit strong personal responsibility as they move between communities or settings, work at the perimeters of institutions and build personal networks that cross organisational boundaries.

I am therefore suggesting that professional agency needs to be strengthened when practitioners who need to collaborate across organisational boundaries or work flexibly with clients without the protection of institutional rituals carry out their work. The strengthening comes when individual actors are connected to 'the wider whole' where at the very least both the interpretations of problems of practice and responses to them are shared responsibilities. This shared agency requires sustaining, but first it requires understanding. The idea of relational agency was developed as one way of describing how such strong forms of agency might arise for and in collaborations that involve working across boundaries between practices; but has, I think, a broader relevance, also informing understandings of relationships between people who are positioned differently within the same practices.

4.3 Relational Agency and Cultural Historical Activity Theory

In Chapter 1 (Section 1.6) I described relational agency as a capacity that emerges in a two-stage process within a constant dynamic, which involves:

(i) working with others to expand the 'object of activity' or task being working on by recognising the motives and the resources that others bring to bear as they too interpret it;
(ii) aligning one's own responses to the newly enhanced interpretations, with the responses being made by the other professionals as they act on the expanded object.

The origins of this description lie within the explanatory frameworks of Cultural Historical Activity Theory (CHAT) already mentioned in previous chapters. There are three reasons for working within CHAT. Firstly, it allows an analysis of action in activities. Secondly, action is seen as part of activities which are object-oriented, i.e. purposeful, reflecting the motives of the practices within which they are located. Finally, CHAT has evolved from a focus on both individual mind and collective action, and offers some scope for examining action with others in relation to the intentions of the others. A brief overview of how I am using the term CHAT may be useful at this point.

The term was created by Cole as a way of bringing together two important aspects of his own experience as a researcher: cultural psychology and the cultural historical

4.3 Relational Agency and Cultural Historical Activity Theory

theory of Vygotsky and his associates (Cole, 1996). Since Cole's original conception of CHAT, it has been taken up as a set of still-developing analytic resources for studying human action in activities. As I have worked with the analytic tools offered by CHAT, I am aware that I have been highlighting two particular strands of work within the cultural historical legacy of Vygotsky because of my own background as a researcher. The strands are different, but are both based on Vygotsky's analyses of how people act in and on the world: sociocultural psychology and activity theory. A quick way of revealing the differences between these two strands is to examine just how each has worked with Vygotsky's legacy (Chaiklin, 2001a; Edwards, 2005b; Engeström, 1999).

Sociocultural psychology has developed out of North and South American and Western European concerns about the inherent separation of mind and world, or self and context, to be found in interactionist descriptions of learning, which at best 'take into account' the contexts which learners experience. Vygotsky's work on mediation and consciousness became attractive to the Western interactionists who disliked an analytic separation of mind and world, because it offered a way of overcoming it by examining the impact of culturally saturated tools such as material artefacts and the concepts carried in language on the formation of mind (Edwards, 2007). In crude summary, the focus in sociocultural accounts, which are based in Vygotsky's work, is on the meditational power of the dialogues, including use of material artefacts, through which one becomes and remains a member of a culture. This strand is particularly strong in the work of, for example, Wertsch and Säljö.

Activity theory, on the other hand, emphasises the dialectical aspects of the creation and use of cultural tools and in particular focuses on the extent to which cultural conditions shape actions in activities. It finds its origins in a Marxist attention to the historical, social and economic foundations of thinking and acting (Chaiklin, 2001b; Kozulin, 1986) and, as developed by Engeström (1999), takes the analytic gaze to the systemic conditions which shape the activities we engage in. The two strands are mutually informing and are compatible, I think, with Cole's intention to develop CHAT as an analytic concept that can deal with sense-making and action in everyday activities.

Relational agency draws on both sociocultural and activity theory accounts of learning. It is a sociocultural concept to the extent that it focuses on the interactional aspects of purposeful action and how they are mediated by the common knowledge generated in boundary practices, but it locates those interactions within an understanding of object-oriented activity (see Appendix A) and systemic affordances that owe a great deal to the activity theory developed by Engeström (Edwards, 2009; Engeström, 1987, 1999).

Let us look at what relational agency means in practice. In Chapter 2 (Section 2.4) I suggested that the object of activity, that is, what is being worked on, in interprofessional collaborations, which are focused on vulnerable young people, might be a child's trajectory. The trajectory will be interpreted differently by different practitioners as their specialist knowledge mediates their interpretations: a health worker will see aspects of the trajectory which will be different from those identified by a social worker. As they work on the trajectory and share their interpretations, they dialogically sustain their joint action for and with the child; and at the same time, by acknowledging what each can bring to bear, they dialectically expand their understandings of the child's trajectory to reveal a more complex picture of the child's life.

They are not working on separate 'bits of a child' as one practitioner once put it, but are working in parallel, seeing the child as a complete person in a complex social world. Parallel work on complex objects of activity needs to be mediated if the mutual alignment which strengthens joint action is to be achieved. There are therefore two processes of mediation in play at the same time in work that can be characterised as relational agency, which explain my emphasis on seeing a capacity for relational agency as a type of expertise that is in addition to a core professional expertise. The two meditational processes are as follows:

(i) The child's trajectory (or any other object of activity) is interpreted in ways which are mediated by the concepts that matter for each profession, with the result that the social worker may focus on safety while the health worker on mental stability. These different concepts contribute to expanding the object of activity for all the professionals involved.
(ii) The mutual attunements of the interpretations of, and responses to, the object of activity that are made by the practitioners are mediated by the common knowledge that has been built up between professionals.

The building of common knowledge between potentially collaborating professionals is therefore crucial to ensuring that when relational agency is needed in the heat of collaborative action, there is no need for translation or transformation of knowledge in order to achieve understandings of purposes and resources. Instead, transfer which, as we saw in Chapter 3 (Section 3.1), ensures a lack of novelty in exchanges across boundaries (Carlile, 2004) can result in quick and purposeful action without lengthy negotiations. Relational agency is therefore more than collaboration. Rather it functions as a strength that is shared between purposeful actors as they draw on their own expertise to work on common objects of activity.

Relational agency is entirely compatible with the CHAT view of selfhood. Vygotsky's child is born social with the result that human development is usually explained in terms of a continuously changing relationship with the historically shaped practices in which one comes to participate, whether in family life or the work place. This account can seem a deterministic approach to the development of selfhood, a point made by Archer when she compares the 'realist' account she offers (Archer, 2000) with the Vygotskian premises on which Harré (1983) develops his analysis of the social basis of the selfhood. She argues, among other points, that Harré only offers an account of the social identity of persons.

For Archer, the self does emerge relationally, but initially through relationships between 'the body, nature and practice' (p. 97), which allows for the development of both personal and social identity, and not through what she dismisses as 'socialisation' (p. 97) or 'society's gift alone' (p. 116). Her powerfully made, though essentially dualist, argument is that we bring the effects of the private encounters between the body nature and the practice to our engagement with the social world and not the reverse. We shall see in Chapter 6 (Section 6.4) that a Vygotskian notion of practice makes the distinction that Archer draws less clear cut, but for the moment let's tackle the assumptions about agency and Vygotsky's legacy in the critique that Archer offers.

Harré's account of the development of self (Harré, 1983) starts with observing initial participation in public practices and the appropriation of what matters in those practices, and moves to discuss a process of private transformation or internalisation which produces individual representations of what is valued publicly, and then proceeds on to recognise public engagement in those practices as an individual who knows how to operate in them. This process can be seen as description of socialisation. However, such an interpretation underplays the dialectical strand in Vygotsky's legacy, which is quite clearly present in the stages outlined by Harré.

Central to Vygotsky's understanding of development through action in and on the world was the notion of externalisation which operates alongside internalisation as we engage in what Vygotsky described as the social situation of development (Vygotsky, 1998). For Vygotsky, internalisation occurs when what is valued in the social situation of development is assimilated into how people think (Harré's second stage); and externalisation of understandings is evidenced in their actions in and on the social situation of their development (Harré's final stage). It is a psychology for a changing world, reflecting one of Vygotsky's intentions: to create a Marxist account of human development. Put simply, minds are shaped by the ways of thinking and concepts that are available in particular social worlds and these ways of thinking are externalised and revealed in actions in and on those worlds: we are both shaped by our cultures and we shape them. As we learn, we therefore find ourselves in new relationships with our worlds; and in doing so we act on them differently and change them. Human agency is therefore central to a version of learning that sees externalisation to be as important as internalisation.

As we saw in Chapter 2 (Section 2.3), expertise is demonstrated in our capacity to manipulate the social practices in which we engage in order to propel us forward in our intentional actions. Far from seeing us as socially determined beings engaged in conventionalised activities, the idea of human agency in our actions on the social situation of development is central to Vygotsky's legacy. Of course, that agency is developed within a sense of what is possible, which we learn alongside others.

This constraint returns us to Taylor's (1991) concern that agency needs to be understood within a framework which includes sets of moral goals that aim at the wellbeing of others as well as ourselves. He nicely outlines what he sees as necessary tensions in modern life if we are simultaneously agentic by acting on and shaping the world and conventionally engaged with what matters:

> Briefly, we can say that authenticity (A) involves (i) creation and construction as well as discovery (ii) originality, and frequently (iii) opposition to the rules of society and even potentially to what we recognize as morality. But it is also true ... that it (B) requires (i) openness to horizons of significance (for otherwise the creation loses the background that can save it from insignificance) and (ii) a self-definition in dialogue. That these demands

may be in tension has to be allowed. But what must be wrong is a simple privileging of one over the other. (Taylor, 1991: 66)

Taylor's account of the necessary tension between creativity and continuity (or dialectics and dialogue) provides a useful counter-argument to Archer's critique of Vygotsky's contribution to understanding agency as merely socialisation. Relational agency can perhaps add to that counter-argument by recognising, as we saw in Chapter 3 (Section 3.2), how mutual awareness and the strength of purpose that it brings can, for example, lead to 'rule-bending' and world-shaping; and by giving particular emphasis to how an awareness of others and their goals becomes part of the process of purposeful action on the world.

4.4 Motives and Relational Agency

But what holds those actions together and how do practitioners keep focused on a shared object of activity? In the previous chapters I have discussed the importance of motives to practices and to the generation of common knowledge. I shall now discuss in more detail how CHAT understandings of motive connect with the idea of relational agency. A key concept here is 'object-motive' which was outline in Chapter 1 (Section 1 3). It was developed by Leont'ev, a major contributor to activity theory. Arguing that 'It is exactly the object of an activity that gives it a determined direction' (Leont'ev, 1978: 62), he proposed that the object motive, that is how the object of activity is interpreted by participants in the activity, calls forth specific responses which reflect the values and purposes of the dominant practices inhabited by participants and the activities in which they engage.

For example, a teacher looking at a child's developmental trajectory may interpret it in terms of academic performance reflecting the practices and activities of schooling, while a social worker looking at the same trajectory may seek signs of vulnerability and risk of harm reflecting her professional activities and practices. The different interpretations of children's trajectories offered by practitioners, and the motives that these interpretations present to practitioners, therefore reflect the dominant activities of their professions and also of the organisations they see as their professional homes. Recognising the object motives of other practitioners to enhance interpretations and responses, as I indicated in the previous section, can make for an enriched response which is likely to benefit the child, but it is not achieved without some effort.

Relational agency is an attempt to conceptualise what is involved in working with the object motives of other practitioners when both interpreting and responding to a complex problem. It is concerned with the 'why' of collaboration as much as the 'how'. It therefore connects directly with Nardi's concern with motives in collaborative work. Criticising studies of collaboration because of their tendency to focus on *how* it is achieved rather than the motives that give shape to participation (Nardi, 2005), she has suggested that we should analytically focus on object motives in order to examine the various motives for collaboration in an object-oriented activity. She argues that more attention needs to be given to *why* people engage in collaboration and what are their 'passionately held motives' (p. 37). Here we return to the importance of values in professional practices indicated in Chapter 2 (Section 2.3). One outcome of thinking about working together in this way is a highlighting of the importance of values. Professional values are woven through the common knowledge that mediate fluid and purposeful responses and are recognised as crucial to how professionals interpret problems in practice.

One of the implications arising from recognising how objects of activity, or professional tasks, elicit different value-laden interpretations and responses from different experts, is that if the object of activity and object motive are not aligned in similar ways for each collaborator, attention needs to be paid to aligning, though not necessarily matching, their different motives as they work with the same client. In other words, as I have already argued, it is not enough to focus only on *how* a social worker and a teacher work with a child, exchange information and so on, we need also to examine *why* they are working with the child. This conclusion is echoed by a practitioner in the National Evaluation of the Children's Fund (NECF) (Edwards, Barnes, Plewis, & Morris, 2006).

> I think the very first step is understanding about what the sort of issues are .... Professions have very, very different ideas about need, about discipline, about responsibility, about the impact of systems on families ... So I think the first step is actually to get some shared understanding about effective practices and about understanding the reasons behind some of them. Understanding some of the reasons why we are seeing these sorts of issues in families. (Practitioner NECF)

4.5 Relational Agency and Demands on Practitioners

In Chapter 3 (Section 3.6) I outlined how the narratives produced in interprofessional conversations can reveal both aspects of the professional knowledge and the motives in play for participants when they discuss practice. By making taken-for-granted aspects of practice accessible to other practitioners participants were able to generate understandings of what matters for them, which I've characterised as common knowledge. In other words, they were learning at those meetings; and engaging relationally with others later in the heat of action takes their learning a little further.

Again I need the language of CHAT to explain what is happening. The premise is that the relationship between the acting subject and the problem being worked on is a dynamic. As practitioners work on the problems that are the objects of the activity, whether they are a child's trajectory or a piece of software, the objects or problems work back on them, confirming their interpretations or revealing unforeseen features. If practitioners work jointly on a problem, the object of activity is itself expanded to reveal unanticipated features for each of the actors. Put briefly, joint interpretations will usually reveal a more complex problem, and the object of activity that works back on the acting subject will offer some novelty and provoke learning (Edwards, 2005a). For example, the software engineer who is working with the accountant to develop a database tool learns about what matters for the accountant, while the accountant picks up more about the potential of the software.

The idea of an expanded object within a joint activity, within practices, is not the same as Engeström's notion of expansive learning, which is a concept that operates at the level of the system and where the expansion of the object is central to systemic change. He explains the collective process which is his focus as follows: 'The expansive cycle begins with individual subjects questioning the accepted practice and it gradually expands into a collective movement or institution.' (Engeström, 2008: 130). I am instead focusing on the object of activity and its impact on the mind-sets and responses of practitioners, reflecting the sociocultural concerns in my work. However, these mind-sets and actions are, of course, embedded in activities in particular professional practices, which may change.

New ways of interpreting the problems of practice can, of course, disrupt comfortable acceptance of established procedures. In Chapter 3 (Section 3.2) I discussed how practitioners involved in inter-professional work with vulnerable children felt they should rule-bend in their organisations to meet the needs of children. But sometimes rule-bending is impossible and instead practitioners experience a sense of personal conflict. In several of the studies discussed in this book, I have heard practitioners describe how they have been told by colleagues that they were betraying their core expertise when they tried to bring back ideas arising from inter-professional collaborations to their home workplaces.

The emotional or affective aspects of reading the figured world of familiar practices in ways which are different from those of the people you work with should not be down-played. In Chapter 2 (Section 2.3) I discussed expertise in terms of an ability to manipulate the practices of a figured world to take forward one's own purposes. However, when the possibilities for action afforded by a figured world are misaligned with one's motives, frustration ensues.

Vygotsky was quite clear that emotion cannot be filtered out of analyses of how we act in the world. In the last year of his life, Vygotsky developed his ideas on the importance of emotion with a new unit of analysis: *'perezhivanie'* (Vygotsky, 1994: 339). *Perezhivanie* can be equated with lived or emotional experience and was, for Vygotsky, central to how we think and engage with the world. *Perezhivanie* has been largely ignored in the development of post-Vygotskian theory. However, it was refined in the writing of Vasilyuk (1991) when he introduced the notion of 'experiencing', which involves living through personal crises in creative ways in order to restore meaning to life. Vasilyuk's examples of critical situations are often quite dramatic. Nonetheless, the attention he has paid to the discomfort of personally experienced contradictions and the questioning of meaning in activities connect with what practitioners have said about the conflicts they feel.

Kozulin (1991), in his review of the English translation of Vasilyuk's book, suggests that his focus on experiencing and crises combines Vygotskian ideas about learning as processes of making sense and meaning as we engage in the world, with 'Western studies of the psychodynamics of the unconscious' (p. 14). By making that connection between thinking and the unconscious, Vasilyuk can help us to see that coping with change is not simply a behavioural response, but also involves a relatively slow process of working through contradictions or 'crises' and gaining new forms of mental equilibrium which enable functioning. The process of working through crises and the repositioning involved, in turn, leads to our interpreting the world differently. New meanings then become clear as we engage with others to work with and reflect on those interpretations.

4.6 Systemic Responses to the Demands of Relational Agency

The rejection of new ideas derived from collaborating with other professionals, which I described a little earlier as betrayal, is more likely to occur in workplaces that are bound together by the bureaucratisation of professional practices that were discussed in Chapter 1 (Section 1.2) than in organisations that are geared to the co-production of solutions such as software engineering. In Chapter 1, I suggested that bureaucratisation provided an institutional safety net for practitioners who made potentially risky decisions during their work with clients, but it down-played what used to be called professional autonomy in client-centred work. Instead, professional knowledge was embedded in routines, and practice in turn became shaped by these routines. Relational agency, the learning it involves and the enhancing of professional agency through joint action that it offers call for a very different organisational structure where rules are set up to support relational engagement.

Although organisations rarely remain unchanged, some organisations are better than others at accommodating the shifts demanded by the integration of new knowledge and realigned motives; or, in activity theory terms, at encouraging an expansion of the object of activity and responding to the outcome of that expansion. To describe this difference between systems, Engeström takes Vygotsky's idea of the 'zone of proximal development' (ZPD), which was developed as a way of assessing a child's capability to learn, and uses it in relation to activity systems (Engeström, 1987) in order to indicate the capacity of a system to learn and change. This version of the ZPD is a way of distinguishing between systems that are adept at learning and those which are less responsive: activity systems which responsively and dynamically evolve are seen to have an almost open-ended ZPD.

These CHAT analyses suggest that systems do not simply mature: changes are stimulated by imbalances which, in turn may lead to systemic change such as a modification in how the work is shared out or the recognition of an entirely new object of activity to be worked on. Sometimes these imbalances are barely discernable, as they arise from small tensions that occur. For example, lack of clarity over whether a form tutor or a head of year in a school makes contact with a child's parent may indicate a tension which may be resolved by a brief conversation; or it may be the first sign of a contradiction in a system where a new emphasis on attainment, which is the responsibility of the heads of year, is beginning to over-ride the school's historically established emphasis on informal relations with children's families through form tutors (Edwards, Lunt, & Stamou, 2010).

Il'enkov, a philosopher who has contributed a great deal to post-Vygotskian theory, helps us to explore the implications of slight shifts for the systems and practices we inhabit in the following way:

> In reality it always happens that a phenomenon which later becomes universal originally emerges as an individual, particular, specific phenomenon, as an exception from the rule. It cannot actually emerge in any other way. Otherwise history would have a rather mysterious form. Thus, any new improvement of labour, every new mode of man's action in production, before becoming generally accepted and recognized, first emerges as a certain deviation from previously accepted and codified norms. Having emerged as an individual exception from the rule in the labour of one or several men, the new form is then taken over by others, becoming in time a new universal norm. If the new norm did not originally appear in this exact manner, it would never become a really universal form, but would exist merely in fantasy, in wishful thinking. (Il'enkov, 1982: 83–84)

While Taylor outlined similar processes in terms of the demands of individual and ethical authenticity and a crucial tension between creative rule-questioning and the normative expectations of being in society (Taylor, 1991) (Section 4.3), Engeström's activity theory framework focuses on the system in order to highlight the contradictions in and between practices that arise through these shifts (Engeström, 1987; Appendix A).

Engeström does not intend to deal with the personal experiencing of contradictions, but his work usefully alerts us to demands that changing systems and the contradictions that give rise to them make on the practitioners who inhabit them. Practitioners who are working relationally on complex problems need to be supported by work systems which make that possible, a point I shall revisit in Chapter 7. In brief, systems need to be set up so that the energies of practitioners are geared to work tasks and not to modifying work systems in order to be able to engage with the object motive of a complex task.

There is a danger that relational agency, as it has been discussed so far, can be regarded as a form of heroism which calls for a capacity to bend rules and work against the grain of both bureaucracy and NPM. I suspect that this may be the case at the moment, but I am proposing a slightly longer-term view towards a time when it is accepted that professional action is driven forward by a strong emphasis on professional motives and values.

The 'goodwork project' at Harvard has, interestingly, examined alignments between professionals' goals and how the importance of these goals is more generally regarded by society at large. Gardner, one of the project leaders, explains:

> As researchers we ask whether professionals can pass the "mirror test"–whether they can look at themselves in the mirror and feel proud of the work that they and their fellow professionals do. We have found that good work is especially difficult to carry out in certain professions at this historical moment when society is changing quickly, market forces are very powerful, and our very sense of time and space is being altered by technology. (Gardner, 2001: 2)

The study focused initially on professionals in the media and bio-technology, and unsurprisingly found different degrees of alignment between personal motivations and what was expected of them. However, it also captured the centrality of values to sustaining a sense of professional purpose:

> Many of our subjects told us that they are working to bring about changes that may take 50 years to come to fruition. So long as individuals like this do not lose heart, we can anticipate that they–and the professions from which they are drawn–will be able to pass the mirror test. (Gardner, 2001: 5)

I shall return to motives and values in professional life in Chapter 6.

4.7 Relational Agency in Practice

While Taylor deals with tensions between intention and possibility in terms of the moral self, for Lave (1988) the institution, activity and person and the tensions within and between them are brought together in practice. It is there that the processes of reproduction, transformation and change, which are reflected in changes in activities, occur. I quote at length to attempt to do justice to her argument:

> Processes of reproduction, transformation, *and* change are implicated in the reproduction *or* transformation or change of activity in all settings and on all occasions. This implies that it is not at the level of cognitive processes that the unique, the nonroutine, the crisis, the exception, the creative novelty, the scientific discovery, major contributions to knowledge, ideal modes of thought, the expert and the powerful, are brought into being and given significance as such. These are all matters of constitutive order in the broadest and most complex sense, and they are constructed in dialectical relations between the experienced lived in world and its constitutive order – in practice. (Lave, 1988: 190 – italics in the original)

The relational turn in expertise may need to wait for an alignment between what matters for professionals and what is more broadly expected of them *pace* the 'good-work' study. However, there are indications of an emergent dialectic between the experienced world of practitioners and the constitutive order of their work, which points towards the relational aspects of that work.

In Chapter 6 I shall discuss the problems faced by workers who are undertaking responsible work with, for example, vulnerable clients. There I shall develop the argument that the relational turn in practice not only reflects the complexity of the problems being tackled and the contradictions that consequently occur but can also offer some counteraction to the wider conditions of work in late modernity.

I shall briefly outline the argument here. These uncertain conditions are summarised in Giddens' observation that currently 'We are left with questions where once there appeared to be answers' (1990: 49). The modern world is a risky place where the social relations that sustained professional work may no longer be embedded in specific situations, yet where professional accountability is high. The worlds experienced by professionals, who are working in systems driven by a management focus on products rather than processes, are structured by systems of strong personal accountability, even when elements of bureaucracy remain. However, the responsiveness and fluidity that the complexities of professional work now demand is giving rise to more relational forms of agentic decision-making that capture both mutually aligned action and, crucially, shared responsibility in activities.

Attention to the relational aspects of work is, of course, not new. Once we accept Lave's view that cognition can be 'stretched over' persons, activities and settings (Lave, 1988: 1) or Bruner's suggestion that as workers we enter communities whose 'extended intelligence' we come to share (Bruner, 1996: 154), we recognise how our thinking and acting are shaped by our participation in systems of distributed expertise to which we also contribute (see Section 2.4). Although I have largely developed the idea of relational agency while examining inter-professional collaborations across organisational boundaries, I believe that the concept may add to the analyses of distributed resources in specific settings offered by, for example, Lave and Bruner. In particular, it can help with conceptualising how practitioners work with the resources, or distributed intelligence, to be found in them and in turn contribute to these resources while engaging in purposeful practices.

In these more boundaried situations the case being made for relational agency connects in some ways with Billett's focus on what he terms 'relational interdependence' in the workplace (Billett, 2006), by arguing, like Billett, for greater attention to agency in explaining relationships between the individual and the social in working life. Offering what he describes as a 'more socially inclusive, engaged and sympathetic view of the individual.' (2006: 65), Billett suggests that changes in people and practices arise from complex relational interdependencies between individual and social 'factors' (p. 66). However, Billett's research programme (for example, Billett & Pavlova, 2005; Billett & Somerville, 2004; Billett, 2004), for all its similarity with the concerns at the core of this book through its emphasis on agency, intentionality, motives and the relational aspects of work, takes as its focus individual agency and its connections with the workplace as a social world. Relational agency works at a different level of detail by attempting to explain how practitioners may sustain joint engagement on a work task to enhance their responses to it.

Relational agency, with its attention to enhancing understandings of problems of practice and its recognition of distributed expertise, has perhaps a stronger resonance with the work of Hakkarainen and his colleagues (Hakkarainen, Palonen, Paavola, & Lehtinen, 2004). Reflecting their focus on reciprocity and the mutual strengthening of competence and expertise to enhance the collective competence of a community, they explain the advantages of creating collective competence discussed in Section 2.6 in terms of the development of new knowledge.

In their work on communities of networked expertise, however, like Engeström, their focus is primarily at the level of system, whether it is a community or a network. Members of Hakkarainen's research team, recognising the usefulness of relational agency have, however, attempted to identify the skills needed for the development of collective competencies in knowledge work in higher education. They conclude that what are required are 'metaskills' which can 'deal with social practices of engaging in collaborative enquiry' (Muukkonen & Lakkala, 2009: 206). If by metaskills they mean skills that are in addition to the core skills that comprise

4.7 Relational Agency in Practice

a specialist expertise, then their analysis comes close to how one might recognise the kind of additional layer relational expertise that was outlined in Chapter 2.

Let us therefore conclude this chapter with examples of how the idea of relational agency is being used in different settings and organisations. The examples are drawn from some of the work of members of the Oxford Centre for Sociocultural and Activity Theory Research (OSAT) over the past few years. They demonstrate how the concept can augment the CHAT analytic tool box when examining how people work resourcefully to accomplish complex tasks and how relational work can impact on one's sense of self.

The first example illustrates its use for participants in web-based systems of distributed expertise. Francis, in his 2007 DPhil (Francis, 2007; in press) examined how masters degree students at Oxford created a 'projective identity' *pace* Gee (2003, 2004), which propelled them forward as a particular kind of person, for example, 'the political guy' or the 'ecological guy'. These identities-in-creation were shaped by how the students wanted to position themselves within both virtual and local networks and, therefore, the job market on graduation. The accounts they offered are complex and this summary, presented in the terminology used in this book, inadequate. In brief, several of the students developed a capacity for agentic relational work within issue-focused web-based communities where people, with a variety expertise between them, discussed common topics such as developments in the US Democratic Party in one case and de-forestation in another. In each case the long-term object of activity for the student in question was his or her own identity. However, they would work towards their developing identity as 'expert' and 'networked' by presenting problems they needed to solve in their studies and by contributing to solving problems for other participants in the on-line groups.

The process mirrors the sequential development of building common knowledge and exercise of relational agency outlined in this book. The students participated relatively passively in these on-line groups until they became versed in the common knowledge in play in them. Once they had the expertise necessary to work the practices of the on-line community, they would engage by both outlining problems they were tackling and asking for advice in interpreting and responding to them and by offering their own expertise. In their case, these extra-mural communities, the learning achieved through them, and the identity confirmations that accrued through their demonstrations of their own expertise, allowed the students to present strong specialist identities as they participated in the socially challenging world of Oxford college life and launched themselves on the job market. At the same time they had honed the additional skills needed for responsive relational engagement that was likely to be a feature of the worlds they were to enter.

An example of the importance of relational agency, as involving a capacity to be attuned to and connect with the knowledge and priorities of others at work, was examined in an ethnographic study of a lengthy collaboration between radiographers, engineers and computer scientists to develop a piece of mammography equipment. Kinti's 2 years of fieldwork identified an initial lack of collaboration, despite an agreed outcome, to create the equipment (Kinti, 2008). She traced these difficulties to differences in object motives for each specialist team. In other words, each team was engaging for different reasons and was working towards accomplishing the task with different motives, which were sometimes in conflict. For example, the computer scientists were based in a university and were therefore located in practices which were shaped by the UK Research Assessment Exercise, through which funds are allocated to universities largely on the basis of the quality of the research-based publications that are produced by faculty. They therefore emphasised published research papers as products of the collaboration, whereas the engineers were heavily focused on the practicalities of design and development. These differences also involved differences in time-scale and the constant managing of team priorities in relation to participants' home organisations. A turning point came with the construction of a separate 'solutions team' which, in terms of the argument I have been presenting, worked with each set of experts to develop common knowledge and to align their motives. The team mediated conflicting priorities and Kinti was then able to observe more fluid forms of relational agency in action as the different experts worked responsively with each other on the development of the equipment.

At the beginning of this chapter I distinguished between forms of working together characterised as inter-subjectivity, where the purpose is that the more expert partner mediates what matters in a culture and supports a novice as she learns to participate as an agentic individual in that culture, and collaborations, where each participant brings relevant resources so that the whole is greater than the parts. Lundsteen's study of internships in an investment bank (Lundsteen, in progress) blurs that distinction by examining a culture where a lack of relational agency in a workplace also impedes the support that novices require when learning to take part in it.

Lundsteen is examining how undergraduate students have experienced summer-long internships in an investment bank, which interestingly did not survive the 2008 recession (see also Section 2.5). Here the concept of relational agency is employed to make sense of the difficulties experienced by students in a workplace dominated by internal competition and a lack of relational work. Each year students were allocated to a work team for the first 6 weeks of their placement and then moved to a different team for the second 6 weeks. The bank regarded these internships as an opportunity to assess the suitability of students prior to the recruitment rounds. The process was successful as the lack of relational engagement on shared objects of activity within many of the work teams meant that students either sank or swam. Interns reported learning not to expect conversations with other team members and to become independent actors within a system of both internal and external competition. For some this lack of relational sharing of resources was too uncomfortable, leading them to decide that banking was not for them.

In another study, Wagstaff (2009) has drawn on the idea of relational agency to understand supervisory relationships over the duration of doctoral study. Like Lundsteen, she is examining a learning situation where one might expect that relationships would move from initial inter-subjectivity in which the novice researcher learns to become a researcher in a relationship with a more expert supervisor which is focused on the thesis, to one where joint work on the thesis mirrors features of relational agency as the student learns to work resourcefully within the broader research community. The study is small-scale, but has indicated that an understanding of relational agency is a useful way of framing apprenticeships for professions, such as social science research, where resourceful practice and relational expertise is useful. In particular, it seems that common knowledge plays an important part in mediating work on the thesis as an object of activity. Efforts are made by to create common knowledge early on in the relationship, and it ultimately becomes a resource through which joint tasks like data analysis are accomplished. Here is a supervisor attempting to build common knowledge very early in the supervisory relationship. He offers an account which reveals what matters for him as an academic:

> A PhD is a strange conglomeration of personal, intellectual and sort of professional agendas. And so, you need to think about where you're going to go with it ... you also need to think about what you've got to offer ... I also think that, my personal interest ... is particularly in the ways in which African societies are being reshaped by their engagements with philanthropies of all sorts of shapes and sizes .... So then I, I'd be ... I think that'd be interesting

In this chapter I have not dealt with potential asymmetries of power in the exercise of relational agency. However, my analyses of inter-professional work suggests that so much depends on how relationships are set up so that the voice of the other is given weight and the extent to which it is recognised that all share strong motives for resourceful work on these complex tasks. If these two features are not in place, then it is difficult to see relational agency in action. Therefore, one cannot ignore the challenges to relational agency presented by differences in standing within the field of action. Nowhere is this more apparent than in relationships between professionals and clients and it is to that topic that we now turn.

References

Archer, M. (2000). *Being human: The problem of agency*. Cambridge: Cambridge University Press.
Billett, S. (2004). *Subjectivity, intentionalities and appropriation at work: Understanding relations between individual and social agency in work and working life*. University of Technology, Sydney. (Oval Research working paper 04–01).
Billett, S. (2006). Relational interdependence between social and individual agency in work and working life. *Mind, Culture and Activity*, 13(1), 53–69.
Billett, S., & Pavlova, M. (2005). Learning through working life: Self and individuals' agentic action. *International Journal of Lifelong Education*, 26(3), 195–211.
Billett, S., & Somerville, M. (2004). Transformations at work: Identity and learning. *Studies in Continuing Education*, 26(2), 309–326.
Bruner, J. S. (1996). *The culture of education*. Cambridge, MA: Harvard University Press.
Carlile, P. (2004). Transferring, translating and transforming: An integrative framework for managing knowledge across boundaries. *Organization Science*, 15(5), 555–568.
Chaiklin, S. (2001a). The institutionalisation of cultural-historical psychology as a multinational practice. In S. Chaiklin (Ed.), *The theory and practice of cultural-historical psychology* (pp. 15–34). Århus: Århus University Press.

Chaiklin, S. (2001b). The category of personality in cultural-historical psychology. In S. Chaiklin (Ed.), *The theory and practice of cultural-historical psychology* (pp. 238–259). Århus: Århus University Press.

Cole, M. (1996). *Cultural psychology: A once and future discipline*. Cambridge, Mass: Harvard University Press.

Edwards, A. (2005a). Relational agency: Learning to be a resourceful practitioner. *International Journal of Educational Research, 43*(3), 168–182.

Edwards, A. (2005b). Let's get beyond community and practice: The many meanings of learning by participating. *The Curriculum Journal, 16*(1), 53–69.

Edwards, A. (2007). Vygotsky and US pragmatism. In H. Daniels, M. Cole, & J. Wertsch (Eds.), *The Cambridge companion to Vygotsky* (pp. 77–100). Cambridge: Cambridge University Press.

Edwards, A. (2009). Agency and activity theory: From the systemic to the relational. In A. Sannino, H. Daniels, & K. Guttierez (Eds.), *Learning and expanding with activity theory* (pp. 197–211). Cambridge: Cambridge University Press.

Edwards, A., Barnes, M., Plewis, I., & Morris, K. (2006). *Working to prevent the social exclusion of children and young people: Final lessons from the National Evaluation of the Children's Fund*. London: DfES. (Research Report 734).

Edwards, A., Lunt, I., & Stamou, E. (2010). Inter-professional work and expertise: New roles at the boundaries of schools. *British Educational Research Journal, 30*(1), 27–45.

Edwards, A., & Mackenzie, L. (2005). Steps towards participation: The social support of learning trajectories. *International Journal of Lifelong Education, 24*(4), 287–302.

Edwards, A., & Mackenzie, L. (2008). Identity shifts in informal learning trajectories. In B. van Oers, W. Wardekker, E. Elbers, & R. van der Veer (Eds.), *The transforming of learning: Advances in cultural-historical activity theory* (pp. 163–181). Cambridge: Cambridge University Press.

Engeström, Y. (1987). *Learning by expanding: An activity-theoretical approach to developmental research*. Helsinki: Orienta-Konsultit.

Engeström, Y. (1999). Activity theory and individual and social transformation. In Y. Engeström, R. Miettinen, & R.-L. Punamäki (Eds.), *Perspectives on activity theory* (pp. 19–38). Cambridge: Cambridge University Press.

Engeström, Y. (2008). *From teams to knots: Activity theoretical studies of collaboration and learning at work*. Cambridge: Cambridge University Press.

Field, J. (2002). *Social capital*. London: Routledge.

Francis, R. (2007). *The predicament of the learner in the new media age*. DPhil, University of Oxford. Available at http://ora.ouls.ox.ac.uk/objects/uuid:0cbd0185-c7ed-4306-b34e-993acd125e96

Friedland, R., & Boden, D. (Eds.) (1994). *NowHere: Space, time and modernity*. Berkley, CA: University of California Press.

Gardner, H. (2001). *Good work in turbulent times*. Accessed July 19, 2009, from http://www.goodworkproject.org

Gee, J. P. (2003). *What video games have to teach us about learning and literacy*. New York, NY and Basingstoke: Palgrave Macmillan.

Gee, J. P. (2004). *Situated language and learning: A critique of traditional schooling*. New York, NY and London: Routledge.

Giddens, A. (1990). *The consequences of modernity*. Cambridge: Polity Press.

Goodwin, R. (2005). Why I study relationships and culture. *The Psychologist, 18*(10), 614–615.

Hakkarainen, K., Palonen, T., Paavola, S., & Lehtinen, E. (2004). *Communities of networked expertise: Professional and educational perspectives*. Amsterdam: Elsevier.

Halpern, D. (2005). *Social capital*. Cambridge: Polity Press.

Harré, R. (1983). *Personal being*. Oxford: Blackwell.

Il'enkov, E. V. (1982). *The dialectics of the abstract and the concrete in Marx's 'capital'*. Moscow: Progress.

References

Kinti, I. (2008). *Balancing at the boundaries of organizations: Knowledge co-configuration between experts*. DPhil thesis, University of Oxford.

Kozulin, A. (1986). *Psychological tools: A sociocultural approach to education*. Cambridge, MA: Harvard University Press.

Kozulin, A. (1991). Psychology of experiencing: A Russian view. *Journal of Humanistic Psychology, 31*, 14–19.

Lave, J. (1988). *Cognition in practice*. Cambridge: Cambridge University Press.

Leont'ev, A. N. (1978). *Activity, consciousness and personality*. Upper Saddle River, NJ: Prentice Hall.

Lundsteen, N. (in progress). *Learning between university and the world of work*. DPhil study, Department of Education, University of Oxford.

Muukkonen, H., & Lakkala, M. (2009). Exploring metaskills of knowledge creating inquiry in higher education. *Computer Supported Collaborative Learning, 4*, 187–211.

Nardi, B. (2005). Objects of desire: Power and passion in collaborative activity. *Mind, Culture and Activity, 12*(1), 37–51.

Seddon, T., Henriksson, L., & Niemeyer, B. (Eds.) (2010). *Learning and work and the politics of working life*. London: Routledge.

Taylor, C. (1977). What is human agency? In T. Mischel (Ed.), *The self: Psychological and philosophical issues*. Oxford: Oxford University Press.

Taylor, C. (1991). *The ethics of authenticity*. Cambridge, MA: Harvard University Press.

Vasilyuk, F. (1991). *The psychology of experiencing: The resolution of life's critical situations*. Hemel Hempstead: Harvester.

Vygotsky, L. S. (1994). The problem of the environment. In R. Van der Veer & J. Valsiner (Eds.), *The Vygotsky reader*. Oxford and Cambridge, MA: Blackwell.

Vygotsky, L. S. (1998). In R. W. Rieber (Ed.), *The collected works of L.S. Vygotsky: Child psychology* (Vol. 5). New York, NY: Plenum Press.

Wagstaff, S. (2009). *Relational agency within dyadic doctoral supervisory relationships*. MSc Dissertation, Department of Education, University of Oxford.

Chapter 5
Working Relationally with Clients

5.1 Personal Responsibility

The relational theme I have been pursuing is also central to how clients are being positioned within policies that aim at their wellbeing. Room, writing quite critically of the new concept of social exclusion, observed that it directs attention to 'relational issues, in other words, inadequate social participation, lack of social integration and lack of power' at the expense of attention to, for example the more equal distribution of resources (Room, 1995: 5). As welfare policies aimed at preventing social exclusion emerged during the late 1990s, responsibility was consequently placed on the individual, as a potential participant in society, to engage with what society had to offer. Where disadvantage made participation difficult, the solution for the UK Labour government from 1997 was to build individual resilience and develop personal capabilities that would enable participation and lack of dependency.

Lister summarised that agenda as the intention to create 'an 'active' welfare state that promotes personal responsibility and individual opportunity, as opposed to what is characterised as a 'passive' welfare state that encourages dependency and lack of initiative' (Lister, 1998: 224). I shall be suggesting that the polarisation of being either active or dependent in one's engagement with the welfare state, reported by Lister, is unfortunate, as it does not allow for the strengthening of individuals and social groups that might be afforded by the exercise of relational agency within relationships of shifting and mutual dependency.

One example of how services were being reoriented to encourage the active engagement of users was the Children's Fund. Set up in 2000 by Children and Young People's Unit (CYPU) to prevent the social exclusion of children aged between 5 and 13, it was premised on the three 'Ps': *prevention* through *partnership* between service providers and the *participation* of children and families in the design, delivery and evaluation of services. The idea was that services, which were to be reconfigured through partnership arrangements between the main providers, would also be developed in response to feedback from those who were using them. As the Prime Minister's 'Office of Public Service Reform' put it in 2002, public services 'have to be refocused around the needs of the patients, the pupils, the passengers and the general public rather than the problems of those who provide the services' (OPSR, 2002: 8).

This reorientation towards a client-centred provision was a dilution of the participatory intentions outlined by Room, for all their limitations, and was presented in terms of a new 'customer focus' (OPSR, 2002: 9), which connected with new public management's attention to targets and indicators for professional practice. The weaknesses of a customer focus did not go unrecognised: Sennett is one of several commentators who have pointed to the dangers of welfare reforms that privilege 'the more independent consumers of welfare' (Sennett, 2003: 187) over those who are passively dependent. The turn away from service-led welfare to a more negotiated form of service provision was limited by the new consumer focus that drove it. The main limitation was that potential users had to be in a position to consume what was on offer, while the problems of, for example, the engagement of those potential users who are frequently termed by service providers 'hard to reach' persisted.

Therefore, although the slow and careful work which focuses on strengthening individuals and families remains a challenge, service improvement, a consumer orientation and the building of user responsibility are all intertwined in welfare reform, as the 2004 Education *Five Year Strategy for Children and Learners* (DfES, 2004) illustrated:

> The central characteristic of such a new system will be personalisation – so that the system fits to the individual rather than the individual having to fit to the system.
>
> The learner is a partner in learning, not a passive recipient – and this means that (especially as they grow older, leaving compulsory education) they have a stake in and a responsibility for their own learning. (extracts from Charles Clarke's introduction to the *Strategy*, DfES, 2004)

In this chapter I shall tease out some of the versions of participation that can be seen in the welfare professions and discuss how relational agency, and the Vygotskian ideas in which it has originated, can offer a framework for understanding how participation may be more than exercising consumer choice or involvement in evaluating services. My central argument will be that Vygotsky's view of development offers a fresh way of thinking about how people engage with their worlds. To reiterate the discussion in Section 4.3, the dialectic of internalisation and externalisation that makes up the process of learning results in qualitative changes in people's relationships with their worlds. In terms of participation in order to prevent social exclusion, I suggest that it is vital that we see participation as developing people's abilities to act on the social situations of their development in order to improve them. I shall therefore attempt to work through what Sennett (2003: 176) has described as one of 'the great bureaucratic dilemmas' for welfare states: allowing for autonomy within dependency.

I shall draw my examples of how relationally oriented work can help support externalisation almost exclusively from interactions between practitioners and clients in the welfare and education professions. I will therefore need to address the questions of discrepancies in power that were not tackled in Chapter 4. Also, once again, I suggest that the discussions of relational working with clients will have relevance for fields such as software engineering where there are expert client relationships in which there may be a difference in power arising from differences in expertise.

5.2 Participation

One of the strands in the development of a policy focus on social exclusion was economic. The 1990s saw a growing fear that there were soon to be too few skilled workers to support the rapidly increasing number of elderly. During that period the idea of a child 'at risk' of not being able to contribute to society began to replace the notion of disadvantage. From the OECD perspective, children and young people who were 'at risk' were likely to fail in the school system and be unlikely to enter work (OECD, 1998). As Levitas (1998) has observed, inclusion had become an individual obligation that needed to be actively performed.

Social inclusion was therefore becoming recast, with the idea of entitlement to integration into society as both an individual right and a societal necessity. The intention was to prevent detachment from society from occurring through engaging those at risk of exclusion in the processes of democratic life. However, that intention seemed quite rapidly to be reduced to a matter of being able to make choices, rather than an emphasis on the responsibilities that co-exist with democracy.

A report on extended schools, i.e. schools that form the hub of educational and social care provision in a neighbourhood, illustrates the point:

> At Our Lady, Star of the Sea, pupils discuss during their breakfast club the choices they have made for that day. There is much haggling between friends over what they should do at lunchtime and after school. As a result, the young pupils seem to have become quite astute consumers, increasingly taking responsibility for managing their own time. (DEMOS-Hay, 2004: 19)

While these discussions might involve students in being active in managing their own time by acting as consumers and selecting from the range of 'choices' available to them, the description does not really capture Room's points about 'inadequate social participation, lack of social integration and lack of power'.

The CYPU did attempt to go much further when setting up the Children's Fund, giving three reasons for their emphasis on the participation of children and young people in its Guidance to service providers:

> **Better services:** 'the involvement of children and young people is central to all service development that aims to meet their needs'.
>
> **Promoting citizenship and social inclusion:** 'the more children and young people are encouraged to participate the more that the process will itself make a contribution to their increased social inclusion'.
>
> **Personal and social education and development:** 'initiatives will not last if children and young people do not benefit through new friendships, learning opportunities and the on-going chance to express their views and ideas'. (CYPU, 2001: 59)

These intentions reflected a growing policy emphasis on participation in developing local services and systems in a raft of government initiatives established to prevent social exclusion (Willow, 2002). However, participation as part of a process to engage those who were likely to be detached from society was not without its difficulties. Prout described early initiatives as 'local, scattered, ad hoc, fragile and experimental' (Prout, 2000: 309). Kirby with Bryson, writing in 2002, suggested that they were not achieving an impact on local policy-making. While, very much in line with the findings of the National Evaluation of the Children's Fund (Edwards et al., 2006; Spicer, Broughton, Evans, & Smith, 2004), Danso et al. concluded that:

> ... despite the expansion of participation activity, there is much still to learn about making participation inclusive and meaningful to children and young people; about ensuring participation is not simply an end in itself but as a means to change; and about the importance of evaluating the impact of participation – on children, on professionals, on decisions and on services. (Danso et al., 2003: 13)

By identifying the need to assess the impact of participation, as an activity, on children, this statement gets to the core of how participation and prevention are connected through developing a sense of personal effectiveness. At the same time, by pointing to the potential impact on professionals and services, of children's participation in the development of services, it raises questions about changes in professional practices arising from the relational work that is focused on improving services so that they better meet the need of users.

However, I do not intend to pursue an analysis of participation as a service-led activity which prepares children for evaluating and improving the services that are provided for them, even though that focus frequently demands that professionals work relationally with service users to enhance the quality and fit of services. I instead intend to focus on Sennett's 'dilemma' and examine how practitioners work relationally with clients on more personal and client-led objects of activity such as a child's developmental trajectory or the life trajectory of a victim of domestic violence, so that they might be configured towards engagement and social inclusion rather than disengagement. The Vygotskian line I am taking will, as I have already indicated, highlight how clients may also find that they can shape the social situations of their development.

In Sections 4.3 and 5.1 I have observed that Vygotsky's learners do not simply take in or internalise what is valued in society, they also externalise or act on the world. Their learning and development are therefore revealed in how they externalise understandings in their actions and relate in fresh ways to what is going on. Elsewhere (Edwards, 2007), I have examined resilience as a quality that is promoted as an insurance against social exclusion. There I suggested that the CHAT attention to externalisation alongside internalisation means that we should find evidence of growing resilience in a person's ability to act on and shape what Vygotsky called the social situations of their development. I argued that a CHAT view of development can help to counteract concerns that attention to resilience in welfare policies places too much emphasis on individual responsibility and personal adaptation and not enough on the affordances of the environments in which they are developing.

Once policies recognise that the exercise of responsible agency, which involves acting on the social situation of one's development, might be an aspect of building resilience, we might be able to develop practices which lead to the development of clients own agency and expertise in taking control over their own life trajectories and the conditions that give rise to them.

Attention to involving children in the reconfiguring of their own trajectories also reflects recent policy concerns with a rights-based approach to welfare arising from 1990 UN Convention on the Rights of the Child. Article 12 of the Convention indicates that children have the right to make their views known when matters that concern them are discussed: consequently they are regarded as people who have the right to influence decision-making about their lives. Seeing resilience in terms of externalisation and a shaping of the conditions of one's own existence also counteracts a notion of children as 'objects of concern' (Mason, 2005: 92), which can be an outcome of inter-professional work (Edwards, 2009), and gives new confidence to adult clients as they learn to act on and shape their worlds (Edwards & Mackenzie, 2005, 2008). Let us therefore now turn to the implications for practice of joint work with clients on their life trajectories as objects of activity.

5.3 Joint Work as Co-configuration

In the LIW study (Edwards, Daniels, Gallagher, Leadbetter, & Warmington, 2009) we examined the capacity of children's services to learn to work flexibly for social inclusion and drew on analyses of learning and the transformation of work emanating from the Harvard Business School (Victor & Boynton, 1998) to map and label the work practices we found. Elsewhere we discussed these analyses in relation to inter-professional work (Edwards & Apostolov, 2007). Here I shall use the framework to consider what the co-configuring of a trajectory might mean for relational engagement between professionals and service users. In brief, Victor and Boynton identified five types of work in the history of industrial production: craft, mass production, process enhancement, mass customization, and co-configuration (Fig. 5.1).

Each type of work generates and requires a certain type of knowledge which is produced in different kinds of relationships. Victor and Boynton suggest that progress in practices occurs through learning and the leveraging of the knowledge produced into new, and arguably more effective, types of work. They explain that what craft workers know about products and processes rests in their personal intuition and experience of the customer, the product, the process and the use of their tools. When these practitioners invent solutions, they create knowledge that is rarely made explicit and is tightly coupled with experience, technique and tools. This kind of work is often regarded as intuitive. However, the articulation of that tacitly held knowledge may lead to the next stage shown in Fig. 5.1, where it can become reified as 'good practice' with the expectation that it is mass produced to becomes the norm for all.

Fig. 5.1 Historical forms of work (adapted from Victor & Boynton, 1998)

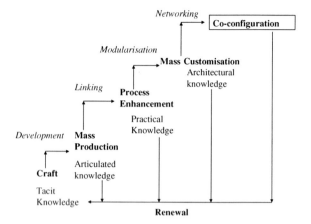

Learning is an important driver for movement through each of the stages represented in Fig. 5.1. Mass production workers follow instructions yet also learn about work through observation, sensing, and feeling the operations. They learn where the instructions are effective and where they are not. This learning leads to a new type of knowledge, which Victor and Boynton call practical knowledge. Practical knowledge is in turn enhanced through linking processes. For example, these processes may involve setting up a team system in which members focus on process improvement, which promotes the sharing of ideas within the team and which fosters collaboration across teams and functions. As we can see, progression through the stages involves increasing transparency and clear articulation of the knowledge being brought into play.

The move to mass customization, they suggest, brings greater precision. To take an example from children's services, it would involve the careful shaping of a specific service, through creating modules or tailored forms of provision which can be specifically targeted at particular groups. In the Children's Fund we saw this occurring in the provision of services, which were targeted at particular groups of children, perhaps from one ethnic background or with a specific disability.

One difference between this work and what happens in the activities to be labelled co-configuration is that with mass customization there is little opportunity for the continuous fashioning of provision to meet individual strengths and needs, whereas the emphasis of co-configuration work is on the continual development of the product or service in a close relationship with the user. Victor and Boynton outline what is involved as follows:

> The work of co-configuration involves building and sustaining a fully integrated system that can sense, respond, and adapt to the individual experience of the customer. When a firm does co-configuration work, it creates a product that can learn and adapt, but it also builds an ongoing relationship between each customer-product pair and the company. Doing mass customization requires designing a product at least once for each customer. This design process requires the company to sense and respond to the individual customer's needs. But co-configuration work takes this relationship up one level – it brings the value of an intelligent and 'adapting' product. The company then continues to work with

5.3 Joint Work as Co-configuration

this customer-product pair to make the product more responsive to each user. In this way, the customization work becomes continuous. (...) Unlike previous work, co-configuration work never results in a 'finished' product. Instead, a living, growing network develops between customer, product, and company. (Victor & Boynton, 1998, p. 195)

Although this model of changing practices originated in the Harvard Business School and does not discuss the provision of welfare services, it resonated strongly with the senior staff responsible for reconfiguring children's services in local authorities in England when the team discussed it with them at the start of the study. Our subsequent analyses of multi-professional working in that project (Edwards, Daniels, Gallagher, Leadbetter, & Warmington, 2009) have shown that co-configuration is currently emerging in some complex multi-professional settings.

The connection between co-configuration and the distributed expertise and relational agency at the core of this book is strong. Co-configuration in responsive and collaborating services requires flexible working in which no single actor has the sole, fixed responsibility and control. It requires participants to have a disposition to recognise and engage relationally with the expertise distributed across rapidly changing work places and to work in new ways with the expertise of those who hitherto had been seen mainly as clients. It is therefore more than listening to clients in order to adjust how to work with them, as is often the case in studies of the impact of pupil voice in schools (McIntyre, Pedder, & Rudduck, 2005). Rather, it has the potential to involve children and families in externalising their own knowledge and repositioning themselves in, and thereby reshaping, the social conditions of their development as they work on them and change them. It therefore echoes the Children's Fund emphasis on participation as a route to the prevention of social exclusion.

When examining evidence from both the Children's Fund and the LIW study, we found that there were two ways of interpreting co-configuration work in children's services. Much depended on what was seen as the object of activity, i.e. the problem space that was being worked on in the process of co-configuration. When the problem space or joint task was service-led, the problem was usually seen as improving existing provision. However, when the object of activity was client-led, such as a child's developmental trajectory with the intention to disrupt a trajectory that was propelling the child towards social exclusion, co-configuration became far more professionally challenging, requiring practitioners to follow a trajectory with the child and family and work on it relationally and flexibly with the family to alter its course. Here relational agency begins to include working with the knowledge and intentions of families and other support networks around vulnerable clients to co-configure their trajectories towards engagement with what society has to offer.

A child's trajectory out of being at risk of social exclusion, for example, will change constantly as practitioners, the child and her family re-shape it. It will come to resemble what Engeström (2005) describes as a 'runaway object' racing ahead of those who are working on it. As we shall see, this more client-centred version of co-configuration work was more likely to engage children and families as partners in configuring and negotiating their own pathways away from social exclusion. These two readings of co-configuration in preventative work, re-shaping services or trajectories, become useful benchmarks in both NECF and LIW for examining how practitioners are working with service users in conditions which encourage their participation.

Both readings of co-configuration allow a focus simultaneously on the individual and the social situation of their development, but the service-oriented version works with one transitory aspect of a client's world, a service which is provided for them, while the focus on a developing trajectory offers a longer-term investment in enabling clients to learn how to act on their worlds and shape their own lives. The more challenging reading of co-configuration was evident in Children's Fund approaches to prevention through participation, so let us look at them in a little more detail.

Here I draw primarily on extensive evidence gathered from service users during the National Evaluation of the Children's Fund (Evans, Pinnock, Beirens, & Edwards, 2006). As I have already indicated, the initiative was established with a service-led perspective, with targeted service provision as the object of activity and focusing on shaping services for specific groups. In many cases its participatory approach to changing provision became diluted. For example, local partnerships did consult children about what they wanted services to do when they commissioned provision and children were involved in evaluating what was provided; but these processes were more a matter of the initial shaping of targeted provision, a feature of mass customization, than ongoing negotiations of co-configuration work.

When we examined professional practices which involved working with parents and carers on disrupting their own children's trajectories towards exclusion, we began to see some glimmerings of co-configuration work which involved families and developmental trajectories. Some practices, however, fell short of engaging families in negotiating their ways out of exclusion. The Children's Fund family worker's description of her practice which follows gives some indication of how a practice that is driven by a service-led sense of expert care cannot always recognise the expertise that a family might be able to bring into negotiations about their own futures:

> I think that the only strategy I have got is empathy...when I go out to see a family I try very hard not to be judgmental in anyway and to put parents at ease in the hope that they will engage on a one to one basis with me...(in) most of the self-referral families...parents do engage, but overall it is recognised that it is quite difficult to get the parents involved. (Family worker in the National Evaluation of the Children's Fund)

But there were some services which tried to get beyond positioning their practitioners as more powerful expert carers who did not need to work with the expertise of clients. These more far-sighted services created possibilities for a co-configured relational approach, which more clearly brought the families into the negotiations and enabled them to achieve a greater sense of responsibility and efficacy. A practitioner outlined one such project:

> ...the main participation is in the individual packages we do with families, which are very much family-led really. It's around their description of the understanding of their needs-the targets that we all agree to work towards, and their evaluations of the things at the end really.

The involvement of families in both setting targets and evaluating whether they had been achieved echoed Taylor's definition of agency (Taylor, 1977), which proposed that we are only truly agentic when we not only set our own goals but are able to evaluate that we have achieved them.

Parents responded with enthusiasm to being treated as partners in working on their own children's trajectories. Talking of how she and her 13-year-old son worked with a family support worker, one mother explained, 'All three of us have worked together. I'm not told you do this, try that. It's "what do you think we should do?" '. Another described how she worked with practitioners in a project for excluded children attended by her sons 'they talk to you, involve you, so you feel you as though you're involved, they will ring your phone, actually talk to you, tell you what's going on, ask advice'.

Examples like these call to mind Dreier's work on the trajectories of patients in psychotherapy as they move across everyday settings where he argues that clients, not therapists, are the primary agents of therapy (Dreier, 1999, 2000). His research focuses on the way that patients order and configure their everyday practices so that they can manage to function well in different contexts. Sennett too has pointed to the need to recognise the expertise of clients. Suggesting that welfare bureaucracies tend to deny the autonomy of service users, he gives the counter example of the police team who worked with the expertise of homeless children in Chicago:

> What impressed me about the cops in the squad car was that they indeed seemed to have learnt from the homeless kids. Though they were hardly credulous or sentimental students, these two men thought they could only deal with these kids by giving them some mental credit. (Sennett, 2003: 177)

Involving parents and children in disrupting their own pathways towards social exclusion has the potential to help them to develop expertise in these everyday negotiations as they take control of their own lives. A CHAT understanding of these negotiations highlights the extent to which they are evidence of an externalisation of understandings and have the potential to contribute to and shape the systems in which they occur. In summary, co-configuration which includes working relationally with children and their carers can provide an opportunity for the kind of dialectic between individual and the social situation of development that was at the core of Vygotsky's developmental psychology.

5.4 Externalisation Co-configuration and Relational Agency

In a recent study of informal learning in an inner-city drop in centre used by women with a range of problems and vulnerabilities, we examined how their trajectories of exclusion were disrupted (Edwards & Mackenzie, 2005, 2008). The accounts we gathered during that study illustrated how engaging the agency of the women who used the centre in co-configuring their own trajectories was sustained by opportunities for them to act on and contribute to the centre and other aspects of the social situations they inhabited. We summarised what was happening by drawing

Fig. 5.2 Steps in a pathway of participation

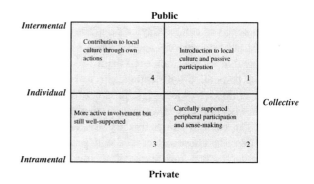

on Harré's Vygotskian framework for tracking the development of identity which was discussed briefly in Chapter 4 (Section 4.3). The model is shown in Fig. 5.2. The attractions of this model include its capacity to show change over time and a recognition of externalisation as part of the processes of learning and relating to the world.

The model assumes that in the process of learning and identity development, individuals move from quadrant 1 through 2 and 3 to 4 where externalization occurs as people contribute to the social situations they inhabit by acting on them. Harré acknowledges that the model is merely a heuristic and that distinctions between quadrants are not clear-cut. For example, there is a dynamic to-ing and fro-ing between 1 and 2 and it is clear that at the time at which he produced the model (Harré, 1983), too little was known about movement between 2 and 3. The model is enriched by subsequent sociocultural analyses. For example, enhanced understandings of the conversational bases of learning and intersubjectivity, offered by Shotter among others (Shotter, 1993), suggest that quadrants 2 and 3 are sites of relational support for individual interpretations and actions. That is, the other is always in some way part of one's learning trajectory. Nonetheless, the model, together with these more recent insights, has proved a useful framework for raising questions about and informing our analyses of individual learning trajectories.

In exploring the trajectories of the users of the centre two of the questions were:

(i) Was there a pattern of participation over time, which suggested that there may be stages in modes of participation? and
(ii) How was any movement through these stages supported?

Here I shall take the trajectories of Tracey and Maggie, two users of the drop in centre, as examples. We explored with them their entry into the centre, why they stayed, what and how they learnt there, what and how they learnt elsewhere, how they related currently to the centre, and what their future plans as learners were.

The Hollybush centre had a long history of engagement with the community it served and a primary focus on the needs of women. The workers, who were all

5.4 Externalisation Co-configuration and Relational Agency

women, offered a drop in facility and a range of services which included support for mental health problems, money advice, a credit union, child care and short-term learning projects in collaboration with, for example, adult education and community arts services. Workers in the centre came from backgrounds in social services, housing, money advice and volunteering, but worked fluidly and collaboratively across roles and responsibilities.

Although the centre aimed at helping women to reposition themselves within their worlds so that they were able to deal with the complex demands of relationships, childcare and economic viability, it did not have as a primary concern either the creation of good mothers or the production of a capable workforce. Workers refused to intervene with children if their mothers were present and adult education opportunities were a far lower priority than short 'trips', which enabled participants to see the world beyond the confines of their housing estate. Rather, the centre aimed at helping participants to deal with breakdowns in social networks and to build up new networks of social support though encouraging mutually supportive relationships within the centre. The workers liked to see themselves as friends to users and aimed at creating an open and accepting family ethos:

> ... it's the same for every individual. If you've got a friend who doesn't judge you and you know is supportive, then that can make a big difference. (centre worker)

The importance of non-judgmental support resonated throughout our interviews as exemplified by this centre worker, describing the drop in element of their work:

> I think that purpose is having somewhere to go that is open, you can go in at any level really. Go in for a cup of coffee. Go in for advice. You don't need a reason to step over the door, you know in terms of using the professionals here...you might be meeting your friend, seeing what is going on for the kids, somewhere where you can take the kids and we don't mind if they make a mess.

The development of this capacity to support each other was also evident in our focus group discussions and interviews with individual participants. As we have already indicated, a capacity to use the resources available does not simply apply to making use of physical resources, such as how to get a loan from the credit union. It also involves a capacity to offer support to and ask for support from others. This attribute is an important aspect of relational agency, where one's ability to engage with the world is enhanced through doing so alongside others. What the centre was doing was creating an open enough system for that kind of fluid form of relational agency to emerge. The fluidity of such relationships is important, as it was clear that what was being encouraged was not dependency, but a capacity to both seek and give help when engaging with the world. We can see the impact of those strategies on both Tracey and Maggie.

Tracey was in her mid thirties and the single parent of three children. Her mother left home when she was ten and she left school with no formal qualifications. She started to attend the centre because it was located within the local community centre building which she was already familiar with. She became a regular user because 'All the staff are very friendly and helpful. It is a nice place to go if you need support and advice'. She was, however, becoming frustrated with other users of Hollybush:

'not enough people turn up for classes so they don't run' and 'some people in the drop in aren't friendly to new ones'.

When she discussed learning, familiarity and emotional support remained strong features of her descriptions. For example, her art class was '....a nice group of women and we all supported each other'. Supporting and not supporting was a salient construct for Tracey. When describing her friendships she explained:

> There is a lot of support. I get a lot of support because I give a lot of support. But there's lots round here that don't give any support. So it makes it awkward to live here. But I don't take no notice of them ones.

She explained the importance of this degree of independence and difference from other women in her world in terms of being a role model for her daughters. Most of her attempts at engaging with more formal modes of learning such as an internet class were given the rationale that they would help her to help her children:

> It [learning internet skills] is very hard .... I found it really frustrating. But I'm doing it because we've got a computer here and I need to learn it for the kids and help them.

Tracey's trajectory appears to have achieved its impetus from a reflective desire to be different from her sisters and many of her neighbours. That impetus was sustained through a number of relationships within which she was variously supported or supporting. Hollybush offered her a new way of being. Her initial engagement in the activities of the centre was relatively passive (quadrant 1, Fig. 5.2). And even after 7 years she did not appear to be making a contribution to its collective life. That is, she was not operating in quadrant 4. But she was operating in quadrants 2 and 3 and engaging in forms of relational agency both in and outside the centre and, particularly within her family, was operating as a supporter in quadrant 3.

The interactions she had with Hollybush workers led her to art classes in the centre and internet classes outside it. It gave validity to her reflections on her own education and that of her children and encouraged the help she gave them as learners. The centre, by emphasising mutual support, helped her develop her capacity to use local resources so that she moved from the in-centre art classes to the external internet class.

We did not trace a linear trajectory of individual learning and mastery over environmental constraints. Rather we observed Tracey's learning as a capacity to recognise and use what was available to support her actions and an ability to acknowledge the purposes and direction of those actions. The trajectory was therefore not a simple one of steady progress through the quadrants. Though as she became more actively in control of her life, recursive loops taking her back to quadrant 1 became less necessary. Tracey had reflected on her own identity shifts, felt pride in her capacity to make them and recognised how they were supported in relationships in which she was variously the supporter and the supported. If we look at Fig. 5.3 we can see that Tracey has made enough movement to be able to operate in quadrant 3 in active ways within the fairly safe private or semi-private arena of friendly classes, immediate family and friendships. Tracey's trajectory therefore nicely illustrates that working relationally with the agency of clients may be a slow

5.4 Externalisation Co-configuration and Relational Agency

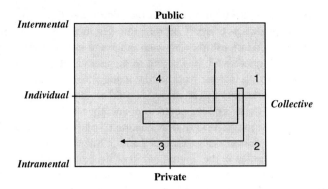

Fig. 5.3 Tracey's steps towards participation in the drop in centre

process, but a necessary one if they are to function within world where being able to use, and ultimately contribute to, available resources is a sign of inclusion in society.

Maggie had not grown up with the huge disadvantages that had faced Tracey. She was in her late twenties and lived with the father of her two children. Her mother was a single parent, who returned to Jamaica to run her own business. Maggie left school with a low-grade leaving certificate and undertook a chef's training course. When interviewed she was a part-time silver service waitress and was taking pre-degree courses in early childhood with a view to eventually becoming a teacher. Both of these were relatively recent developments for her and marked a growing confidence. Currently, because of her studying, she saw herself as different from friends and neighbours and had started to identify with the teachers in her son's school where she helped out 1 day a week and where she was beginning to navigate this new figured world:

> Yeah, I think I am a lot different from the people I hang around with ... she [a friend] doesn't really understand my need to study.

> I'm there[at the school] 24/7. They all call me Maggie. I know all the teachers. I'm always invited to all the teachers' meals. I've been to the pub with the teachers.

Maggie had started to attend Hollybush 8 years earlier because she needed the support it offered her. She was still visiting regularly but was aware of how far she had moved on and how she could help others:

> [When you see someone there who is continuously depressed] you think to yourself, well I was lower than that and I've come to this stage now ... you have to approach them first, because they won't approach you. ....you know that because you have been there.

She still got support from the centre:

> I walk straight into the kitchen ... and it's nice, they give you a hug and you know it like a proper hug as Luke [her son] does. I am really close to at least five of the women here and probably closer because of that common ground thing [i.e. they have all at times had considerable problems].

Her view on successful initial entry into the centre was the ability to 'humble yourself' (i.e. accept that you won't be integrated immediately). People were in established supportive relationships with each other and it would take time to integrate: participation in quadrant 1 was bound to be passive. Her role now extended beyond mutual support, to include work on the management committee, helping to paint the centre and scrubbing the kitchen. She told us that 'You appreciate places once you contribute to them' and the centre remained her 'safety net'.

In the centre she no longer operated in quadrant 1, but still benefited from the relationships that were features of quadrants 2 and 3. She then operated in quadrant 4, externalised her expertise in the figured world of the centre and contributed to its collective life, drawing on the common knowledge built up there. At the same time she was beginning to develop expertise in engaging with the figured world of her son's school. Again, as with Tracey, we are not observing a linear trajectory even in the modes of operation within the centre. Instead her work in quadrant 4 is sustained by the support she gets and gives in 2 and 3. We can see the pattern in Fig. 5.4.

It does seem that there was a pattern of progression between the four quadrants shown in Fig. 5.2. But that progression was not straightforward, rather there was a shifting back and fore in order to gather resources for action in a more advanced mode of participation. There is therefore a recursive movement through the quadrants with generally supported passive participation in 1 and forms of relational agency in operation in 2, 3 and 4, which allow for shared expansion of the objects of activity and joint action on them.

These two trajectories illustrate the demands for professionals of Sennett's dilemma of allowing for autonomy within dependency. Firstly, agency has to be encouraged in relationships which are also premised on offering professional support. As a result of the study, the staff wrestled with their role as 'friends' and rapidly recognised that was not the best description of their positions. They were working at informality, flexibility and accessibility, yet they came to acknowledge their specific expertise in housing problems, dealing with domestic violence and so on. Their

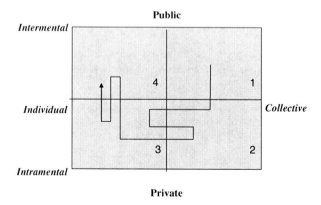

Fig. 5.4 Maggie's steps towards participation in the drop in centre

expertise, however, also included the ability to work with and strengthen the agency of users as they in turn offered each other help and support.

Enhancing the agency of centre users involved taking a pedagogic stance while working with them to co-configure their pathways out of debt and distress. It meant giving a high degree of support and modelling what could be done in interactions with rent offices or schools in the early stages (quadrant 1) and a gradual withdrawing of support and increasing of expectations in quadrants 2 and 3, while at the same time providing a space in which agency could be exercised in action to reconfigure their own lives and in doing so work on and change the social situations of their development.

Including the most vulnerable in negotiations, as so many professionals recognise, takes time. In another study of a short-term intervention with 'hard to reach families' (Evangelou, Sylva, Edwards, & Smith, 2008), we found that experienced workers were unwilling to seek out and work with these families which were labelled in that way because of the need for a lengthy period with them, while the short-term nature of their funding would mean that they would raise expectations and ultimately 'let the families down' by walking away when funding ended. Relational work, with those who need it most, cannot be done quickly.

5.5 Working with the Expertise of Those Who Use Services

Respecting and engaging the expertise of clients is of course not a new concept. It has underpinned a great deal of work on disability (Barnes, Davis, & Tew, 2000; Russell, 2003; Shakespeare, 2006) and is central to approaches to social work that strengthen family and other local networks (Folgheraiter, 2004; Hunter & Ritchie, 2007; Morris & Burford, 2007), while the idea of engaging patients in the resolving of their own problems has long been at the core of a raft of therapeutic practices. However, I am suggesting that the processes of relational agency that were outlined in Chapters 3 and 4 may offer, at the very least, a set of principles against which practitioners may be able gauge or develop their relational work with clients.

These processes include the establishing of common knowledge in which values and expertise are made explicit and motives are brought into a degree of alignment so that later interactions do not need justifications and explanations. Folgheraiter describes this phase in developing the networks that are so important to what he terms 'relational social work' as creating a '*social* task' (p. 192): people need to recognise that there is a task to work on and it is one that is important for them. This process involves recognising the different expertises that are in play. Professionals are therefore not positioned as friends. As Sennett observes, 'Very few friendships could or should bear the weight of providing sustained or effective help' (2003: 195) and indeed the development of intimacy would create a bond which would increase the dependency of the client. Rather they are experts who are also interested in making explicit and helping to mobilise the expertise of those who are clients in order to co-configure their life trajectories. Again I turn to Sennett's argument for mutual recognition and respect. His way forward is by:

> ... honoring different practical achievements rather than privileging potential talent; by admitting the just claims of adult dependency; by permitting people to participate more actively in the conditions of their own care. (Sennett, 2003: 261)

The negotiations that result in this way of working are more demanding than the suggestion by Nixon and his colleagues (Nixon, Martin, McKeown, & Ranson, 1997), that professionals now need to recognise that their expertise cannot be taken for granted so professional standing needs to be negotiated with clients. Instead, the suggestion here is that relevant professional expertise needs to be made explicit, but that the expertise of clients also needs to be recognised. In a similar vein, Hunter and Richie use the term 'co-production' (Hunter & Ritchie, 2007: 15) and echo the description of relational agency given in Chapter 4 (Section 4.3). They argue that co-production requires new thinking and behaviour between 'problem holders' or clients and professionals in both defining the problem and developing solutions to produce 'a dynamic process with each actor or dancer influencing each other' (p. 15). However, unlike Hunter and Ritchie, I am avoiding a link which they, at least partially, accept between agency and consumer power. A Vygotskian emphasis on externalization and development as acting on and shaping one's world, brings me closer to Sennett's concern with both individual agency and the reduction of the structural inequalities which have given rise to experiences of disadvantage and social exclusion.

My argument therefore does not deny power differentials in negotiations between professionals and clients, nor the importance of the statutory responsibilities of welfare professionals. Rather, it represents an attempt to recognise, and allow, the exercise of agency within dependency, as part of the process of defining and reacting to problems. I am therefore, once again, suggesting that relational forms of expertise require an awareness of one's core expertise and the ability to make that clear to others. Also, as I've argued in previous chapters, it demands a capacity to recognise and work with the expertise that others have to offer in both interpreting and responding to complex problems. When the exercise of relational agency involves working with the agency of those who are not expecting the opportunity to exercise it, then a pedagogical element is added which will include eliciting and negotiating the motives of clients and often working slowly to support them as they develop a capacity for agentic action on their own life trajectories.

References

Barnes, M., Davis, A., & Tew, J. (2000). Valuing experience: Users' experiences of compulsion under the Mental Health Act 1983. *Mental Health Review Journal*, 5(3), 11–14.
CYPU. (2001). *Children's Fund guidance*. London: DfES.
Danso, C., Greaves, H., Howell, S., Ryan, M., Sinclair, R., & Tunnard, J. (2003). *The involvement of children and young people in promoting change and enhancing the quality of social car* (Research Report). London: National Children's Bureau.

References

DEMOS-Hay Group. (2004). *Schools out: Can teachers, social workers and health staff learn to work together?* London: DEMOS.

DfES. (2004). *Five year strategy for children and learners.* London: HMSO.

Dreier, O. (1999). Personal trajectories of participation across contexts of social practice. *Outlines, 1,* 5–32.

Dreier, O. (2000). Psychotherapy in clients' trajectories across contexts. In C. Mattingly & L. Garro (Eds.), *Narratives and the cultural construction of illness and healing* (pp. 237–258). Berkeley, CA: University of California Press.

Edwards, A. (2007). Working collaboratively to build resilience: A CHAT approach. *Social Policy and Society, 6*(2), 255–265.

Edwards, A. (2009). Relational agency in collaborations for the wellbeing of children and young people. *Journal of Children's Services, 4*(1), 33–43.

Edwards, A., & Apostolov, A. (2007). A Cultural-historical interpretation of resilience: The implications for practice. *Outlines: Critical Social Studies, 9*(1), 70–84.

Edwards, A., Barnes, M., Plewis, I., Morris, K., et al. (2006). *Working to prevent the social exclusion of children and young people: Final lessons from the National Evaluation of the Children's Fund.* London: DfES. (Research Report 734).

Edwards, A., Daniels, H., Gallagher, T., Leadbetter, J., & Warmington, P. (2009). *Improving inter-professional collaborations: Multi-agency working for children's wellbeing.* London: Routledge.

Edwards, A., & Mackenzie, L. (2005). Steps towards participation: The social support of learning trajectories. *International Journal of Lifelong Education, 24*(4), 287–302.

Edwards, A., & Mackenzie, L. (2008). Identity shifts in informal learning trajectories. In B. van Oers, W. Wardekker, E. Elbers, & R. van der Veer (Eds.), *The transforming of learning: Advances in cultural historical activity theory* (pp. 163–181). Cambridge: Cambridge University Press.

Engeström, Y. (2005). Knotworking to create collaborative intentionality capital in fluid organizational fields. In M. M. Beyerlein, S. T. Beyerlein, & F. A. Kennedy (Eds.), *Collaborative capital: Creating intangible value* (pp. 307–336). Amsterdam: Elsevier.

Evangelou, M., Sylva, K., Edwards, A., & Smith, T. (2008). *Supporting parents in promoting early learning.* London: DCSF. (Research Report 039).

Evans, R., Pinnock, K., Beirens, H., & Edwards, A. (2006). *Developing preventative practices: The experiences of children, young people and their families in the Children's Fun.* London: DfES. (Research Report 735).

Folgheraiter, F. (2004). *Relational social work: Toward networking in societal practices.* London: Jessica Kingsley.

Harré, R. (1983). *Personal being.* Oxford: Blackwell.

Hunter, S., & Ritchie, P. (Eds.) (2007). *Co-production and personalisation in social care.* London: Jessica Kingsley.

Kirby, P., & Bryson, S. (2002). *Measuring the magic? Evaluating and researching young people's participation in public decision making.* London: The Carnegie United Kingdom Trust.

Levitas, R. (1998). *The inclusive society: Social exclusion and new labour.* London: Macmillan.

Lister, R. (1998). From equality to social inclusion: New Labour and the welfare state. *Critical Social Policy, 18*(2), 215–225.

Mason, J. (2005). Child protection policy and the construction of childhood. In J. Mason & T. Fattore (Eds.), *Children taken seriously* (pp. 91–97). London: Jessica Kingsley.

McIntyre, D., Pedder, D., & Rudduck, J. (2005). Pupil voice: Comfortable and uncomfortable learnings for teachers. *Research Papers in Education, 20*(2), 149–168.

Morris, K., & Burford, G. (2007). Working with children's existing networks – Building better opportunities? *Social Policy and Society, 6*(2), 209–217.

Nixon, J., Martin, J., McKeown, P., & Ranson, S. (1997). Towards a learning profession: Changing codes of occupational practice within the new management of education. *British Journal of Sociology of Education, 18*(1), 5–28.

OECD. (1998). *Co-ordinating services for children and youth at risk: A world view*. Paris: OECD.
Office of Public Services Reform. (2002). *Reforming out public services: Principles into practice*. London: Office of Public Services Reform.
Prout, A. (2000). Children's participation: Control and self-realisation in British late modernity. *Children and Society, 14*, 305–319.
Room, G. (1995). Poverty and social exclusion: The new European agenda for policy and research. In G. Room (Ed.), *Beyond the threshold: The measurement and analysis of social exclusion* (pp. 1–9). Bristol: Policy Press.
Russell, P. (2003). Access and achievement or social exclusion? Are the government's policies working for disabled children and their families? *Children and Society, 17*, 215–225.
Sennett, R. (2003). *Respect: The formation of character in an age of inequality*. London: Allen Lane.
Shakespeare, T. (2006). *Disability rights and wrongs*. London: Routledge.
Shotter, J. (1993). *The cultural politics of everyday life*. Buckingham: Open University Press.
Spicer, N., Broughton, K., Evans, R., & Smith, P. (2004). *Children, young people, parents and carers' participation in Children's Fund case study partnerships*. Birmingham: DfES, University of Birmingham. (RR602).
Taylor, C. (1977). What is human agency? In T. Mischel (Ed.), *The self: Psychological and philosophical issues* (pp. 103–135). Oxford: Oxford University Press.
Victor, B., & Boynton, A. (1998). *Invented here: Maximizing your organization's internal growth and profitability*. Boston, MA: Harvard Business School Press.
Willow, C. (2002). *Participation in practice: Children and young people as partners in change*. London: The Children's Society.

Chapter 6
Being a Professional

6.1 Working in Relation

In Chapter 1 (Section 1.2) I described the conceptions of being a professional as unclear and called for a refreshed vision. I explained that I would be taking a broad view of what is professional work, by examining expertise in practices that have some claim to being considered professional by virtue of their need to do more than simply follow routine procedures or tackle prescribed tasks. In the chapters that followed, I have discussed work where engaging responsively with others enhances the expertise available. In those chapters I outlined the extent to which the relational forms of expertise, which are at the core of this book, are given direction by ethical commitments that involve recognising the expertise and priorities of others and engaging in value-laden practices.

While pursuing these themes, it has been impossible to ignore the impact of the legacies of bureaucratic conditions and NPM on the development of more relational practices in the public sector. These organisational tensions will be explored in Chapter 7, but in the present chapter I shall be examining the responsive and negotiated open-ended work with other practitioners and with clients that characterises relational agency. My focus will therefore be decision-making in the heat of action and, in particular, the part played by professional knowledge in those fluid and responsive decisions.

Knowledge-based decisions that are negotiated rapidly with others are, of course, not only to be found in the welfare professions. I have already made several references to software engineers, the importance of knowledge to them and their need to work flexibly with each other and their clients in the kind of problem-solving that can also generate new knowledge. Another area, where heat of the action collaboration which is not structured by stable team working, is hospital theatre work (Bleakley, Hobbs, Boyden, Allard, & Walsh, 2006; Healey, Undre, & Vincent, 2006). Bleakley and his colleagues have summarised the need to rethink collaboration in the operating theatre in ways which indicate the need for attention to relational expertise and to an understanding of relational agency in surgical work. The distinction between 'multiprofessional' and 'interprofessional' that they make reveals the precarious nature of practices where the capacity to take the standpoint of the other and recognise their expertise is lacking.

> Operating theatre teams characteristically model multiprofessional rather than interprofessional practice, where conventional hierarchical activity and intra-professional 'adhesion'...tend to dominate over intentional collaborative practices .... A symptom of this conservatism is the stereotyping of the 'other' professional(s) by a member of any professional group in the OT (nurses, surgeons, anaesthetists, anaesthetic assistants....).
> (Bleakley et al., 2006: 462)

Their observations suggest that specialist knowledge without attention to relational expertise can lead to othering and separation rather than to mutually attuned responses to a complex problem.

The more established professions can find a breaking down of their exclusivity quite challenging. Hoyle's work on Family Justice Centres dealing with, for example, domestic violence (Hoyle, 1998) also points to the need for the legal profession to develop a capacity for working relationally alongside the specialist knowledge they bring to the centres. These examples suggest that even those professions, which are typically seen as autonomous, may find themselves considering how to develop the additional expertise necessary to working with and contributing to the intelligence that in Lave's terms can be 'stretched over' persons, activities and settings (Lave, 1988:1). However, my own work on local systems of expertise is a little more optimistic. It has found that general medical practitioners in the community are not only delivering services through systems of distributed specialisms within multidisciplinary health centres, but they are also beginning to contribute to local expertise as part of wider local systems of preventative practice.

The interplay between expert knowledge and relational expertise, therefore, requires teasing out. In this chapter I consider how professional work is currently being constructed and the implications of current developments for the relative importance of the specialist knowledge and the responsibility and trust which have contributed to the notion of professionalism. In doing so I shall pursue the argument started in Chapter 2 (Section 2.5) that the relational expertise that I have been describing, with all its attention to commitment and values, cannot replace the specialist knowledge that is contributed to the collective intelligence in use in complex activities.

6.2 Knowledge and Commitment in Professional Work

Evetts' extensive analyses of changes in professionalism (for example, Evetts, 2003, 2006, 2009) trace broad themes which resonate with those in this book. In a 2006 overview article, she indicates how, in 1951, Parsons' observed the normalising effects of the inter-relatedness of capitalism, the rational-legal social order and the modern professions in 'mutually balancing in the maintenance and stability of a fragile normative social order' (p. 517). There the authority of the professions rested on what Weber has called the 'dehumanized' aspects of work (Weber, 1968: 975), which included the limited power afforded non-professionals and professional impersonality. Apparently, the qualities that have given professions their authority

6.2 Knowledge and Commitment in Professional Work

are the antithesis of those needed for the exercise of relational agency with other practitioners and with clients.

Nonetheless, I am not advocating an anarchic breakdown of the normative social order. Rather, I am arguing for a relational turn in professional practices, which will erode the unquestioned power of the dynamic outlined by Parsons, and which will need replacing by a stabilising concern with expert knowledge, its use and construction in practices. Knowledge that stabilises is not stable knowledge. Indeed, a Marxist attention to refining both knowledge and the tools available for refining knowledge should, I suggest, be a central strand in professional practices. As I have already indicated, the idea of relational agency arose from an attempt to develop concepts that might capture the nature of complex relational work. Analyses of professional work, I suggest, call for conceptual tools, which allow engagement with, and revelation of, knowledge, its use and its generation. We need to open up what Stehr described as the 'black box' that is knowledge (1994:163).

Knorr Cetina's work on epistemic cultures (1999) and on experts' engagement with epistemic objects gets beyond the notion of knowledge as a mystery hidden in a black box. What she describes as 'exteriorized theories of science and expertise' (Knorr Cetina, 1997: 23) have much to offer understandings of professional knowledge that is far from 'dehumanized'. They nuance the centrality of knowledge in practices and its potentially stabilising effects for the experts who seek a relationship with the knowledge that is embedded in what they do. She explains as follows:

> ... objects serve as centering and integrating devices for regimes of expertise that transcend an expert's lifetime and create the collective conventions and the moral order commutarians are concerned about. Object worlds also make up the embedding environments in which expert work is carried out, thus constituting something like and emotional home for expert selves. (Knorr Cetina, 1997: 9)

Here she is not talking about objects as instruments which are 'ready to hand' (p. 10): these should be seen as tools rather than knowledge objects. The latter, in contrast, are problematic and need to be worked on to refine them, rather than worked with on routine tasks. Objects of knowledge, she explains are 'the goal of expert work' (p. 12), where the expert self becomes bound to the knowledge object through a sense of 'lack' and the creation of a 'structure of wanting' (p. 16), which sustains the connection. The outcome is a 'state of subjective fusion with the object of knowledge' (p. 18).

Her work has been developed in relation to accountants, nurses, software engineers and teachers in the ProLearn project at the University of Oslo (Jensen, Lahn, Nerland, in press). Jensen, for example, has drawn on the ideas of lack, desire and the binding power of knowledge to explain how seeking knowledge in research activities ties nurses to their concern with developing knowledge in and on nursing (Jensen & Lahn, 2005; Jensen, 2007)

I shall only touch on some of these ideas in relation to my concern with knowledge in expert practices. In Chapter 1 (Section 1.4 and 1.5) I observed that Knorr Cetina's (1999) notion of 'engrossment' with knowledge is an important part of those professional practices which are not merely a matter of rule-following without engaging with what matters professionally. The idea of engrossment is elaborated in her study of how traders in investment banks work with the market as an object of 'attachment' (Knorr Cetina & Bruegger, 2002). There the market is seen as an object of knowledge which is unfolding and engaging those who work on it, not just to understand it, but also to test, move and manipulate it and be stimulated by its capacity to generate questions. Engagement arises through practitioners' need to continually work on the object of knowledge and define it. Knorr Cetina and Bruegger also describe this engagement in terms of 'lack' or incompleteness in the traders' understanding of it and their desire to pursue a better grasp of what is there.

Throughout the previous chapters I have worked with the term 'object' as it is understood within CHAT discourses, where it is a problem space which is worked on, shaped and transformed. For example, in Chapter 4 (Section 4.4) I described a CHAT object of activity as a feature of an activity, such as a child's trajectory. There the trajectory becomes the object of the actions of participants who are engaged in the activity of reconfiguring it in order to prevent that child's social exclusion. As I explained there, each practitioner's interpretation of the trajectory and the response that is invoked is based on the 'object motive' (Leont'ev, 1978) that is inherent in his or her interpretation of the object. There is therefore some common ground between the object motive and an object of activity in a CHAT analysis and Knorr Cetina's notion of engrossment in a knowledge object.

I refer to Knorr Cetina's work primarily because it alerts us to the importance of knowledge in professional activities which are open-ended and which call for professional engagement with the problems that are revealed. But knowledge does not get forgotten in CHAT: the importance of mediation of what matters in a culture, through the use of cultural tools such as language, means that knowledge is a central element in the theory. But the idea of an epistemic object as an unfolding entity that is open to scrutiny and is made and remade in knowledge-rich practices that comes from Knorr Cetina's work is a useful one when examining how professions adapt to new resources and new demands.

CHAT analyses also recognise that interpreting a professional task and manipulating resources to work on it are actions that are imbued with professional knowledge, which includes values and a recognition of possible outcomes. In responsive professional work CHAT 'objects of activity' are also marked by their unfolding nature as they are worked on and their complexity increasingly revealed. As this happens, professionals are pulled forward in their work, for example, by a commitment to pushing knowledge boundaries in the case of software engineers, or by the ethics of care in so many of the welfare professions. Miettinen and Virkkunen (2005) have also seen similarities between CHAT and epistemic objects and, from their activity theory concerns with organisational change, have argued that practice itself should be treated as an epistemic object and in particular practitioners should focus on the institutional contradictions that become evident in it as practices need to change.

6.2 Knowledge and Commitment in Professional Work

Therefore, despite the allure of Knorr Cetina's writings, I shall persist with CHAT analyses because, as useful as an emphasis on the attraction of epistemic objects is, CHAT can take us a little further for two reasons. The first is the inherent dynamic between conceptual tools and the object of activity that it presents. If we return to Vygotsky's interest in how concepts are revealed in how we act on the world, the conceptual resources that are brought in to play when the object of professional action is identified and worked on can tell us a great deal about the professional knowledge in use. Middleton made a similar point when he focused on language as a resource for action in his analyses of inter-professional talk in DWR settings in the LIW study and created an analytic protocol that revealed the concepts discussed in Section 3.2 (Middleton, 2009) (See also Section 8.4 and Appendix B).

Wagstaff's study of doctoral supervisions outlined in Section 4.7 illustrates the point being made here. The analysis distinguishes between the mediational means employed by supervisors and by students when they work on shared objects of activity, such as the data that have been gathered by the student. The dynamic between object of activity and conceptual tools reveals the extent to which supervisors use abstract and potentially generalisable conceptual tools such as 'identity project' or 'division of labour', while the students will often draw on situated knowledge that is not evident in the data, such as their personal knowledge of the respondent's background.

This distinction between what was mediating analyses of data in supervisions takes us to the second reason for staying with CHAT: Vygotsky's concern with the relationship between what he termed everyday and scientific knowledge. The distinction allows us to distinguish between everyday knowledge, which is situation-specific such as 'she went to a good school' or 'her grandmother has always cared about her' and that which has more generalisability such as 'identity project' or 'strengthening family networks can lead to longer term support for a vulnerable child'. The pedagogic task in doctoral supervisions, for example, is to take everyday understandings out of their specific situations and assist students in developing them into testable concepts, or higher forms of mental functioning as Vygotsky put it (Vygotsky, 1997). When researching knowledge in practices, the distinction provides access to the extent to which the knowledge employed in practices is situated and everyday, or more generalisable and open to reasoned contestation. Later in this chapter I shall return to both of these CHAT resources for studying knowledge in action in Section 6.3 when I discuss responsive relational work where recognisable professional knowledge is lacking.

Here I want to pursue the importance of moral commitment to work that is central to both Knorr Cetina's notion of engrossment and the idea of object-oriented activity which underpins relational agency. Evetts, in her 2009 discussion of how the professions are changing in relation to the constraints of NPM, distinguished between 'organizational professionalism' and 'occupational professionalism' (2009: 248). The former is characterised by a discourse of professionalism as a form of organizational control within hierarchical structures, and is a feature of NPM in public service sector work. The latter emphasises relationships over structures, and demonstrates an orientation to work where 'the needs and demands of audiences, patients, clients, students and children are paramount' (2009: 252).

Evetts suggests that there may be a connection between NPM, 'organizational professionalism' and a possible decline in trust in professions evidenced in, for example, media responses when behaviour is seen as unprofessional. She is rightly cautious about declaring a causal link between how professionalism can be used as a way of monitoring behaviour in public sector organisations and an erosion of the trust that is so important to activities where professional discretion is possible. However, I suspect she may be right about how 'organizational professionalism' is eroding a public sense that professions are driven by a set of intrinsic values. Our studies of public service workers while they were adapting to operating outside the work practices of their home organisations (Edwards, Daniels, Gallagher, Leadbetter, & Warmington, 2009) revealed just how important professional values were once practitioners could think beyond the rule-bound practices that had previously shaped their responses. Indeed these values led to their rule-bending within these organisations in order to accomplish value-laden tasks such as rapidly marshalling help for a child.

Relational agency clearly works against the grain of 'organizational professionalism' by asserting that professional practices are driven by professional values and involve paying attention to relationships and trust in the expertise of others and the quality of the resources, both conceptual and material, that they can bring to bear on problems. The quality of the resources, for example, the specialist help a social worker can offer a housing officer when dealing with a homeless family, is crucial. As I indicated in Chapter 1 (Section 1.6), Nowotny (2003) has pointed to how the current ease of access to information makes it possible for it to seep beyond the boundaries of specialist expertise so that people can believe they have expert knowledge. Yet information is not knowledge in the way that Stehr has described it as 'a capacity for social action' (1994: 95), and specialist knowledge and engagement with it is central to the exercise of relational agency in professional practice.

6.3 Expert Knowledge and Relational Agency

Stehr makes it clear that knowledge as a capacity for action is not simply a matter of applying scientific knowledge. Rather its production and use are intertwined with the social organisation in which it originates. One problem that arises from Stehr's observation for practitioners who work across boundaries is that relational inter-professional work occurs at the margins of organisations, bringing the risk that those who engage in it may lose touch with the specialist knowledge that shapes their professions and the identity as expert which goes with it. Jack (2006), as we have already seen, has observed how social workers who engage in community programmes are not accorded the professional status within the profession which goes with 'heavy-end child protection work' (2006: 338).

In the study of how secondary schools adjusted to inter-professional work, which was mentioned in Chapter 2 (Section 2.5), I found the danger of a disconnection

6.3 Expert Knowledge and Relational Agency

between specialist knowledge, which is intertwined with the social organisation in which it is developed, and relational work at the margins of those organisations, to be starkly illustrated. The potential problem of waning expertise as a result of working at the margins of the professions had been amplified by the use of employees, with no specialist professional expertise, to support vulnerable children outside the core functions of the school. A major part of their work involved liaising with professionals such as social workers, community police and health professionals to weave support around vulnerable children. Lacking specialist expertise, relational knowledge, which we formulated as 'know who' to distinguish it from the 'know what', 'why' and 'how' of specialist knowledge, was all important for these workers.

The study had set out to examine how secondary schools were adjusting in order to engage in inter-professional collaborations to support their pupils. However, rather than an opening of teachers' practices to embrace more relational engagement with other practitioners, we found that inter-professional work was pushed to the margins of the school and carried out by these unqualified staff who were paid as teaching assistants (TA) (see Edwards, 2009a; Edwards, Lunt, & Stamou, 2010 for extended discussions of these phenomena). The study therefore brought us to processes of workforce remodelling. Workforce remodelling, in English public sector children's services, aims at creating a 'multi-skilled team to provide effective learning opportunities for children' (from the National Remodelling Team website, cited in Yarker, 2005). TA were often initially employed to take over mundane tasks from teachers (Bach, Kessler, & Heron, 2006). However, they have increasingly become part of teaching teams working alongside qualified teachers and are 'ever more significant contributors to pupils' learning' (Cajkler et al., 2007:72), despite their lack of core knowledge.

As I have already outlined in Chapter 2 (Section 2.5), we described the new welfare-oriented roles carried out by TA level staff by the generic title of 'welfare manager'. Teaching staff justified the new role because the welfare managers were 'completely there for the children' as they were untrammelled by the timetable and the curriculum: in every school their flexibility was the main reason given for introducing the role. However, although the external liaison work which linked the schools with other services for children was increasingly falling on them, we found that welfare managers were highly dependent on being able to access the specialist professional knowledge that was available locally, and were not contributing to it with their own. Welfare managers identified what they saw as the problems the children presented, by drawing on their situated everyday knowledge of the children, their families and the neighbourhood, then exercised their 'know who' by asking for help. One welfare manager explained her developing network and the importance of 'know who' to how she operated:

> I've got the sort of rapport with social services that I can ring them up for advice....now I would automatically ring them ...can you give me some advice. And if it is not you who should I go to?

The welfare managers were doing high-level, potentially risky, work. However, they lacked an engagement with knowledge that was beyond their everyday situated understandings of the locality in which they lived and worked. Consequently, their engrossment was with individual children and perhaps the children's families, and their accounts of their practices were anecdotal tales from the field about specific problem children and families.

When we compare them with the traders in the investment bank studied by Knorr Cetina and Bruegger (2002), we find that the knowledge object in play was not at the more generalisable level of 'the prevention of social exclusion' or even ' the local system of support for children' but their everyday understandings of the child with whom they were working. To give a CHAT analysis, they were working on a recognisable problem space, i.e. a child's trajectory, but that work was mediated by everyday understandings and not by the more powerful knowledge that is derived from experience of working across cases with well-founded specialist knowledge.

In terms of relational agency we can see that, driven by a sense of care for individual children, they could operate as advocates for the children and their families, but they had no distinctive professional knowledge to bring to bear on a child's trajectory and they could not contribute to reshaping it through helping to expand understandings of it that were mediated by specialist understandings. Instead, they often found themselves taking on the role of caring parent.

Cameron, Mooney, and Moss (2002) have similarly observed that child care work in England is closely associated with mothering, which in turn is leading to the development of services and workers 'as providers of substitute mothering' (p. 575) where around 98% of the workforce are women and the levels of qualification are low, even when compared with the population as a whole. The welfare managers had no initial preparation for their posts; were marking out new practices so were not involved in apprenticeships; variously received brief training on assessing needs and attended day courses on domestic violence and safe-guarding children and so on. As a result they did not have a robust professional knowledge base which gave them generalisable knowledge that would distinguish their contributions to local systems of distributed expertise. The following account from one welfare manager gives a flavour of the *ad hocery* of the training received:

> Something I'm going to in a couple of weeks is the (name of project) which is a group of people who used to self-harm so they can be telling welfare officers this is how you should be dealing with it...that's quite good because we have got self-harmers here...because you don't know until you are told. You think you are doing the right thing, but you know, you don't know until you are told.

Their expertise was context-dependent and based on everyday local knowledge, 'know who' was therefore crucial to how they carried out their work. Consequently, they were keen to learn as much as possible about the resources that were distributed locally. Describing the range of short courses she had attended with practitioners from other agencies, another welfare manager explained:

> I think it is good to keep in with these people. And also it keeps me involved with who these people are and who I can turn to for support, because I think we need it as well.

Their work therefore appeared to have an ephemeral base. It was described as 'mushrooming', yet it was difficult to discern what attributes were expected of them apart from being 'very good with children'; 'bringing other qualities (other than teaching)'; and being 'good at filtering out' problems or 'fact-finding'. Of course, they were relatively inexpensive staff. One senior teacher explained their appointment on the grounds that she could 'not afford five non-teaching heads of year *(i.e. qualified teachers)'* to undertake the pastoral work that was being done by the welfare managers.

A similar extended role for under-qualified staff was also to be found a 2008 examination of an initiative aimed at developing the capacity of the Voluntary and Community Sector workforce to help parents, whose children were at risk of learning delay, to become educators of their own children (Evangelou, Sylva, Edwards, & Smith, 2008). There we found practitioners who were working responsively in complex settings with little training and with short-term funding. These practitioners were reconfiguring their settings-based or home-visiting practices so that they could model for parents what they could do to help their young children to learn. The practitioners had a wide range of backgrounds and qualifications and included volunteers alongside paid workers. What they all had in common, as well as like the welfare workers being mainly women, was that the initiative required them to shift the focus of their practices either from working with young children, as was the case for nursery nurses, or from supporting vulnerable adults, as was the situation for family support workers, in order to work with adults to help them promote their children's learning.

The new practices were complex, involving constant professional judgments. Practitioners were required to assess parents' readiness to engage as educators of their young children; parents' current understandings of what they might do; the practical possibilities of the adults carrying forward the ideas that were being passed on to them; the most appropriate material resources and ideas to use with them; and how to work with professionals from other agencies. The practitioners, who attended short training events of 1 day to a week in length, were given access to resources and, in the best situations, found themselves working alongside other practitioners who might support their learning. They learnt quickly and we found almost consistent examples of sensitive responsive work. However, there was considerable frustration about lack of knowledge among staff, arising from their position as what Gunter (2007: 6) has described as a 'flexible and endlessly trainable' workforce. Of course, short-term funding was a major obstacle to developing their work, but also there were concerns about their own need for specialist training.

The initiative that we were examining had made staff development a central theme, but could only offer short doses. Nonetheless, these workers were better prepared than were the welfare managers, whose patterns of training lacked coherence and who were never put into an apprenticeship position where they could become familiar with the knowledge embedded in established practices. These short doses alerted practitioners to what they did not know. The workers in the 'parents as educators' initiative therefore demonstrated what we described as a 'thirst for knowledge'. They knew that they did not know enough to work in the most beneficial ways with parents.

When the development of expertise is described in terms of building local networks through attending courses, as was the case with the welfare managers, we may be fast approaching a point where creating networked support is what counts. If so, this is a worrying development. Relational agency, as a pre-requisite for inter-professional work or responsive work with clients, demands more. It is premised on (a) informed interpretations of, for example, a child's trajectory as an object of activity and (b) the capacity to make those interpretations explicit. Some element of the exclusive knowledge is therefore important. Relational agency requires that practitioners are not only able to recognise and draw on the expertise that is distributed across local systems, but also to contribute to it. It involves both a core expertise and a relational expertise and the latter cannot be a substitute for the former.

That observation about the centrality of core knowledge also means that relational work does not, for example, turn a social worker into a generalist practitioner. Here a social worker in an experimental multi-professional team explains how working relationally with others and their specialist knowledge has allowed her to concentrate her energies on her areas of professional strength. She had become clearer about her contribution to ensuring children's wellbeing and finds that it is enhanced by no longer needing to take on aspects of tasks that are outside her expertise:

> It's about being clear in our roles, about when we're doing a team around the child meeting, actually saying, they're easy meetings to do because we break up our tasks. In statutory work you would come away with a huge list of tasks for the social worker. Any minutes from a care team meeting or a child protection review meeting will have a list of tasks for the social worker. A lot of them crossover into health or into education, but the expectation is, is that you manage that part; whereas I think now that sustaining a relationship is part of it, I think it is about people accepting their responsibility in their role.

That division of labour had allowed her and the other social workers in the team to work in more satisfyingly in-depth ways with families. She explained:

> But I think when you move into this kind of work you need a commitment to say, "I'm going to go further." You have different relationships with professionals. You have an open relationships with ... with professionals, a better understanding of each other's roles. I think I understand the limitations, the frustrations and some of the other issues impacting on, for example, health visitors, learning mentors better than I did when I was in statutory social work and ... I don't know, I guess probably most of us feel the same. I think it's about the depth of that relationship. That's brought in by the work we do with our families because the trust that we build with our families.

These extracts are from discussions with a team who were working with vulnerable families and who were selected because of their specialist expertise. The team leader explained that she had worked hard to persuade senior colleagues that she needed specialist experience in the team: 'it took a lot of convincing people that if we're really serious about working with families we need a team, we need experienced workers'.

Throughout this chapter I have referred to professional knowledge, expertise and now experience. These are concepts that regularly over-lap. Here is a head teacher in another city describing what the social worker who is attached to her school brings to the school.

> Well as far as I can see there are two different kinds of expertise. There's the straightforward child benefit ... and all those bits of benefit and housing and the sort of stuff, if you had lots of time you could go away and read about. Over the years before we had a social worker I used to muddle my way through and think well ... But she (the social worker) has that. She knows where to go, so there's ... there's that. I think the other expertise is an understanding of the law around child protection and what is and what isn't possible because I think sometimes and it happens sometimes particularly with very young new teachers who are concerned about the children and sometimes think, "Well, you know, a child's come into school 3 days running without socks. You know, is this a child protection ...?" She (the social worker) comes in and can discuss actually there are certain procedures that you need to go through.

The head teacher was making a distinction between the knowledge, which is the province of the social worker, but is within her grasp as a teacher, and the more specialist knowledge of child protection. In the case of child protection the social worker draws on her exclusive knowledge and exercises her specialist expertise in the sense that I described expertise in Chapter 2 (Section 2.3), *pace* Holland, Lachicotte, Skinner, and Cain (1998), as being able to manipulate practices to take forward one's intentions.

Early definitions of who could be called professional made much of their initial training and exclusive knowledge base (Wilensky, 1964). However, as Evetts (2006), among others, has argued that concepts of stable professional authority based on exclusive knowledge have needed to be rethought as professions have learnt to adapt their practices to changing societal conditions. Knowledge, but also learning, is therefore integral to practices which involve more than simply following routine procedures or tackling prescribed tasks. I do not intend to argue that knowledge is simply situated in historic practices and all learning is therefore apprenticeships: such a line would deny the human agency that is central to my discussion of the relational turn. However, we cannot think about adaptation without turning to the practices themselves, how they connect with activities and are imbued with knowledge.

6.4 Knowledge in Practices

Echoing Stehr's (1994) observation about how the production and use of knowledge is intertwined with the social organisation in which it originates, Tsoukas (2005) asks the following questions:

> What is organizational knowledge and what forms does it take? What are the forms of life within which different kinds of knowledge are embedded? How is new knowledge created? How do individuals draw on different forms of organizational knowledge and for what effects? What are the representational and social practices through which organizations construct and communicate their forms of knowledge? How are knowledge claims justified and legitimated within organisations? (Tsoukas, 2005:3)

The welfare managers discussed in the previous section demonstrate the importance of these questions to an understanding of professional work and its development. They were positioned outside the core practices of schools, and we were told frequently that these core practices were strengthened because the welfare managers took on the welfare work so that 'teachers can teach'. They operated in different communication systems from those in place for passing information about children's academic performance. They were seen as 'plugging a gap' between systems and were therefore creating practices where the knowledge in use needed to be borrowed from elsewhere and where their own claims to knowledge were heavily situated and were 'everyday' in the Vygotskian sense (Edwards, 2009a; Edwards et al., 2010).

Tsoukas's questions are therefore perhaps best tackled by examining what happens at the level of practice rather than at the level of organisation. That is, if practices are seen as collective, purposeful, knowledge-laden, imbued with cultural values, emotionally freighted and open to change. Practices, as I have just described them, occur within institutions such as families, schools and hospitals and consist of activities which are intentional in some way. Settings within institutions may differ, as may the activities within them, and participants will experience activities differently depending on, for example, the division of labour within them. The accident and emergency departments of hospitals involve different activities and different professional experiences from those found the operating theatres described by Bleakley et al. (2006), yet they operate within a broad set of institutional practices which are aimed at making sick people well and which, potentially at least, interconnect.

In my definition of practices I have drawn heavily on Hedegaard's cultural historical analysis of relationships between societal norms and expectations, institutional practices, the opportunities for action that they create and individual actions in activities. Figure 6.1 is an adaptation of the figure produced in her 2009 text, as Hedegaard has recently revised the original (Hedegaard, personal communication).

Hedegaard's framework usefully emphasises the part that motives and values play in shaping the practices we inhabit, how opportunities for action in the social situation of development are interpreted by individual actors, and how we work in activities. As well as reading across the rows to recognise that an activity setting might comprise several social situations of development, experienced differently by different actors but reflecting similar motivations, we can also read up and down the columns. Here we can see that the values and motives that are carried in institutional

Society	Tradition	Conditions
Institution	Practice	Values/Motive Objects
Activity setting	Social situation of development	Motivation
Person	Activity	Motives/Engagement/Intentions

Fig. 6.1 Levels of analysis (after Hedegaard, 2009: 17)

6.4 Knowledge in Practices

practices are reflected in the social situations of development that arise in particular practices, and in how people engage in activities in these social situations. Hedegaard has developed the framework to analyse differences between children's experiences of home and school, but I suggest that it is a useful analytic heuristic for examining practices elsewhere. My addition to the framework would be to add knowledge to values and motives. As I have already indicated, engagement with knowledge is central to my discussion of being a professional.

Cole (1996) suggests that the terms 'activity' and 'practice' are replacing 'context' and 'situation', in part because they offer a way out of the dualistic separation of person and environment that is not part of CHAT. In the framework I am offering, people inhabit practices laden with the accumulated knowledge necessary to undertake activities and they engage in activities which demand that knowledge. As a result of taking part in activities that are collectively recognised as representing a practice, they *become* members of that practice as social workers or teachers. When they engage in the often more complex activities to be found at the margins of their institutional practices, they also work with the knowledge of other specialists. They may then find that the knowledge they encounter there is not collectively recognised as a legitimate part of mainstream practices and, as I indicated in Chapter 4 (Section 4.5), their sense of who they are as professionals is threatened.

Barnes' analysis of practices as 'a collective accomplishment' (Barnes, 2001: 23) suggests that the relational turn is central to established practices as well as to those that cross professional boundaries, and points to why new knowledge may destabilize practices. Taking the example of horses being ridden in formation, he makes the point that practices should not be thought of as a collectivity of individuals all held together by a single object: rather, we should attend to how actors are attuned to each other. For him practice is therefore not simply a matter of shared motives:

> What is required to understand a practice of this kind is not individuals oriented primarily by their own habits, nor is it individuals oriented by the same collective object; rather it is human beings oriented to *each other*. (Barnes, 2001: 24 *italics in the original*)

This attunement is unarticulated, but assumes a collectively held, tacit understanding of core knowledge and expectations. Understanding or changing practices, therefore, involves engaging with the collective and the tacit knowledge that exists there.

Knowledge in practices, and by extension in activities, is rarely made explicit, but that does not mean it is merely the kind of intuitive craft knowledge that Victor and Boynton see as tacitly held and not articulated (Victor & Boynton, 1998 and Chapter 5 Section 5.2). Polanyi was clear that tacit and explicit knowledge are inseparable (Polanyi, 1962), and that tacit knowledge offers a background awareness of phenomena which allows us to foreground and focus on specific features. For example, years of working on piano scales mean that a pianist can focus on a piece of complex fingering without needing to make her tacit knowledge of scales explicit. One of the problems of practice is that so much knowledge becomes tacit as expertise grows and the complexities of professional tasks are revealed. Polanyi was primarily examining personal or individual knowledge. But the interconnection of tacit and explicit knowledge also holds true if we see practices as collective endeavours.

The importance of tacit knowledge to expert practices can prove problematic when tackling Tsoukas's knowledge claims question. This is certainly so in the case of teaching in England and elsewhere, where competing claims for its knowledge base has made it a battleground which has finally left it vulnerable to 'organizational professionalism' of a deeply inhibiting kind. For example, teachers have been trained simply to deliver a prescribed curriculum and not to think pedagogically about children as learners (Edwards & Protheroe, 2003, 2004; Edwards, 2009b, 2010).

One aspect of the battle over claims to the knowledge base has been to assert the importance of the practitioner knowledge (Clandenin & Connelly, 2000; Elbaz, 1991), which arises in response to the demands of practice and is heavily situated within specific local practices. Hiebert, Gallimore, and Stigler (2002), while recognising the virtues of teachers' practitioner knowledge, nevertheless suggest that it makes an inadequate basis for strong knowledge claims and offer criteria for a knowledge base which focuses attention on the explicit aspects of practitioner knowledge. These are that the knowledge should be public, storable, shareable and open to verification and development. They explain what that means for teachers' knowledge work, in ways that echo Knorr Cetina's concern with engrossment with epistemic objects. '[Teachers] must operate in a system that allows them to treat ideas for teaching as objects that can be shared and examined publicly' (Hiebert et al., 2002: 7).

In the next chapter I shall discuss how important it is that knowledge which is generated in practices is made explicit in order to influence strategic planning in the institutions or 'systems' which shape the practices. Here I shall explore what attention to knowledge objects means for how we think about knowledge in practices. To return to more of Tsoukas's questions: how is new knowledge created and what are the representational and social practices through which organisations construct and communicate their forms of knowledge? Seeing knowledge objects as open to verification and development within collective practices is more than responding to the demands of practice with well-tuned adjustments. It means attending to the knowledge in play and working on developing it. Hiebert and his colleagues suggest it requires expertise in accumulating and sharing evidence about practice, making judgments about the quality of the evidence and evaluating its general relevance. They also indicate that it involves looking beyond the situated knowledge of local practices and examining other publicly available evidence about the phenomena of interest.

I agree. However, their proposals do not mean that all practitioners should become researchers of practice. Instead, my argument, echoing a little the points made by Miettinen and Virkkunen (2005) (Section 6.2), is that if knowledge in practices is to be seen to be of value beyond the place and the moment, practitioners need to work not only on improving practice, but also on the tools that help them to make visible and work on the knowledge in use. They need to be interested in the knowledge they bring to bear in activities and to be able to question it, make connections and develop it. This expectation is entirely in line with the Vygotskian notion of externalisation discussed in previous chapters. Vygotsky's view of learning recognises the continuous refining of the conceptual tools which we use to act on the world. As I said in Section 6.2 when discussing the need for a stablising concern with expert knowledge, it is important to attend to refining both knowledge and the tools available for refining knowledge.

Working at the level of practice allows a purchase on the questions about organisational knowledge that Tsoukas poses. In particular, once we see practices as collective cultural experiences with pasts and futures that are open to scrutiny, we can begin to tease out connections between knowledge, values and relationships. Without taking seriously the knowledge in practices, professions are in danger of finding 'organizational professionalism' their only option.

References

Bach, S., Kessler, I., & Heron, P. (2006). Changing job boundaries and workforce reform: The case of teaching assistants. *Industrial Relations Journal, 37*(1), 2–21.
Barnes, B. (2001). Practice as collective activity. In T. Schatzki, K. Knorr Cetina, & E. von Savigny (Eds.), *The practice turn in contemporary theory* (pp. 17–28). London: Routledge.
Bleakley, A., Hobbs, A., Boyden, J., Allard, J., & Walsh, L. (2006). Improving teamwork climate in operating theatres: The shift from multiprofessionalism to interprofessionalism. *Journal of Interprofessional Care, 20*, 461–470.
Cajkler, W., Tennant, G., Tiknaz, Y., Sage, R., Taylor, C., Tucker, S. A., et al. (2007). *A systematic literature review on the perceptions of ways in which teaching assistants work to support pupils' social and academic engagement in secondary classrooms.* London: EPPI Centre.
Cameron, C., Mooney, A., & Moss, P. (2002). The child care workforce: Current conditions and future directions. *Critical Social Policy, 22*(4), 572–595.
Clandenin, D. J., & Connelly, F. M. (2000). *Narrative inquiry: Experience and story in qualitative research*. San Francisco, CA: Jossey-Bass.
Cole, M. (1996). *Cultural psychology: A once and future discipline*. Cambridge, MA: Harvard University Press.
Edwards (2009a). Understanding boundaries in inter-professional work. *The Scottish Educational Review, 41*(1), 5–21.
Edwards, A. (2009b). Becoming a Teacher. In H. Daniels, J. Porter H. Lauder (Eds), *Educational theories, cultures and learning* (pp. 153–164). London: Routledge.
Edwards, A. (2010). How can CHAT help us to understand and develop teacher education? In V. Ellis, A. Edwards, & P. Smagorinsky (Eds.), *Learning teaching: Cultural historical perspectives on teacher education and development* (pp. 63–77). London: Routledge.
Edwards, A., Daniels, H., Gallagher, T., Leadbetter, J., & Warmington, P. (2009). *Improving inter-professional collaborations: Multi-agency working for children's wellbeing*. London: Routledge.
Edwards, A., Lunt, I., & Stamou, E. (2010). Inter-professional work and expertise: New roles at the boundaries of schools. *British Educational Research Journal, 30*(1), 27–45.
Edwards, A., & Protheroe, L. (2003). Learning to see in classrooms: What are student teachers learning about teaching and learning while learning to teach in schools? *British Educational Research Journal, 29*(2), 227–242.
Edwards, A., & Protheroe, L. (2004). Teaching by proxy: Understanding how mentors are positioned in partnerships. *Oxford Review of Education, 30*(2), 183–197.

Elbaz, F. (1991). Research on teacher's knowledge: The evolution of a discourse. *Journal of Curriculum Studies, 23*(1), 1–19.

Evangelou, M., Sylva, K., Edwards, A., & Smith, T. (2008). *Supporting parents in promoting early learning*. London: DCSF Research Report 039.

Evetts, J. (2003). The sociological analysis of professionalism. *International Sociology, 18*(3), 395–415.

Evetts, J. (2006). Introduction – Trust and professionalism: Challenges and occupational changes. *Current Sociology, 54*(4), 515–531.

Evetts, J. (2009). New professionalism and new public management: Changes continuities and consequences. *Comparative Sociology, 8*, 247–266.

Gunter, H. (2007). Remodelling the school workforce in England: A study in tyranny. *Journal for Critical Education Policy Studies, 5*(1), 1–11.

Healey, A. N., Undre, S., & Vincent, C. (2006). Defining the technical skills of teamwork in surgery. *Quality and Safety in Health Care, 15*(4), 231–234.

Hedegaard, M. (2009). A cultural-historical theory of children's development. In M. Hedegaard & M. Fleer (Eds.), *Studying children: A cultural-historical approach* (pp. 10–29). Buckingham: Open University Press.

Hiebert, J., Gallimore, R., & Stigler, J. (2002). A knowledge base for the teaching profession: What would it look like and how can we get one? *Educational Researcher, 31*(5), 3–15.

Holland, D., Lachicotte, W., Skinner, D., & Cain, C. (1998). *Identity and agency in cultural world*. Cambridge, MA: Harvard University Press.

Hoyle, C. (1998). *Negotiating domestic violence: Police, criminal justice and victims*. Oxford: Oxford University Press.

Jack, G. (2006). The area and community components of children's well-being. *Children and Society, 20*(5), 334–347.

Jensen, K. (2007). The desire to learn: An analysis of knowledge-seeking practices among professionals. *Oxford Review of Education, 33*(4), 489–502.

Jensen, K., & Lahn, L. (2005). The binding role of knowledge: An analysis of nursing students. *Journal of Education and Work, 18*(3), 305–320.

Jensen, K., Lahn, L., & Nerland, M. (Eds.) (in press). *Professional learning in the knowledge society*. Rotterdam: Sense.

Knorr Cetina, K. (1997). Sociality with objects: Social relations in post-social knowledge societies. *Theory Culture Society, 14*(1), 1–29.

Knorr Cetina, K. (1999). *Epistemic cultures: How sciences make knowledge*. Cambridge, MA: Harvard University Press.

Knorr Cetina, K., & Bruegger, U. (2002). Traders' engagement with markets: A postsocial relationship. *Theory Culture and Society, 19*(5–6), 161–185.

Lave, J. (1988). *Cognition in practice*. Cambridge: Cambridge University Press.

Leont'ev, A. N. (1978). *Activity, consciousness and personality*. Englewood Cliffs, NJ: Prentice Hall.

Middleton, D. (2009). Identifying learning in inter-professional discourse: The development of an analytic protocol. In H. Daniels, A. Edwards, Y. Engeström, & S. Ludvigsen (Eds.), *Activity theory in practice: Promoting learning across boundaries and agencies* (pp. 90–104). London: Routledge.

Miettinen, R., & Virkkunen, J. (2005). Epistemic objects, artifacts and organizational change. *Organization, 12*(3), 437–456.

Nowotny, H. (2003). Dilemmas of expertise. *Science and Public Policy, 30*(3), 151–156.

Parsons, T. (1951). *The social system*. New York, NY: Free Press.

Polanyi, M. (1962). *Personal knowledge*. Chicago, IL: University of Chicago Press.

Stehr, N. (1994). *Knowledge societies*. London: Sage.

Tsoukas, H. (2005). *Complex knowledge*. Oxford: Oxford University Press.

Victor, B., & Boynton, A. (1998). *Invented here: Maximizing your organization's internal growth and profitability*. Boston, MA: Harvard Business School Press.

Vygotsky, L. S. (1997). Analysis of higher mental functions. In R. W. Rieber (Ed.), *The collected works of L.S. Vygotsky, vol 4: The history of the development of higher mental functions* New York, NY: Plenum Press.
Weber, M. (1968). *Economy and society*. New York, NY: Bedminster Press.
Wilensky, H. (1964). The professionalization of everyone? *The American Journal of Sociology, 70*(2), 137–158.
Yarker, P. (2005). On not being a teacher: The professional and personal costs of workforce remodelling. *Forum, 47*(2–3), 169–174.

Chapter 7
Working Upstream

7.1 Systemic Learning from Operational Practices

So far the relational turn has been examined as a phenomenon that can enhance the work of practitioners who are tackling complex problems and are working at and across the vertical boundaries that exist between organisations or parallel units in organisations. In this chapter the focus shifts to relationships at the hierarchical boundaries in organisations or broader systems, and in particular to the opportunities for the upstream flow of the knowledge that is being generated and refined in operational practices.

The relational turn in the professional practices discussed in previous chapters involves responses that collaborating practitioners can bring to a professional task and also, as a prior to action, an expansion of the interpretations that are made of the tasks so that their complexity can be recognised. In some cases the expansions of interpretations and responses have been achieved rapidly and operational practices have, as a result, raced ahead of the organisational systems where the practices are primarily located. For example, as we have already seen (Section 3.2), in the LIW study (Edwards, Daniels, Gallagher, Leadbetter, & Warmington, 2009), we found that practitioners had to 'rule-bend' in their home organisations in order to work responsively to support vulnerable children alongside other professionals. This rule-bending signalled responsible professional decision-making and, for example, involved cutting through established channels of communication to make immediate contact with the person who could help a child or family.

In this chapter, I attempt to weave together some of the themes set out in discussions of the relational aspects of professional practice in order to consider their implications for how knowledge not only moves across boundaries between organisations or sub-units but also moves upstream from operational practices to inform strategy. My focus is, therefore, the problem of 'sticky' knowledge which moves with difficulty within systems rather than the 'leaky' knowledge that can seep through the boundaries within and between organisations (Seely Brown & Duguid, 2001, 2002).

However, this is not a chapter about the practice of strategy (Mintzberg, 1994), nor is it about the learning organisation *pace* Nonaka and Takeuchi (1995). Rather, the focus is what happens when attempts are made to move knowledge upwards at hierarchical boundaries and the themes are familiar. They include working at boundaries; engagement with knowledge; recognising motives in practices; building common knowledge; and exercising relational expertise. Attention to practices remains central, with strategy seen as a distinct practice which sits in a hierarchical relationship above operational practices in many of the organisations in which professionals find themselves working.

The strategic practices that are most relevant are those that have the potential to shape the conditions under which operational practitioners are able to carry out their work. These strategic practices include, for example, control over the flexibility of the working day and the local mediation of national policy priorities. While NPM with its target-led methods might offer some freedom of movement to practitioners, the bureaucratic legacies to be found in so many of the systems which sustain organisational forms of professionalism can, I suggest, act as a drag which inhibits systemic responses to changes in operational practices.

A lack of attention to what can be learnt from operational practices is not new. Yanow, for example, has outlined case studies of the almost wilful ignoring by senior staff of the knowledge available at operational levels within their organisations (Yanow, 2004). However, some see a growing tension between the strength and the relevance of the knowledge of professionals who are in direct contact with clients and the organisations in which they work. For example, Shaw, Morris and Edwards (2009) observe that 'Social workers, computer programmers, teachers and accountants work with human capital and their greater accredited knowledge is [therefore] thought to bring greater power.' We cited Darr and Warhurst who suggest that the relevant knowledge held by the workforce is at last being recognised, bringing a potential change in the relations between 'labour' and employers.

> [T]he balance of power within the employment relationship is assumed to have shifted decisively in favour of labour. The reason for this shift is that the knowledge that is now critical for firms resides intangibly within workers' heads: it is the inherent property of the producer. (Darr & Warhurst, 2008: 32)

Yet in the welfare professions in the UK, one of the most striking paradoxes in the current development of services is that, at a time when service providers are being urged to recognise democratic accountability and to work closely with potential service users through stronger engagement with the strengths and priorities of local communities (Mulgan, 2009), knowledge generated among practitioners who work in the same communities is still not being mobilised in the formulation of local policy.

However, there are lessons to be learnt from analyses of economic performance and knowledge management. The potential benefits of learning from the sites of operational practices are central to an argument made by Lundvall in a 2005 paper on social capital and economic performance. There he proposes that the learning economy needs to be able to draw on the broad range of experiences of those who contribute to it and the key to achieving this is what he terms 'learning by interacting'. Learning by interacting, he argues, 'has the effect of transforming local learning into general knowledge embodied in, for instance, new machinery, new components, new software-systems or even new business solutions' (2005: ∫5). The learning he proposes is characterised by a form of 'vertical disintegration', which allows the diverse experiences of, for example, users, suppliers and designers to be 'absorbed' and therefore used by the company.

Lundvall's arguments bring together the advantages of working across boundaries between organisations and within organisations for the recognition and mobilisation of useful knowledge. However, a prerequisite for the successful disintegration, or at least the eroding, of boundaries is the strength and type of social capital available, as that will affect who is trusted and, therefore, who can be worked with. This point returns us to the importance of common knowledge discussed in Chapters 3 and 4 and to the extent to which the boundaries that may inhibit knowledge flows, wherever they are, connect with the identities of those who inhabit the practices on either side of them.

7.2 Distinctly Different Practices in Organisational Hierarchies

My own work has shown quite clearly how practices and the identities they sustain help create the hierarchical boundaries that impede creative strategic responses to changes in operational practices. For example, the National Evaluation of the Children's Fund (NECF) (Edwards, Barnes, Plewis, & Morris, 2006) found that the meetings of the strategic Partnership Boards, which commissioned Children's Fund services in each local authority, frequently consisted of strategic staff who waded through piles of papers which were rarely read in any detail but which contained action points for which the Board members were accountable. Operational level practitioners were occasionally invited in to present a success story to the Boards, but the Board meetings were time-limited, preventing discussions of what led to the success in operational practices. Indeed, the stories were often pushed off the agenda at the last minute as the accounts that were offered were not recognised as immediately relevant to the strategic concerns of the Boards.

The analytic framework which was presented in Fig. 6.1 (Section 6.4) would suggest that the institutional practices represented by the Boards were focused on different objects of activity and worked with different motives from those which were represented by the practices of operational level practitioners. In Section 6.4, I suggested that the model given in Fig. 6.1 might be augmented by examining the knowledge in use and how it is worked with at each level. Differences in engagement with knowledge were clear when we looked at how the Boards discussed their work. These differences allowed the NECF research team to distinguish between how Board members constructed their roles and purposes and how they separated themselves from the operational practices they commissioned.

The major distinction between the Boards was between what we termed 'Developing Boards', where there was some, often heated, discussion of what the prevention of social exclusion meant and how it connected with the services being commissioned, and 'Stable Boards'. These were Boards which saw their purpose as simply dispensing money to maintain existing services; and where there was much harking back to previous experiences of similar initiatives and no discussion at all of what was meant by the new concept of the prevention of social exclusion. The Developing Boards were far more likely to see how the new services that were being funded were opening up a new field of preventative activity, while the Stable Boards were more preoccupied with drawing on their previous experiences to tackle the immediate tasks of meeting current funding criteria.

The motives driving strategic practices in the different types of Boards were, unsurprisingly, reflected in the approaches taken by the services they commissioned and the practices to be found at the operational level. Developing Boards were far more likely to commission new services which grasped the opportunity to offer well-thought-out preventative provision, while the Stable Boards were more likely to commission existing services with little evidence of significant attempts to consider how the services might be adjusted to work in more responsively preventative ways.

However, despite taking the material resources offered by the Children's Fund and working with them in different ways on the problem of preventing social exclusion, the discursive practices in both types of Board, although different from each other, were also different from those to be found in the settings where practitioners engaged with service users. The differences created a boundary between the Boards and the operational practices of the services they commissioned, which in turn separated the knowledge being drawn on and generated in their practices from that which was in play at the operational levels.

The different discursive practices at each level within the Children's Fund sustained quite different identities, which made breaching the hierarchical boundaries impossible. Here are just a few examples from Children's Fund practitioners, but similar statements were also made by practitioners involved in the later LIW study (Edwards et al., 2009):

> I'm not very good at feeding up to the key strategic players. I tend to just get on with my job. I am not a glory seeker and that I think at times is a negative thing for myself.
>
> The learning happens on the ground and people felt frustrated, they wanted to take that somewhere but actually it didn't really seem to go anywhere.
>
> Reports go up the line, but I am not sure what happens to them.

In NECF and other evaluations of government interventions, we have observed how wasteful the consequent lack of learning from practice is for organisations and have suggested that interventions like the Children's Fund, which aim at reshaping practices, should include a pedagogic framework which attempts to assist the movement of knowledge upstream to inform strategy. Here we have simply been echoing Lundvall's suggestion, in his discussion of the 'learning economy', that the mobilisation of knowledge within and across systems should be thought of in terms of learning. He concludes that economists cannot tackle the problems of economic development on their own. Rather there is 'a need for extensive

7.2 Distinctly Different Practices in Organisational Hierarchies

co-operation between economists and experts in pedagogical and sociological disciplines' (Lundvall, 1996: ∫19) and a need to recognise the 'social dimension of strategy' (∫20).

The pedagogical challenge for organisations is, of course, increased when the changes in practices also involve horizontal cross-boundary collaborations between operational staff. Vertical co-ordination across hierarchical boundaries is much more easily achieved, through for example performance management, in tightly bounded single purpose organisations. However, upstream learning to respond to the challenges of inter-professional collaborations is crucial if professions are to respond to complex societal problems.

Christensen and Lægreid (2007) have argued that joined-up policies aimed at tackling these kinds of problems depend on action being taken on the ground and 'cannot be easily imposed from top down' (p. 1063). They note that developing a public sector system that can accommodate a cross-government approach to policy will take time: 'new skills, changes in organizational culture, and the building of mutual trust relations needs patience' (p. 1063). The pressure on strategic practices is, therefore, coming from two directions: horizontally, from potential partners at a strategic level, and vertically, from below from operational staff who are already involved in inter-professional collaborations. While both are important, the vertical pressure from below, perhaps, needs to be tackled before adjustments are made with other organisations.

Schulz's (2001, 2003) analysis of organisational knowledge flows distinguished between horizontal flows between parallel subunits and vertical flows from sub-units to supervising units. He suggested that vertical knowledge flows reveal the risks and possibilities that can arise when knowledge from different sub-units are combined and they need to occur quickly so that the relevance of new knowledge and their implications can be assessed at a strategic level. Barley and Kunda (2001: 76) made a similar point when they argued that when the nature of work in an organisation changes, 'organizational structures either adapt or risk becoming misaligned with the activities they organise'. This is perhaps particularly the case in organisations shaped by NPM and which need to deal with complex problems such as social exclusion. Ordóñez, Schweiter, Galinsky and Bazerman (2009), in a swingeing attack on aggressive top-down goal-setting in organisations, have proposed that performance goals can lead to unethical behaviour by altering an organisation's culture; and they suggest that learning goals should replace performance goals in order to allow, in their argument, business organisations to adapt to changing environments and new knowledge.

We should not, however, underestimate the difficulties of organisational adjustments based on the need for one set of practices to learn from knowledge being generated in another. I am not alone in highlighting how knowledge is specific to particular practices. Howard-Grenville and Carlile (2006) have suggested that the difficulties lie in different 'knowledge regimes' which they define as:

> ...the nested connections between the material realities engaged by work practices, the work practices themselves, and the larger collective conventions that reflect and account for the appropriate use of such practices. (2006: 434)

In cultural historical terms *pace* Fig. 6.1 and Hedegaard (2009), these knowledge regimes may interpret seemingly similar objects of activity somewhat differently, depending on their position within the accounting system of the organisation. In the case of the Children's Fund Boards, their accountability to the central government department that funded each partnership was different from the accountability experienced by the service providers, who felt primarily accountable to the users of the services they offered. Consequently, the motives each group recognised in the objects of activity – or problems they were working on – reflected these differences.

Howard-Grenville and Carlile (2006: 481) identified three features of practices which they suggest allow a comparison across knowledge regimes:

- the causal specificity of knowledge (i.e. the relationship between cause and effect) in the development of new knowledge;
- the temporal cycle needed to develop knowledge; and
- the representation of knowledge through clear and shareable measurement artefacts.

Their focus on measurement artefacts as boundary objects may be a function of their study of manufacturing processes, in their case semiconductor production. Nonetheless, their argument for the need for unambiguous representations of what counts as success that can be used at the boundaries between knowledge regimes would seem to have broad relevance.

For example, another way of presenting their suggestion to organisations driven by value-laden knowledge objects of activity, such as children's wellbeing, would be to propose a sharing of values and motives across boundaries. However, they also observed that even potentially useful boundary objects cannot connect systems if the gaps between the two sets of practices are too wide and, unsurprisingly, given Carlile's attention to common knowledge in his 2004 paper, the solution they proposed is the development of common knowledge 'grounded in the material realities' of the work. Although their study focused primarily on how two organisations sought ways of achieving productive collaborations, their analyses offer a framework for exploring some of the challenges of upstream learning within organisations.

7.3 Differences in Engagement with Knowledge Between Hierarchical Practices

Howard-Grenville and Carlile's attention to how knowledge is mobilised across practices did not attempt to privilege one form of knowledge tie over another. Yet once one turns to practices which are related hierarchically, the relative status of knowledge becomes a concern that was reflected in the frustrations about upstream knowledge flows identified by NECF in the previous section. Yanow has made a distinction between the local knowledge of operational workers and what she describes as rational-scientific- technical expertise that is to be found further up the organisation hierarchy (Yanow, 2004), arguing that each represents very different knowledge practices.

Indeed, her distinction echoes the Vygotskian differentiation between everyday situated knowledge and the more generalisable scientific concepts discussed in the previous chapter (Section 6.2). She described the knowledge of the operational staff in the case studies she reviewed as carried within context-rich narratives which often contained vital information about the interface of the organisation and those who used its services or products. She compared the knowledge embedded in narratives with the knowledge of organisational decision-makers who need the knowledge gleaned at the interface with users, but frequently underplay or even disparage the knowledge of operational staff which is so often embedded in narratives of particular events. Her argument was that these differences are bound up with the politics of expertise and a privileging of university-based knowledge over practical knowledge with the result that attempts made by lower status workers at moving knowledge upwards and across boundaries may appear transgressive and 'disturbing the 'natural' organizational-structural order of things' (2004: ∫18). Yanow suggested that the danger is that categorisations employed by operational staff may 'pollute' strategic categorisations and erode the boundaries that separate them. Here we can see how identity maintenance gets in the way of opportunities for learning.

A Vygotskian view of individual learning can reveal the problem of upstream knowledge movement for organisations in pedagogic terms. The Vygotskian line on individual learning is that it is the outcome of a dialectic between everyday situated understandings and the more powerful concepts that are valued publicly and are not situation specific, and it is the role of education to create a dialectic that brings these two kinds of understanding into an interplay that allows conceptual development. The outcome of the dialectic for the learner is the capacity to employ the more powerful concepts as they act on the world. However, the concepts may also be refined in the dialectic: they are not necessarily fixed.

I suggest that this dialectic account of learning can also be used when considering how organisations learn, i.e. recognise and use available knowledge. If that suggestion is taken up the need to encourage a dialectic between the situated knowledge offered by operational staff and the more general concerns of strategists becomes clear. It does seem that impermeable boundaries within organisations, both between subunits of operational work and between workers, managers and strategists, can inhibit more collective versions of a learning dialectic that might help organisations respond to changing features of the world in which they operate.

Yanow's arguments go a long way to explain the unease and lack of welcome from local strategists that was experienced by Children's Fund and other staff who had important messages from the user interface to take forward. They also help us to recognise how hierarchical boundaries have a stabilising function within organisations and are therefore discursively sustained to protect identities and positions. However, although the higher one is placed in an organisation, the more likely it is that one is dealing with the general rather than the particular in decision-making, it is also clear (as anyone who has listened to an account of how insider information can be gathered over dinner will recognise) that strategic knowledge is also carried and shared in narratives through which the concepts and values that count are revealed and reiterated. The knowledge regimes themselves, therefore, may not be so different, with contextual knowledge embedded in narratives being of value at every level of practice.

7.4 Differences in Temporalities

A core difference between the timelines of operational work in responsive and the interactional professional work and those of decision-making at an organisational level lies in the constant negotiations and adaptations that characterise responsive professional practice. It is not at all surprising that systemic adaptations that arise from changing patterns of responses to clients are achieved only slowly and may be first felt as forms of 'rule-bending' rather than as easily discernable shifts in incentives and expectations. An English report that summarised progress on the development of joined-up services for vulnerable children (Laming, 2009) captured the problems that arise when the work of motivated professionals runs ahead of the organisational arrangements which should support them:

> Joint working between children's social workers, youth workers, schools, early years, police and health too often depends on the commitment of individual staff and sometimes this happens despite, rather than because of, the organisational arrangements. (Laming, 2009: 11 Section 1.6)

In situations of this kind, where 'organizational professionalism' prevails over 'occupational professionalism' (Evetts, 2009), the values-driven responses of front-line workers can appear transgressive rather than creative.

However, in fields where being creative is crucial, developments made in direct work with the users of services can become part of a recognisable and supported process of product development. Mørch, Nygård and Ludvigsen, for example, have analysed the interplay between the adaptations that occur when software is developed with users to meet their specific needs and what they term the processes of generalisation. Generalisation occurs as some of the ideas arising from these adaptations are taken up more broadly and lead to organisational adjustments which reflect their wider relevance. They explain as follows:

> The difference between the two levels of development [adaptation and generalisation] is related to the timescales involved and in which direction the software as emerging objects goes. Adaptation at the most specific level is in most cases part of the short cycles of activities, but if they address increased specification and adaptability towards specific user-groups we can also talk about extended timescales on this level. Generalisation, however, is about long cycles of activities based on co-configuration between the customers and the company and mediated by the software (products and knowledge management support). Innovations are initiated as local adaptations to the products during a short development cycle and may be brought forward to all customers (at another time scale of development). (Mørch, Nygård, & Ludvigsen, 2009: 201–202)

The relationship between adaptation and generalisation that they trace is connected with a process of aggregation which occurs when a specific solution is integrated into a general solution at the organisational level. They work with an Engeströmian activity theory framework (see Appendix A) and see this process of generalisation as a way of resolving the tensions and breakdowns in the broader systems that arise through the evolving development of software artefacts. Generalisation is therefore a creative response to a systemic problem that has arisen from creative adaptations at the operational level. The differences in timescales are, however, recognised and the ability to respond is built into systems to enable software engineers to remain responsive and, therefore, at the leading edge of product development. The Mørch et al. study is presented quite tentatively as a single case, but it does connect with work on feedback loops and product innovation more generally (Christiansen & Lundvall, 2004).

7.5 Representations that Work Across Boundaries

There has been a considerable amount of work on the creation of potentially shared objects of activity which allow different systems to configure their practices towards shared purposes, i.e. make the horizontal links discussed Chapters 3 and 4. These have included the use of care agreements that travel with patients as navigate complex health care systems (Engeström, 2001) and assessment portfolios that bring together schools and universities in the shared task of training beginning teachers (Jahreie & Ludvigsen, 2007). But these artefacts assume that compatible knowledge systems and professional identities are to be found in each of the organisations which are oriented towards potentially shared objects, such as the illness of patients or the learning trajectories of student teachers. Where this compatibility cannot be assumed, attention may need to be paid to translating locally embedded knowledge into powerful concepts which can travel and can be aligned with the motives of more powerful practice. As I have already indicated, one cannot assume compatibility between the motives to be found in the practices of operational work and strategy.

One approach to translation is to encourage the articulation of the concepts that drive practice. There is certainly some value, as I have suggested throughout the previous chapters, in clarifying the purposes of practices and how they are interpreted and indicating the resources that specialist expertise can bring to bear. But these processes imply seeing the hierarchical boundaries as sites of intersecting practices where the common knowledge discussed in previous chapters can be built. My own experiences of evaluation studies in the welfare sector suggests that long-term knowledge building at the boundaries that separate hierarchical practices is unlikely to happen in that field. Boundary sites between practitioners involved in strategy and operational staff or local communities do emerge, but are created by the strategic actors when they need advice from, for example, local communities to meet external demands that they tackle local needs. Sometimes there is a willingness to listen and learn more broadly, but it is often accompanied by an impatience, as this statement from a senior local authority officer about the Children's Fund activities in her area illustrates:

> If you search about and see where's the engine room, where all this learning is... [where it] is distilled and disseminated in a form that can really inform development, you can't find it.

Quite understandably, in this example the local authority strategy team wanted operational practices to reveal what are often termed 'key ideas'. However, successful practices are not simply made up of sets of ideas that might be codified and moved across boundaries. Johnson and Lundvall have argued, in a 2001 paper on economics and the developing world, that the answer to the demands of knowledge transfer is not simply to attempt to codify tacitly held knowledge. In line with the points made in Chapter 2, that expertise is to be found in the manipulation of the practices of 'figured worlds' (Holland, Lachicotte, Skinner, & Cain, 1998) to take forward intentions, they propose that not all knowledge can be codified and that some knowledge may be only partially codified. This, they suggest, is particularly the case for what they describe (p.7) as the 'softer knowledge about what is going on in firms'. This knowledge 'skilful human behaviour (quarrelling, flirting, telling stories...)' (p.7) would become less useful once it was codified. It is this knowledge, the intertwined exercise of know-what, how, why, and who, that marks out expertise in a practice and can render a practice a mystery to the uninitiated.

Johnson and Lundvall's arguments are made in relation to the transfer of knowledge from the wealthy North to the developing South rather than to upstream in organisations. But the reservations they hold about codification as a simple solution are relevant to the concerns of this chapter, as is their attention to how appeals for codification can play into the sustaining of distinctions in power in organisations:

> Changing the control of knowledge is often an instrument for changing the power structure and codification and other changes in the structure of knowledge may be better explained as elements in a process of power struggles than as an exercise in equilibrating marginal benefits and costs. (Johnson & Lundvall, 2001: 6)

However, their main argument is that very little knowledge is 'perfectly public' (p.14). I would agree and therefore recognise that even the clearest of representations are rarely amenable to being understood and drawn on as predictable resources for action across differing practices.

7.6 Upstream Learning and Resistance to Change in Organisations

The CHAT line being pursued in this book connects with analyses that see change as organisational narrative (Van den Ven & Poole, 2005). From that perspective change is historically grounded and contextually situated accounts of shifts in purposes and processes over time, woven into organisational structures such as the hierarchical boundaries I have just outlined. The picture presented so far has been of

7.6 Upstream Learning and Resistance to Change in Organisations

how hierarchical boundaries stabilise organisations by working against the grain of organisational change and resisting the knowledge already potentially available to them within the organisation as a system. The narrative account of change, therefore, helps to explain its slow pace in many organisations.

Problems of lack of creative response at an organisational level are not unrecognised. As Tsoukas has observed:

> What is crucially missing from (organisational theory) is...theories of creative action in organizations. This in turn calls for more work on how structure interacts with process over time, how reflectivity functions and how context and contingencies influence action paths. (Tsoukas, 2003: 618)

Tsoukas's concern with a need for reflectivity in the interplay between structure and process takes us back to the unreflective resistance to a dialectic between operational and strategic practices in the examples discussed so far, while his attention to context and contingencies returns us to the motives that shape practices and therefore how activities are approached and carried through at different layers within organisations. A focus on motives in practices and activities means that despite my misgivings in Section 7.2, efforts may need to be made to recognise some degree of compatibility across hierarchical practices, through a building of common knowledge which includes an elaboration of motives.

One might expect that, in the kinds of organisations in which professionals work, motives at different layers of practices are likely to at the very least overlap. Hospitals aim at preventing and curing sickness, welfare services at safeguarding the vulnerable and educational services at educating future generations of citizens and workers. Yet the prevalence of what Evetts (2009) has described as 'organizational' professionalism over 'occupational' professionalism is likely to mean that the motives that drive professional actions are not reflected higher up the system. Hence the need for rule-bending at the operational level already alluded to. The prevailing organisational narratives offered by NPM are top-down models of organisational priorities which are in turn shaped by national policies. Influence that moves up the organisational layers is unlikely. Yet the lack of organisational flexibility that arises can be frustrating for policy makers, too, as the 2009 Laming report has already illustrated.

For Tsoukas the way forward for understanding the interaction of structure and process lies in recognising that organisations are 'constitutively social all the way – discursive practices embedded within discursive practices' and that we should 'look for the discursive practices involved in organizing' (2003: 619). However, it is already clear that what prevents upstream learning is how distinct discursive practices, and their 'ready to hand' (Knorr Cetina, 1997: 10) non-reflective scripts at each layer in organisations, protect particular identities and can therefore make it difficult to talk across boundaries.

We collected a great deal of evidence of the discursive shoring up of boundaries and how these simultaneously shape identities. Here some operational level practitioners, educational psychologists, education welfare officers and social workers, in a multi-professional team in the LIW study, discuss difficulties in taking ideas upstream and so echo the views of practitioners from the Children's Fund offered in Section 7.2.

> Yeah because we're dealing with very senior people who are making the overall strategy of the multi-professional team, you've got people who are operational on the ground floor level who are working hard to move further and further towards it [multi-professional work], and you've got one layer which some where is, I don't know what they do.

Since identities were sustained by peers, attempting to operate at, or across, the boundaries was seen as quite high risk.

> It is very hard in that context to actually be a lone voice and say actually, you know I do think this...but it can...the pressure of being seen to agree with your peers is actually very strong.

> It takes an awful lot of confidence and experience to be able to do that. And it's a very uncomfortable place to be.

> Yeah we just need to know the game...who the players are in the game because that just feels so far removed that you don't even know where they are or anything.

These views reveal an implicit contradiction between operational and more senior practices where the more knowledgeable operational staff were silenced by being positioned without access to the discursive practices of the strategic staff and without the opportunity to build common knowledge that might reveal their expertise as well as the motives and concerns of strategic staff. The contradiction was made evident in the following statement from an operational practitioner:

> I think the strategists need to talk with you rather than talk down to you. Because I've been to so many presentations when, you know you are given this, it seems an unreal world that they are talking about and it doesn't fit with the reality on the ground at all. And you go away at the end of it thinking this is rubbish...but nobody disagrees much with what they are saying.

This is not an easy problem to solve. In one attempt at tackling similar contradictions and developing a discursive practice that might cut through the barriers to be found between operation and strategy, Ahonen and Virkkunen (2003) set up a series of what they termed 'Competence Laboratories', which are based on DWR Change Laboratories (Engeström, 2007; Appendix A), in three different telecommunication call centres in Finland. They outlined their intentions as a form of knowledge management which brought together 'operative and strategic learning' to create new knowledge and they acknowledged that 'the combination is not harmonious' (p. 60).

The Competence Laboratory had two steps. Firstly, operational practitioners identified how their activity had changed over time and the current challenges facing them as learners. In the second step the managers were brought into the Competence Laboratories to present how the organisations' strategy units viewed the same activity. The expectation was that after a dialogue with the management the practitioners would modify their vision and develop some 'concrete innovations' (p. 60), which would capture the interpretations of both operational and managerial staff. Once step two, was reached the empirical question became whether a dialogue that resulted in an expanded understanding of the object of activity, i.e. the vision of the future and its concrete manifestations, would result.

However, it did not happen, as the managers did not engage with the object of activity worked on in the first step. As a result the intervention did not produce a transformation of the organisations' business plans or strategic visions, leading Ahonen and Virkkunen to conclude that a focus on practices and competence in DWR-type change sessions is insufficient.

Reflecting on how managers, in different ways, deflected attention from scrutiny of the visions and associated business plans and prevented the development of a cross-boundary dialogue, they observed that the 'business model that frames the daily practices must be explicated and questioned' and that:

> The strategic learning required for the transformation of business strategies calls for new forms of dialogue between the management's strategy work and the practitioners' pursuit of developing their work practice. (Ahonen & Virkkunen 2003: 82)

Ahonen and Virkkunen felt that the short-term cross-hierarchy dialogues that did occur could be seen as 'potentially expansive preludes to further cross-hierarchical development' (p.82). However, the intervention was not sustained long enough for them to do more than point to the possibility. The discursive practices of organising revealed by the actions of the managers in that study were finally robust deflections of attempts at achieving some attunement between changes in operational practices and organisational vision and were another example of shoring up of the boundaries.

However, patience is a word already used several times in this chapter. Tsoukas, as we have seen, has called 'for more work on how structure interacts with process over time' (2003: 618). Santos and Eisenhardt (2005) make a similar point when they outline a longitudinal research programme of what they term process research which might lead to a better understanding of how boundaries evolve and shape organisations. Hierarchical boundaries which impede relational work between management and operations are so central to sustaining heavily embedded and historically-based organisational concepts such as strategy and management that the reflectivity suggested by Tsoukas clearly cannot be rushed.

7.7 Mediation and Relevance

The strong distinctions made between different types of practices in organisations are in line with the arguments made by Seely Brown and Duguid in their 2001 paper on knowledge in organisations. They, too, draw on Vygotsky to frame their analysis of how practical knowledge, which includes 'know how', and like Lundvall they emphasise the social aspects of knowledge flow. Noting that organisations 'deliberately embrace communities with fundamentally different practices' (p. 207), they argue that the survival of organisations depends on how they co-ordinate knowledge across the practices and divisions of labour they represent. A central argument is that recognising practice distinctions and their epistemic differences, in the way they are outlined in the present chapter, is a necessary starting point for coping with the limitations of sticky knowledge, which they prefer to call tacit knowledge.

They offer a solution which is again compatible with the line pursued here. They observe that 'the challenge of stickiness, [has] hitherto [been] primarily dealt with through the imposition of routines' (p. 209). However, this response presents challenges for organisations 'whose primary asset is the ability to develop knowledge continuously' (p. 209):

> For such organizations, the most important relationship between quasi-autonomous communities within a dynamically structured firm must be one of negotiation – negotiation which allows change, on the one hand, to occur locally and, on the other hand to affect global strategic change if necessary. (Seely Brown & Duguid, 2001: 209)

Apologising for what they describe as an 'anodyne' solution, they nonetheless suggest that it is 'profoundly different from conventional organizational coordination' (p. 209). They are not specifically tackling problems of upstream learning, but of the failure of useful knowledge to circulate in systems. Let us therefore turn to how their advice may be followed to achieve upstream knowledge flows. What is being negotiated and what are the relational attributes involved in negotiating knowledge at and over these boundaries?

Negotiation, of course, presupposes some possibility of affiliation to a proposed outcome: a recognition of the relevance of new knowledge. When discussing the vertical knowledge flows in organisations revealed in his study of flows in 570 subsidiaries of US companies in Denmark and of Danish Companies in the United States, Schulz (2001) emphasised the perceived relevance of new knowledge as a crucial component. While reciprocation was important for horizontal knowledge flows, new knowledge was important for upward knowledge flows as it allowed its implications to be tested efficiently. Schulz explains:

> ...hierarchies can serve as efficient clearing houses for new knowledge with uncertain relevance' and new knowledge can then be exposed to 'a large array of diverse prior knowledge' and therefore uncover new and serendipitous resource deployments. (Schulz, 2001: 677)

He also observed that relevance is often recognised 'on less than rational grounds; sentiments and beliefs play an important role' (677). He therefore concluded that relevance is 'a rather curious but under-explored aspect of organizational knowledge that merits much more attention in future' (677).

Schulz's analyses suggest not only that identity plays a part in acknowledging relevance but also that recognition may need to be negotiated.

There has been a great deal of discussion of relationships in boundary spanning and bridging (Wenger, 1998), and of working jointly with potentially shared boundary objects (Bechky, 2003), all of which can contribute to understanding how knowledge is negotiated as it is mediated across boundaries. But here the focus is the relationships in which knowledge is mediated upstream. The examples are once again drawn mainly from evaluations of large-scale initiatives with children and families.

7.7 Mediation and Relevance

The initiaitives involved the commissioning of services which worked closely with vulnerable clients and at some distance from the strategic bodies which commissioned them and at even greater distance from the central government agencies which directed the initiatives. A system where links are made though commissioning arrangements may offer particular challenges to the upstream flow of knowledge, yet the freedom of movement given to commissioned services often meant that new ideas and ways of working were developed as practitioners responded to the goals they had been set.

NECF, the evaluation of the Children's Fund (Edwards et al., 2006), identified four ways in which knowledge was moved vertically from practice to the more strategic levels in the local partnerships. Two of these were specific roles which focused on influencing strategy by doing different kinds of negotiating. The first role was 'knowledge champion'. These were often local government members on Partnership Boards, who had a strong sense of responsibility to the communities they represented and who played an advocacy role 'I think we are champions of partnership commissioning and for the kids, because kids actually don't get championed'. Being a knowledge champion was therefore part of their identities within their communities. The second role was 'knowledge broker'. These were usually the paid programme manager for each partnership. It was part of their contracted role within the initiative to operate in both sets of discourse practices therefore, like the council members, they were not experiencing identity strain as they functioned almost bilingually in operational and strategic practices. However, as we have seen, these advocacy processes had limited success, leaving practitioners feeling frustrated that important messages from their front line work with families was not getting through to strategists.

There were also two structural responses: 'pillars' and 'over-lapping systems'. Pillars grouped services in cognate thematic areas connecting strategy and practice in, for example, 'access and participation' or 'health and wellbeing'. These smaller more focused thematic structures were places where motives were more clearly aligned across hierarchical practices, but they were able to offer more limited and less joined up responses to the complex problems being faced.

Only two of the eighteen case study sites set up what we termed 'over-lapping systems', which were characterised by sets of vertical trails or networks of 'know who', which enabled a range of people to work at the boundaries between hierarchical practices. These contacts did not occur naturally and involved capacity building to enable operational practitioners to translate their knowledge into terms of relevance to strategists. For example, programme managers helped service providers to develop ideas so that they could be taken forward to develop commissioning. As one programme manager explained: 'You've got to keep the strategy and the operational as close as you can'. We described the meshing that connected the layers as 'complex systems which were geared to taking forward the aims of the Children's Fund' (Edwards et al., 2006). However, it was clear that the translation was being done by operational practitioners and mediation was then explicitly undertaken through formal presentations of these translated ideas.

There were no examples of sustained fora where the 'implicit mediation' (Wertsch, 2007) discussed in Chapter 1 (Section 1.4) and the development of common knowledge discussed in previous chapters could occur over time. However, where Developing Boards did establish short-term single-purpose task groups in which Board members, practitioners and potential service users met to discuss issues of relevance to the Board, they were clearly productive. One Board member described her experience of these groups as 'some of the most interesting and effective discussions I've certainly been involved in'. She elaborated '...you don't get these in the Board...because the agenda's usually too much and everyone is always looking at their watch'.

These fora, though infrequent and short-lived, were boundary spaces where practitioners and users were momentarily brought in from profane status (Edwards, 2009) to inform the sacred concerns of the Boards. They were places where problems such as responsive commissioning could be worked on and the expertise of each participant brought to bear. They also offered spaces where a degree of indeterminacy and uncertainty was possible, where 'what ifs' – *pace* Wartofsky's tertiary artefacts (Wartofsky, 1973) discussed earlier (Sections 4.4 and 3.6), could be employed and 'know-who' developed in discussions where the relevance of practitioner and user knowledge was recognised by everyone. Like the 'quasi-autonomous communities' pointed to by Seely Brown and Duguid (2001: 209), the services which were represented negotiated the knowledge they brought so that it might be recognised as relevant. The motives driving the practices of each participant outside the meetings may have been different, for example, accountability to the national government for the strategists or meeting the needs of refugee children for the operational staff. However, practitioner and service user knowledge that was brought by the operational practitioners was relevant to the motives driving strategy.

For the operational staff, expertise at the boundaries, therefore, lay in looking into the figured world of strategy; recognising ideas of potential relevance to strategic agenda; translating knowledge from operational practice so that it could be recognised as relevant by strategists, and displaying its relevance to problems identified by strategists in the few boundary spaces made available. It was a practitioner expertise that was developed with the help of the 'bilingual' programme managers.

7.8 Knowledge Flows from Research to Policy

The previous two sentences could easily apply to the relationships that obtain between researchers who do policy-related work and the political strategists whose work they would like to inform. These ideas therefore have broader relevance. Pollard, the Director of the UK Teaching and Learning [Educational] Research Programme (TLRP), has consistently connected research quality to relevance (Pollard, 2006), arguing that relevance was enhanced through engaging research users, whether practitioners or policy-makers, at each stage of the research process. Drawing on evidence from a TLRP funded seminar series on user engagement, we

7.8 Knowledge Flows from Research to Policy

have written about knowledge flows between researchers and both groups (Edwards, Sebba, & Rickinson, 2007; Rickinson, Sebba, & Edwards, in press). Here I shall focus only on the problem of moving knowledge upstream from research into the relatively closed discourse practices of policy makers.

Here we find another example of wasted knowledge. The 2003 report on the social sciences in Britain (Commission on the Social Sciences, 2003) observed:

> There are significant problems with the exploitation of social science research in government, local government, commerce, the voluntary sector and the media. These come about through 'interface management' and communication problems, though the caution of some academics towards close engagement with practitioners is a source of great disappointment to many users of social science research. (extracted from the Executive Summary)

Practitioners in this statement include strategists, and the difficultly is defined as a communication one, with the cautious academics who do not want to lose control of the knowledge they might offer as a significant part of the boundary problem. However, a former English Minister of Education has subsequently put it differently, suggesting that the difficulty lies more in different motives in different practices. At the 2006 British Educational Research Association Conference Estelle Morris reminded researchers that policy decisions are usually based on political values and ideology. If we follow that line, relevance to the motives that shape political practices is central to any negotiations that occur in the same way that the relevance of the operational knowledge to strategic practice influences negotiations at hierarchical boundaries in, for example, local authorities.

The TLRP stance on relevance and user-engagement placed it at the centre of debates about expert knowledge in academe and the boundaries produced by the knowledge practices that operate there. The TLRP argument for relevance grew out of earlier discussions about the production of 'Mode 2 knowledge'. Whereas Mode 1 knowledge is produced in universities using tried and tested research processes and may then be applied in practice, Mode 2 knowledge is produced outside academe in partnerships between academics and those doing development work in the organisations where the knowledge is used (Gibbons et al., 1994).

Over the past decade or so, the relationships that sustain the production of Mode 2 knowledge have increasingly influenced how universities think about how they engage with, for example, industry. However, by the late 1990s, some of the broader implications of the blurring of academic boundaries arising from attention to Mode 2 knowledge production were being recognised. While Nowotny, as we saw in Chapter 1 (Section 1.6), has become wary about knowledge seepage and the consequent dilution of expert or specialist knowledge, Gibbons has gone on to make a case for relevance which is based in an erosion of the boundaries between academic study and the world beyond the University. He has argued for 'socially robust knowledge', a view which now resonates strongly with expectations that research should demonstrate 'impact' on for example national wellbeing and the economy:

> ...the more open and comprehensive the scientific community, the more socially robust will be the knowledge it produces. This is contrary to the traditional assumption that there is a strong relationship between the social and intellectual coherence (and therefore boundedness) of a scientific community and the reliability of the knowledge it produces. Reliable

knowledge may have been produced by such cohesive (and therefore restricted) scientific communities. But socially robust knowledge can only be produced by much more sprawling socio/scientific constituencies with open frontiers. (Gibbons, 1999: 16)

Once science enters the open market or meeting place, Gibbons suggests, the safeguards of organisations are left behind and participants need to become self-organising in the joint production of reliable or socially robust knowledge. The argument made so far in this book would suggest that Nowotny's concerns about loss of expertise and Gibbons' call for sprawling constituencies and open frontiers are not the only options if we are concerned about how research has an impact on policy. The core issue instead is the development of some common knowledge about what matters for policy to support the negotiation of relevant expertise across the boundaries of different practices.

Discussions in the TLRP seminar series very much pursued this line. The importance of fora, mediation and negotiation were once again apparent, as were over-lapping systems, which were characterised by sets of vertical trails or networks of 'know who' which resembled those just discussed in relation to the Children's Fund. The idea of over-laps and intricate trails connected strongly with Nutley's view (Nutley, Walter, & Davies, 2007) that researchers should analyse and engage with policy networks, which include think tanks, professional groups and internal analysts, rather than think only in linear terms of direct links between researchers and those most immediately connected with policy making. Here Nutley echoes the early observations of Weiss that 'the process is...a disorderly set of interconnectedness and backward and forwardness that defies neat diagrams' (Weiss, 1979). The interface between research and policy is therefore a complex one. Researchers, like the operational practitioners, were also advised by policy-based contributors to the seminars to translate their knowledge into key messages and to peer into the figured worlds of policy to identify what were termed 'wicked issues' or topics of immediate policy relevance and to be aware of the different time-scales in operation.

There are, of course differences, between the examples of moving knowledge from practice upstream in organisations and mobilising research-based knowledge so that it can inform policy. These include the fact that researchers are quite explicitly knowledge gatherers and knowledge producers – they will have done the distilling; and that university-based researchers need to sustain a degree of independence from policy in order to be able to give advice which is not shaped by political motives. Yet the need to be able to negotiate and to develop common knowledge as a prerequisite to taking knowledge upstream allows us to see yet again the difficulties involved if strong pedagogically oriented frameworks are not established to help the mobilisation of knowledge up hierarchical systems.

This chapter has examined the difficulties involved knowledge mobilisation as practices change in different parts of potentially connected systems. In the next chapter I turn to the difficulties faced by researchers who try to capture changes in these systems as they work in them.

References

Ahonenn, H., & Virkkunen, J. (2003). Shared challenge for learning: Dialogue between management and front-line workers in knowledge management. *Journal of Information Technology and Management, 2*(1–2), 59–84.

Barley, S., & Kunda, G. (2001). Bringing work back in. *Organization Science, 12*(1), 77–95.

Bechky, B. (2003). Object lessons: Workplace artifacts as representations of occupational jurisdiction. *American Journal of Sociology, 109*(3), 720–752.

Carlile, P. (2004). Transferring, translating and transforming: An integrative framework for managing knowledge across boundaries. *Organization Science, 15*(5), 555–568.

Christensen, T., & Laegreid, P. (2007, November/December). The whole of government approach to public service reform. *Public Administration Review, 67*(6), 1059–1066.

Christiansen, J. L., & Lundvall, B.-Å. (Eds.) (2004). *Product innovation, interactive learning and economic performance.* Amsterdam: Elsevier.

Commission on the Social Sciences. (2003). *Great expectations: The social sciences in Britain.* Chaired by D. Rhind. Available at http:www.the-academy.org.uk

Darr, A., & Warhurst, C. (2008). Assumptions, assertions and the need for evidence: Debugging debates about knowledge workers. *Current Sociology, 56*(1), 25–45.

Edwards, A. (2009). Understanding boundaries in inter-professional work. *The Scottish Educational Review, 41*(1), 5–21.

Edwards, A., Barnes, M., Plewis, I., Morris, K., et al. (2006). *Working to prevent the social exclusion of children and young people: Final lessons from the national evaluation of the children's fund.* London: DfES. (Research Report 734).

Edwards, A., Daniels, H., Gallagher, T., Leadbetter, J., & Warmington, P. (2009). *Improving inter-professional collaborations: Multi-agency working for children's wellbeing.* London: Routledge.

Edwards, A., Sebba, J., & Rickinson, M. (2007). Working with users: Some implications for educational research. *British Educational Research Journal, 33*(5), 647–661.

Engeström, Y. (2001). Expansive Learning at Work: Toward an activity theoretical reconceptualization. *Journal of Education and Work, 14*(1), 133–156.

Engeström, Y. (2007). Putting Vygotsky to work: The change laboratory as an application of double stimulation. In H. Daniels, M. Cole, & J. V. Wertsch (Eds.), *The Cambridge companion to Vygotsky* (pp. 363–382). New York, NY: Cambridge University Press.

Evetts, J. (2009). New professionalism and new public management: Changes continuities and consequences. *Comparative Sociology, 8*, 247–266.

Gibbons, M. (1999). Science's new social contract with society. *Nature, 402*, c81–c84.

Gibbons, M., Limoges, C., Nowotny, H., Schwartzman, S., Scott, P., & Trow, M. (1994). *The new production of knowledge.* London: Sage.

Hedegaard, M. (2009). A cultural-historical theory of children's development. In M. Hedegaard & M. Fleer (Eds.), *Studying children: A cultural-historical approach* (pp. 10–29). Buckingham: Open University Press.

Holland, D., Lachicotte, W., Skinner, D., & Cain, C. (1998). *Identity and agency in cultural worlds.* Cambridge, MA: Harvard University Press.

Howard-Grenville, J., & Carlile, P. (2006). The incompatibility of knowledge regimes: Consequences of the material world or cross-domain work. *European Journal of Information Systems, 15*, 473–485.

Jahreie, C.-F., & Ludvigsen, S. (2007). Portfolios as boundary object: Learning and change in teacher education. *Research and Practice in Technology Enhanced Learning, 2*(3), 299–318.

Johnson, B., & Lundvall, B.-Å. (2001, January 18–20). *Why all this fuss about codified and tacit knowledge?* Druid Winter Conference, Korsør, Denmark.

Knorr Cetina, K. (1997). Sociality with objects: Social relations in post-social knowledge societies. *Theory, Culture, Society, 14*(1), 1–29.

Laming, L. (2009). *The protection of children in England: A progress report*. London: The Stationery Office. Accessed September, 2009, from http://publications.everychildmatters.gov.uk/eOrderingDownload/HC-330.pdf

Lundvall, B.-Å. (1996). *The social dimension of the learning economy*. DRUID working paper, ES No. 96–1.

Lundvall, B.-Å. (2005, Jan). *Interactive learning, social capital and economic performance*. Paper presented at the advancing knowledge and the knowledge economy conference, Washington, DC.

Mintzberg, H. (1994). *The rise and fall of strategic planning*. New York, NY: Free Press.

Mørch, A., Nygård, K., & Ludvigsen, S. (2009). Adaptation and generalisation in software product development. In H. Daniels, A. Edwards, Y. Engeström, & S. Ludvigsen (Eds.), *Activity theory in practice: Promoting learning across boundaries and agencies* (pp. 184–206). London: Routledge.

Mulgan, G. (2009). *The art of public strategy: Mobilizing power and knowledge for the public good*. Oxford: Oxford University Press.

Nonaka, I., & Takeuchi, H. (1995). *The knowledge creating company: How Japanese companies create the dynamics of innovation*. Oxford: Oxford University Press.

Nutley, S., Walter, I., & Davies, H. (2007). *Using evidence: How research can inform public services*. Bristol: Policy Press.

Ordóñez, L., Schweiter, M., Galinsky, A., & Bazerman, M. (2009). *Goals gone wild: The systematic side effects of over-prescribing goal setting*. Harvard Business School working paper 09-083.

Pollard, A. (2006). Challenges facing educational research: Educational Review Guest Lecture 2005. *Educational Review*, 58(3), 251–267.

Rickinson, M., Sebba, J., & Edwards, A. (in press). *Improving user-engagement in educational research*. London, Routledge.

Santos, F., & Eisenhardt, K. (2005). Organizational boundaries and theories of organization. *Organization Science*, 16(5), 491–508.

Schulz, M. (2001). The uncertain relevance of newness: Organizational learning and knowledge flows. *The Academy of Management Journal*, 44(4), 661–681.

Schulz, M. (2003). Pathways of relevance: Exploring inflows of knowledge into subunits of multinational corporations. *Organization Science*, 14(4), 440–459.

Seely Brown, J., & Duguid, P. (2001). Knowledge and organizations: A social practice perspective. *Organization Science*, 12(2), 198–213.

Seely Brown, J., & Duguid, P. (2002). *The social life of information*. Boston, MA: Harvard Business School Press.

Shaw, I., Morris, K., & Edwards, A. (2009). Technology, social services and organizational innovation *or* how great expectations in London and Cardiff are dashed in Lowestoft and Cymtyrch. *Journal of Social Work Practice*, 23(4), 383–400.

Tsoukas, H. (2003). New times, fresh challenges: Reflections on the past and future of organization theory. In H. Tsoukas & C. Knudsen (Eds.), *The Oxford handbook of organization theory: Meta-theoretical perspectives* (pp. 607–622). Oxford: Oxford University Press.

Van den Ven, A., & Poole, M. S. (2005). Alternative approaches for studying organizational change. *Organization Studies*, 26, 1377–1404.

Wartofsky, M. (1973). *Models*. Dordrecht: Reidel.

Weiss, C. (1979). The many meanings of research utilization. *Public Administration Review*, 39(5), 426–431.

Wenger, E. (1998). *Communities of practice: Learning, meaning, and identity*. Cambridge: Cambridge University Press.

Wertsch, J. V. (2007). Mediation. In H. Daniels, M. Cole, & J. V. Wertsch (Eds.), *The Cambridge companion to Vygotsky* (pp. 178–192). New York, NY: Cambridge University Press.

Yanow, D. (2004). Translating local knowledge at organizational peripheries. *British Journal of Management*, 15, ʃ9–ʃ25.

Chapter 8
Researching the Relational in Practices

8.1 Finding the Object of Enquiry

In this chapter we move on to identifying what it is that we attempt to capture when examining features of the relational turn in expertise. In other words, what are the objects of enquiry and how do we get to grips with them as researchers? It is all too easy to talk of resourceful practice and negotiating expertise but where do we look for these phenomena? How do we know we have found them? How do we know we are keeping up with them as they change and move away from us? Let us therefore revisit some of the main ideas in this book in order to identify the problems they present for the researcher.

I have argued that professional expertise involves engagement with what matters. Expert practices are shaped by value-laden goals and as we inhabit these practices we display what Yanow and Tsoukas (2009), following Taylor (1995), call 'engaged agency'. The goals of professional practices are not idiosyncratic. Rather they are, in part at least, the culturally formed products of what Holland et al. have labelled 'figured worlds' (1998). I have already suggested that the idea of figured worlds is helpful because it allows us to see that increasing expertise in a professional world is evident in a qualitative change in the relationships between people and the practices they inhabit. That change, as I outlined in Chapter 2 (Section 2.3), is the capacity to exercise some control over the practices of that world in order to take forward one's intentions.

A recognition of intentionality also acknowledges that the goals to be found in the figured worlds of professional practices are not entirely culturally pre-determined. The view of learning that has threaded its way through discussions sees learning in Vygotsky's terms, as a continuous process of internalisation and externalisation through which we are both shaped by and shape the worlds we inhabit. As actors in practices, we therefore work towards culturally formed goals and contribute to shaping these goals as we act creatively on the tasks that embody them; though, of course, the freedom of movement we have for creative action and shaping goals will vary across settings. Capturing the exercise of expertise in a research study, therefore, calls for attention to motives, agency, historically formed practices, the potential for action in settings, and the changes that occur while we are in the research site. This long and complex list leads to the need to be clear about what should be fore-grounded to become the primary object(s) of enquiry in a particular study.

Then the relational turn itself adds another dimension of expertise to be studied. The core concept here is the idea of distributed expertise which is stretched across systems. That kind of expertise can be brought into play in negotiations to accomplish tasks within common practices: for example, when a senior and a junior social worker collaborate to support the different needs of a vulnerable family. Alternatively, as in the focus of much of this book, it can be a resource for the inter-professional work which is to be found at the sites of intersecting practices. When examining these phenomena, we start with the list in the previous paragraph and add the following two points to it: attention to how working relationally with other professionals can expand understandings of phenomena and responses to them, and how joint interpretations of tasks and responses are mediated. These objects of enquiry again demand attention to the actual processes of negotiation and of learning. They also move us on from only tackling the *who, where* and *how* questions, and, in addition, raise questions about *what* is being negotiated, that is, what is the knowledge to be found in practices.

Like Orlikowski (2002, 2006), I have taken a practice view of knowledge. From this perspective, knowledge is seen as 'not static or given, but as a capability produced and reproduced in recurrent social practices' and 'always in the making' (Orlikowski, 2006: 460). The emphasis on capability reflects the view of knowledge put forward in this book. However, I am not offering a relativist account which sees all knowledge as potentially equally robust, neither am I suggesting that knowledge is located only in practices and that practitioners are merely swept along in pre-determined ways of acting. Indeed, I have been taking a securely cognitive approach focusing on how knowledge is recognised and worked with in negotiations to accomplish professional tasks. I have, therefore, argued that professional expertise involves using specialist knowledge to work towards the goals of the professional.

The Vygotskian line on cognition that I have been following suggests that, when specialist knowledge in use is the object of enquiry, analyses of talk in and about practice is a useful way forward (Makitälo & Säljö, 2002; Middleton, 2009; Tsoukas, 2005). Though as we shall see, there are yet more questions to be asked before deciding on the final unit of analysis in a study, including whether the focus is on what people know or on how they come to know. These questions also apply to how we recognise and examine the common knowledge which is generated where practices intersect and which acts as a mediating resource for work that straddles different practices.

What about practices themselves? So far in this chapter I have talked about inhabiting historically formed practices, observed that they are shaped by value-laden goals and argued that, as we work within them, we learn to manipulate them in order to take forward our intentions. Expertise, I have suggested, is evident in our abilities to work with practices to achieve our goals. When we take practice as an object of enquiry we, therefore, once again face a choice of focuses, including how

8.1 Finding the Object of Enquiry

history plays into present practices, the motives that shape them, and how people operate within them.

Säljö has made an important distinction between the object of enquiry in research and the unit of analysis, and has argued for attention to what he called their congruence:

> In rationalist and idealist traditions, for instance in mainstream cognitivism and in differential psychology, this notion of the correspondence between what is in fact studied and what is conceptualised has always been deeply problematic, although it may not have appeared so. In such dualist perspectives, the object of inquiry that is of real interest is the intellectual machinery and the thought processes that allegedly produce behaviour, language and human action more in general. These objects of inquiry, referred to as cognitive structures, mental models or something similar, are inferred from people's performance on various kinds of tasks, but they can never be observed in themselves. Even concepts such as the various types of memory, short-, intermediate- and long-term memory, working memory etc. that have been suggested in the literature belong to this class of entities. The unit of analysis in research is always something more concrete and down to earth, such as performance in experiments or interviews that have generally already been structured on the basis of the theoretical perspective which the researcher uses. (Säljö, 2007: 7–8).

In other words we should not delude ourselves that the ready-to-hand phenomena that we may find easy to examine do capture our intended object of enquiry. For example, can we get at expert knowledge in use merely through observations of practices?

As Säljö goes on to argue, lighting on a unit of analysis is particularly difficult for those of us who work with Vygotsky's legacy, whether following a socio-cultural, cultural historical or an activity theory line. All three slightly different but strongly connected approaches have inherited a recognition that mind and world are recursively interconnected in relationships that change over time. As a result, the unit of analysis is in danger of expanding not only to include every aspect of a social world that might be of interest but also to be impossible to define as elements are in a continuous process of change.

This continuously shifting intertwining of mind and world demands far more of researchers than do individualist or interactionist approaches which simply 'take context into account'. Rather, it calls for careful questioning of what is the focus of the study and what can be taken as the unit of analysis. Sociocultural researchers like Säljö focus on, for example, what people say as they solve work or classroom problems but augment these analyses with analyses of the practices in which these conversations occur, their histories, broader motives and so on (Makitälo & Säljö, 2002; Makitälo, 2003, 2006; Mercer, 2004). The intertwining of mind and world in such work therefore demands a primary focus on the talk and frequent iterations between the talk and institutional practices in which they occur.

Cultural-historical researchers (Hedegaard, 2009a, b) also tend to keep an eye both on institutional practices as historically formed and on how they are experienced and manipulated by the actors within them, but give more weight to the practices and how they are worked with than to the language in use. The work of Holland and her colleagues on figured worlds (Holland et al., 1998) would therefore also fit here, regardless of whether they would accept the cultural-historical label.

Hedegaard's work (see Table 6.1), for example, calls for attention to the motives that shape both practices and actions within activities within practices. While one might finally focus on the historically shaped practices, the activities or the actions, Hedegaard's attention to motives means that one is always examining one phenomenon and its purposes in relation to the others. The object of enquiry in her own work tends to be the child's experience of practices as social situations for their development, but that focus is far from narrow. Taking the child's – or a beginning professional's – experience of different social situations of development as an object of enquiry demands a comparison of motive-driven practices as well as of how the activities are experienced within them.

The concrete unit of analysis in this kind of work is not the knowledge that is revealed in fine-grained analyses of talk, rather it is how talk and other behaviours reveal how people work with the purposes of different practices to take forward their intentions, how they accomplish the kinds of identities that fit with the worlds they inhabit. Hedegaard's research with Fleer, for example, illustrates very clearly how advantaged middleclass children are as they move between home and school (Hedegaard & Fleer, 2009). While Hedegaard's work has focused on children, the ideas, as I suggested in Chapter 6 (Section 6.4), also connect to how adults experience opportunities for professional development and the moves they make between different activity settings.

At first sight, Engeström's work on activity theory (Engeström, 1999) seems to have solved the unit of analysis question: it is undoubtedly the activity system, or connected systems brought into interaction by objects of activity which have the potential to be shared by each system. An example of a potentially shared object of activity might be an assessment system to grade beginning teachers that is being developed by both a school and a university department.

Activity systems, as bounded units of analysis, overcome the problems of the changing relationships that occur as people externalise what they know as they work on their worlds. For example, objects of activity, such as assessment proforma, can become tools that are used on tasks which may then become embedded in rules as aspects of work that become second nature. The notion of a changing system is fundamental to Engeström's work, as working with systemic contradictions to expand interpretations of an activity system's object of activity can lead to quite dramatic shifts in the configurations of the system itself. This would be the case if the assessment proforma were worked on as objects of activity and changed in function from being instruments for summative assessment to being used for formative feedback. Such a change, from object to tool, would lead to shifts in the rules that shaped the activity system and in the division of labour. But the system itself would still remain the unit of analysis (see Appendix A). Engeström's framework also allows for the emergence of new activity systems. However, as Engeström himself recognises, the very bounded completeness of an activity system means that attention is rarely paid to the individual and interactional moves that occur with them and lead to the expansion of the object of activity or of the emergence of new systems.

My own work on relational agency as a unit of analysis is at a middle layer of relational action, located between the system and the individual. Initially, the

8.1 Finding the Object of Enquiry

object of enquiry in this programme of work was the relationships between people within systems. It emerged as a focus from a desire to capture the kinds of joint action within systems that can lead to expansion of the object of activity and therefore changes at the systemic level (Edwards, 2005, 2009a). However, as I began to examine the object-oriented relational work that occurred outside established activity systems I began to shift the object of enquiry and as a result started to take the object-oriented relational dynamic as a discrete unit of analysis, placing slightly less emphasis on changes within specific systems (Edwards, 2009b).

Nonetheless, my growing interest in the knowledge that was brought into these object-oriented professional relationships meant that I needed to connect the dynamic that was giving rise to relational agency in action back to the systems where participants had developed their core expertise. The idea of common knowledge helped, as it not only evidently served as a meditational means assisting the exercise of relational agency, but connected the knowledge in use outside established practices back to the core practices in which it had been developed. That attention to knowledge-laden practices and to fluid and responsive work outside established activity systems meant that I became more interested in the emerging inter-professional practices, and their capacity for knowledge generation, than in discrete activity systems and how they change.

Relational agency as my unit of analysis has therefore remained fairly consistent, but my object of enquiry has shifted from systemic change to knowledge generation and its use in the negotiation of task accomplishment, though I hope I have not entirely lost sight of Barley and Kunda's concern for articulating changes in roles and relationships 'with an image of organisational structure' (2001: 89).

My own attempts at trying to track congruence between object of enquiry and unit of analysis, I hope reveal that it is not an easy task, but is one that researchers need to attend to. Säljö in his 2007 paper outlined the complexity of the research task and the need to modify the unit of analysis as, for example, cultural tools change:

> So, to understand learning as a sociocultural phenomenon we must at some stage, as Merlin Donald (2000, 2001) has pointed out, turn to culture, history and institutionalized patterns of communication and action. We must seek to understand how intellectual and physical tools change over history and what this implies for human knowing and skills. As Jim Wertsch (1991, 1998) has forcefully argued, we need to understand the co-ordination between people and external tools that is the centre of gravity in human skills and learning. (Säljö, 2007: 11–12).

Of course, the Vygotsky line is not the only approach to examining practices. In previous chapters I have pointed to the work of, among others, Barnes, Bourdieu, Collins, the Dreyfus brothers, Jensen, Knorr Cetina and Nerland. However, with the exception of Collins (2004), the proponents of the Vygotsky line have found themselves more explicitly tackling methodological issues than have others working in this area. Here, for example is Valsiner making very similar points to Säljö. Also coming from a Vygotskian starting point, Valsiner is arguing that regardless of whether social science research is seen as involving quantitative or qualitative analyses, the extent to which the data are themselves social constructions needs to be continuously questioned:

> The issue of the representativeness of the data – qualitative or quantitative – remains the central unresolved question for the methodology of social sciences. Errors in representation can be diminished by correction of methods through direct (experiential) access to the phenomena, guided by the researcher's educated intuition. (Valsiner, 2000: 99).

Those of us working within the field framed by Vygotsky's attention to mind and culture, continue to struggle, often explicitly, with the interconnectedness of our units of analyses and with their changing nature. Professional expertise as an object of enquiry is therefore not a special case, but its overt concern with working on the world in relationships with others makes it a useful exemplar of some of the challenges facing the social science that bases itself on Vygotsky's legacy. Let us therefore turn to the implications of a quest for congruence for the design of research studies.

8.2 Background and Foreground in Research Design

Once one has identified the object of study – for example, knowledge-in-use; coming to know; negotiating an interpretation of a task; or manipulating a practice – the next step is to place limits on it. The Vygotskian attention to the intertwining of mind and world can make that difficult to do, as there is often a strong temptation to try to capture as much as possible: actions, activities, practices, social systems and political environment. Selecting what to foreground and what to position as relevant yet background presents the researcher with dilemmas.

Writing of the need to see human functioning in terms of the engaged agency of actors in settings, Taylor draws attention to the difficulty of making the selection since the 'very fashion in which we operate as engaged agents within such a background makes the prospect of total explicating incoherent' (Taylor, 1995: 70). He went on to explain why, nevertheless, some kind of attention to background is important.

> One of the features that distinguishes a view of human agency as engaged from the disengaged view is that the former has some place for this kind of background. On the disengaged view, and in particular the mechanistic theory that often underpins it, there is of course, no explicit rejection of this notion, but the entire issue to which it provides some answer doesn't arise. Intelligibility is assumed from the start and doesn't need a context to provide it. (Taylor, 1995: 70).

Objectivist researchers who succeed in convincing themselves that the social world can be studied without attention to human agency, therefore, appear to have an easier time, but do not necessarily answer the most useful questions. Taylor's argument is that what he describes as 'the dominant rationalist view' (p. 63) ignores notions of engaged agency or knowing agents and has led to a simplistic information processing account of disengaged human functioning that, for example, separates facts from values. Engaged agency, on the other hand, is made intelligible

8.2 Background and Foreground in Research Design

in relation to the background which is the starting point for their intentional engagement with the world. The common knowledge that mediates relationally oriented inter-professional work can, from this perspective, be seen as derived from a mutual revealing of what matters in the professional 'backgrounds' of each participant.

Professional decision-making, even of an 'organizational' kind (Evetts, 2009), cannot be explained as information processing with no engagement with purposes and no professional hinterland from which alternatives are evaluated. The arguments presented in this book suggest that the relational turn in professional work calls for even more attention to the engagement of agentic practitioners with the goals and values that give purpose to their actions. The background is therefore important, but, if the focus is, for example, professional decision-making, then the background cannot be the object of enquiry. The engaged researcher has to identify her purposes and select a focus that sustains the compatibility of the object of enquiry with the unit of analysis and uses the unit of analysis as a starting point from which to reveal connections with the background in which they have arisen. Mäkitalo and Säljö outline the problem, from the perspective of their particular methodological interests, as follows:

> Analysts interested in institutional talk, and other communicative activities in such settings, face an interesting dilemma when it comes to the problem of how to account for the relationship between the structural and enduring features of institutions and interactional dynamics. (Mäkitalo and Säljö 2002: 58).

Their approach is to attend to how the institutional context is revealed in talk at work by focusing on the categories used to structure exchanges about work. They argue that language 'contributes to shaping collective practices that precede individual reasoning' (p. 63). In other words, the categories that are revealed in workplace talk not only reveal professional knowledge but also themselves structure the institution, limiting and affording particular ways of thinking and acting. Mäkitalo and Säljö propose a focus on the language-in-use as participants accomplish the tasks they are committed to within the institution. The focus is, therefore, on how categories are invoked to fulfil the purposes of the organisation.

There are, however, three broad approaches to studying expertise in action in practices that are compatible with the way expertise has been discussed in this book: discourse analysis in naturally occurring settings over time; narratives and personal trajectories; and interventionist research. As ever the boundaries are blurred, as interventionist research can include ethnographic data; while one can easily argue that any research, even the most sensitive and discrete ethnographies, is a form of intervention in a setting. All three approaches acknowledge the interplay between background and foreground and each requires discipline in selecting and working with the objects of enquiry, while at the same time offering enough flexibility to allow the researcher to follow objects of enquiry as they change over time. Let us look at them in turn.

8.3 Discursive Approaches to Researching Relational Aspects of Professional Practices

This book has examined how the relational turn calls for attention to the knowledge to be found in practice; how it is made evident to others; recognised, accessed and worked with against a background of institutional affordances and expectations. Within discrete lifeworlds, such as social work or software engineering, the background is comfortably assumed to be shared with common knowledge and shared forms of categorisations already mediating how tasks are accomplished. Research on institutional talk – for example, Sarangi and Roberts (1999) and the programme of studies undertaken at the Linnaeus Centre at Gothenburg where Mäkitälo and Säljö are based – is showing us how we can access knowledge in use in practices.

In their 2002 study of talk in a Swedish employment office, Makitälo and Säljö examined how institutional categories are deployed in talk. Their purpose was to reveal the meanings in practices. They distinguished their aim from ethnomethodology, arguing that the latter involves parcelling off the cultural in order to focus on how participants perceive their worlds, a legacy of ethnomethodology's origins in phenomenology. They concluded that:

> The use of the category [in workplace talk] must be understood in terms of its *sociocultural genesis* and the manner in which it invites and restricts meaning potentials and constituting possibilities according to institutional rules, routines and patterns of reasoning. But at the same time it must be understood in terms of the production of *situated sense*. (Maakitälo & Säljö 2002: 74–75).

The categories in use in their case study included the 'thoughts and plans' of the clients and work training schemes which, when invoked, signalled a change in status for clients. Categories like these represent the restrictions and possibilities for action available within institutions and at the same time are employed to accomplish tasks within institutional practices.

But what does this analytic method offer analyses of inter-professional work and the accomplishing of tasks at sites of intersecting institutional boundaries? The Gothenburg team have also tackled work in this area, looking at the work of public health teams working in and with schools (Hjorne, Larsson, & Säljö, 2010).

They argue that, in order to work together, the participants, who are from different professional backgrounds, have to re-present problems and events in their discussions about particular children. They explain: 'Issues such as deciding on what is the nature of a pupil's difficulties, and what interventions and resources are reasonable and productive in a particular situation, rely on discursive work' (Hjörne et al., 2010: 82). In these practices, categories which are used when understanding what happens in school, are brought into use to attend to pupil health.

Their study examined the kinds of categories employed by the members of a pupil health team to identify and act on the problems presented to them. The following extract from their data serves as an example:

> In the next excerpt the team members discuss [6 year old] Muhammed, who is claimed to have some difficulties in school that need to be attended to.

8.3 Discursive Approaches to Researching Relational Aspects of Professional Practices 145

1.	Teacher:	concerning Muhammed, it's difficult but it works you can say he is attending every day, he likes it very much here in our school he ... but (.) what we have noticed is that he needs very much (.) much clarity he needs
2.	Schoolnurse:	excuse me, in what class is he?
3.	Teacher:	he is a pre-school child, in grade zero we can say, he has difficulties to concentrate, he has difficulties, but I don't know really, it's difficult to get a handle on what his difficulties are, but I don't know really, but what we think then is that he cannot manage, you soon observe that he certainly can, so, what you think at first is turned upside down, but definitely he has big, big, big concentration-problems to sit, he has very (...) sometimes you wonder if he understands what you mean, he has great problems with that

(Hjorne et al., 2010: 85)

The research team comment that:

In spite of the fact that the teacher has first-hand information of Muhammed's activities in school, she does not include issues of instruction, pedagogy or classroom activities in her analysis of his problems. Instead her accounting strategy implies that the problems are placed inside the child, which may be seen as accommodating to the social language[of psychology] that dominates the meetings. (Hjorne et al., 2010: 86)

This form of analysis can therefore quite powerfully capture the discursive shifts that mark inter-professional collaboration as the categories of one group begin to dominate. In another piece of work in the same programme (Hjörne & Säljö, 2004), drew on an earlier study by Mehan (1993) to show how the more powerful knowledge in inter-professional team meetings would dominate, with the result that children with minor problems could be labelled with relatively serious medical terminology. Mehan observed that 'When categorizing a student [the educators in his study] reproduced the status relations among the different discourses that exist in society' and that the higher status meanings were 'read into the child' (1993:264). The relational turn in cross-boundary work is, therefore, not a neutral act, and negotiations aimed at task accomplishment are likely to reflect the more powerful knowledge and the priorities of the practices in which it has been developed.

In my own work we have traced the negotiation of common knowledge in interprofessional meetings (Edwards & Kinti, 2009). The following is a set of comments from an educational psychologist in a meeting with teachers and social workers already discussed in relation to implicit mediation in Sections 1.4 and 3.6. The psychologist categorised the problems and then offered new ways of recognising the situation:

What we need to be doing is to be looking perhaps far more carefully at precisely what difficulties exist, why we think they exist and what support might actually be appropriate to help. And then recognise the paradigms that a whole range of professionals and voluntary sectors want to work from. There's you know, education has its particular paradigm, medicine has a particular paradigm and the voluntary social work. And those sort of paradigms inform how people operate and their expectations. So when you get people into a room...there's a different expectation and different way of working. Accepting all of that what we're attempting to do, and it is an attempt, is to begin to support schools in coordinating this performance out there. And what I'm particularly interested in is, because I've been seconded to that role, so we'll be actually taking on the, the coordination role. It's about opening schools up, making the boundaries more permeable and it's not just about you know people coming in and people going out. But I need clear purposes to what we're about, it has to be about making a difference for children and young people and their families.

He used the categories that impede inter-professional working, 'particular paradigm', 'sectors', 'different expectation', 'different way of working' and counter-posed the new way forward: 'begin to support schools', 'opening up schools', 'boundaries more permeable', 'clear purposes', 'making a difference for young people and their families' and began to set out the categories that would enable him to carry out the role that he had recently taken on in the new world of integrated children's services that was opening up.

An hour later in the same meeting the teacher, who defended the status quo and the tight boundaries around the school in the extract discussed in Chapter 3 (Section 3.6), offered a second story (Ryave, 1978). This was a device which allowed her to echo the categories of the educational psychologist which aimed at opening up school boundaries without criticising those categories currently in use in her school which aimed at maintaining the boundary around it:

I mean something that just.... sorry, something that just came into my head is many years ago I worked in [name of city] for the child guidance service. And the way they worked it there was that the child guidance service... there were offices in each areas. I think there were eight offices altogether. And each office then had its own schools and the schools referred to child guidance. In that team, I was a teacher in the team, we had weekly meetings where all the children that were referred by those schools were discussed with the paperwork obviously. That team consisted of psychiatrist, Ed Psych, social worker, teacher and I can see a couple of others but I'm not sure what agencies they were. So then the child is discussed, the presenting problem is discussed and it was decided at that weekly meeting which agency was actually going to be dealing with them, at that time, was going to initially. And then obviously the presented one would come back if it was felt, you know, there need to be more. I actually look back on that system – it doesn't exist any longer in [the city] – but I looked on that system as being a very good one at the time.

These are all no more than illustrative extracts to indicate the potential of this approach to examining what is going on within what I have been describing as knowledge-laden and values-driven practices. However, they point to how examining both *what* language is used and *how* and *why* it is used – i.e. to accomplish what purpose within an organisation, or to stake a claim to a position within a new space that is opening up – is a fruitful approach to analyses of the relational in and across practices.

8.4 Narratives and Personal Trajectories

When one shifts one's gaze to what happens at the personal level when a protagonist negotiates the discursive possibilities available to them, one gets glimpses of what might be called 'the intentional self' as it propels itself forward in a process of what

8.4 Narratives and Personal Trajectories

Kozulin (1998: 136) has described as 'life as authoring'. The idea of self-authoring, Kozulin argues, is necessary if we are to face the demands of cultural pluralism brought about by modernity, as we can no longer sustain a notion of self as cultural reproduction. While he does not discuss professional practices and the changing demands on them, his ideas nonetheless resonate with how the teacher in the previous extract responded to the opportunity to intentionally reposition herself in the emerging practices of inter-professional collaboration, which were being offered by the educational psychologist.

There are, of course, methodological implications. Kozulin draws heavily on Bakhtin's work to argue that the self needs to be seen as a construction that occurs over time and is not simply a phenomenon which is a mere product of its immediate culture. It is therefore something that cannot be 'reduced to its here and now characteristics but can be reconstructed through its synchronous and diachronous projections' (1998: 153). From this perspective, selves may be offered new possibilities for meaning making (in his argument these opportunities are characterised by literature) which produce a verbal consciousness that can allow a process of life as authoring rather than one of life as reproduction.

Self as projection also echoes Gee's work on projective identity (Francis, in press; Gee, 2003, 2004) and takes us towards questions which are central to understanding relational agency, such as how engaged agency is experienced in relations with others: practices are navigated; actions supported and understandings negotiated. Bruner's work on narratives and identity (Bruner, 2004) echoes Taylor's argument for a social science that deals seriously with human agency and, like Kozulin, emphasises both self-construction and time. He explains his narrative project in the following way:

> ... autobiography (formal or informal) should be viewed as a set of procedures for life making". And just as it is worthwhile examining in minute detail how physics or history go about their world making, might we not be well advised to explore in equal detail what we do when we construct ourselves autobiographically? Even if the exercise should produce some obdurate dilemmas, it might nonetheless cast some light on what we might mean by such expressions as "a life". (Bruner, 2004: 692)

But how do these notions of agency connect with the accounts of practices as forms of historically shaped figured worlds that have been offered throughout this book? Holland et al. (1998) outline the problem as follows:

'...persons...are caught in the tensions between past histories that have settled in them and the present discourses and images that attract them or somehow impinge on them' (p. 4). They do, however, also offer a way out of the impasse. Like Kozulin, they suggest that semiotic mediation opens up possibilities of agency which can cut across the pre-determining powers of rigid practices:

> Persons develop more or less conscious conceptions of themselves as actors in socially and culturally constructed worlds, and these senses of themselves, these identities, to the degree they are conscious and objectified, permit these persons, through the kinds of semiotic mediation described by Vygotsky, at least a modicum of agency or control over their own behavior. (Holland et al., 1998: 40)

The discursive formulations that characterise the common knowledge about what matters, which is built where practices intersect and which is used to mediate relational task accomplishment, are, therefore, as I have already argued, pivotal to the emergence of relational agency in action on complex professional problems. For an account of how to analyse the development of common knowledge in inter-professional meetings that was discussed in Chapter 3, see Edwards, Daniels, Gallagher, Leadbetter, and Warmington (2009), Middleton (2009) and Appendix B.

The analytic framework in the LIW study that was used on the social action which took place in the inter-professional conversations we recorded in DWR sessions was developed by Middleton, one of the members of the research team. He drew on his earlier studies of talk in hospital work teams and the use of common knowledge, which was based on previous experiences within the team, to bring some sense of stability to within-team deliberations (Middleton, 1996). The framework, when applied to inter-professional conversations where common knowledge had to be created, captured how the common understandings that were needed to accomplish the newly complex task were first recognised and then worked on until they became resources for realising inter-professional collaborations to support vulnerable children. In brief, Middleton's analytic protocol revealed what mattered for professionals from different backgrounds as they expanded the objects of activity they were beginning to work on. He explained that:

> [The protocol was used] as a unit of analysis for examining the sequential organisation of session talk in terms of identifying distinctions that make the difference for participants in learning to do multi-agency work. It provided a basis for tracking the emergence of what-it-is-to-learn as an analytic focus of concern across sessions at each site. Its cyclical use application enabled: reading, reviewing, interrogating, collating and comparing all the audio-visual evidence from the intervention sessions in order to identify the emergent strands of learning. (Middleton, 2009: 102)

As a result, this unit of analysis of communicative action allowed an examination of the sequential and contingent development of concepts over time. At the same time the talk that was studied made explicit what was of consequence for participants in the newly emerging relational practices of inter-professional collaboration, giving them 'at least a modicum of agency or control over their own behaviour' (Holland et al., 1998: 40).

Let us return, therefore, to the people who are navigating practices and resourcefully drawing on the support they find available as they propel themselves intentionally forward over time. Here, trajectories are the object of enquiry, but not trajectories as clear, linear, pre-determined pathways. Rather, they are seen analytically as complex units of analysis which are situated within configurations of possibilities which may or may not support dispositions to engage with opportunities. Importantly, as Gorard and Rees (2002) have observed, trajectories should be seen as 'embedded' in social relationships. The reconfiguration of local opportunities and attempts at interagency collaboration I have been discussing mean that we also need to follow the negotiating participant across activity settings and, to echo Gorard and Rees, examine the nature of relationships which sustain particular

8.4 Narratives and Personal Trajectories

trajectories. Dreier's (1999, 2000) analyses of how forms of participation and dispositions to participate are supported by social practices, therefore, offer a useful starting point, as they recognise the challenge of the recursive interconnection of mind and world outlined by Säljö. Dreier, like Kozulin and Bruner, advises us to examine how selves are formed and identities negotiated over time and like Hedegaard (2009b) keeps an eye on both practices and the negotiating person. Arguing that we need to conceptualise subjects as participants in structures of ongoing social practice, he highlights possibilities for action as well as the sense-making involved in personal and inter-personal projects:

> ... social contexts may be arranged for particular trajectories of participation in them and through them, e.g. by virtue of an internal structure of divisions and stations or an array of social contexts for the unfolding of personal life trajectories, with transitions and changing constellations of personal social practice and configurations of personal significance. (Dreier, 1999: 8)

Trajectories for the Vygotskian researcher, therefore, do not simply trace the identity projects of individuals. They also allow us to examine how participation in and across practices is negotiated in small an often nuanced steps; and, where the focus is on the agency that emerges in object-oriented interactions, it permits an analysis of how a capacity for it might be developed in particular configurations of practices.

One of the first studies I undertook while refining the concept of relational agency (Edwards & Mackenzie, 2005, 2008) followed the trajectories of women who used an inner-city drop in centre (see Section 5.4). There they experienced non-judgemental support from both workers and fellow service users, which built their capacity to re-engage with the resources available locally. The relational agency we observed developed initially through strong forms of inter-subjective support, as workers and other users took the standpoint of the women who needed help. They worked alongside them to develop their capacity for negotiating and working in and on the practices that shaped the problems they were dealing with, which ranged from arrears with electricity bills to mental health problems.

The agency was relational in the sense that agentic action on these problems occurred in the relationship between, for example, a user of the drop in centre and one of the workers or, as users became less in need of support, between the users of the centre. The trajectories we traced were, as I demonstrated in Section 5.4, far from being linear moves from vulnerability to competent participation in local practices. Rather, the centre functioned as a safe place where people could return to seek help and recharge. The emphasis on mutual responsibility that was engendered by the workers set up possibilities for the reciprocity that produced relational strength. The narrative accounts of their lives and aspirations which were offered by the women who used the centre reflected the reciprocity offered there as they positioned themselves as people who could both accept and offer support.

Nonetheless, there is still work to be done to broaden notions of narrative and trajectory to reflect the interplay of self, other and the affordances of practices. Here, the crucial next step is to develop a unit of analysis that might capture the interweaving of object-oriented actions as participants from different 'backgrounds' come to foreground, at different times, the same object of activity while remaining reciprocally engaged with each other. This approach to analysing the relational turn is likely to be fruitful as well as being in line with the arguments pursued in this book.

8.5 Interventionist Research

Social research, as Giddens (1990: 15–16) observed of sociology, 'spirals in and out of the universe of social life, reconstructing both itself and that universe as an integral part of that process'. Giddens' argument is that sociology is therefore complicit in the development of modernity because of the part it plays in analytically disembedding social systems so that they become objects of analysis, with the result that nothing is certain and all is open to revision. He explains as follows:

> In conditions of modernity the social world can never form a stable environment in terms of the input of new knowledge about its character and functioning. New knowledge (concepts, theories, findings) does not simply render the social world more transparent, but alters its nature, spinning off in novel directions. (Giddens, 1990: 153)

The solution for Giddens, to what he sees as an undesirable outcome of such a reflexive yet unreflective form of social research, is to 'keep to the Marxian principle that avenues of desired social change will have little practical impact if they are not connected to institutionally immanent possibilities' (1990: 155). His call for what might be termed a socially responsible social science resonates strongly with those who work close to practice in fields like pedagogy, where one finds oneself regularly seeking and engaging with the intentions of participants in the field to the extent that pedagogic research in education can be seen as 'an engaged social science' (Edwards, 2001, 2002).

Chaiklin pursued a similar point, while summarising the papers that made up his 1993 edited collection with Lave on Vygotskian approaches to practice. He observed that 'An important common thread [in the papers] ... is the expectation that social scientific research will contribute to the improvement of practice' (1993: 388–389). He went on to suggest that 'social science research has the potential to illuminate and clarify the practices we are studying as well as the possibility to be incorporated into the very practices being investigated' (1993: 394).

Chaiklin was implicitly identifying a practical solution to Giddens' concerns about the impact of social research on society and suggesting a way forward for research. His suggestion is entirely consistent with Vygotsky's super-ordinate aim, which was to create a psychology which could provide the conceptual resources to allow humankind to transform the world for the better. Here, Vygotsky teases out the relationship between conceptual awareness, agency and practices that informed the Holland et al. (1998) way out of the agency/practice impasse discussed in Section 8.4

8.5 Interventionist Research

The person, using the power of things or stimuli, controls his own behaviour through them, grouping them, putting them together, sorting them. In other words the great uniqueness of the will consists of man having no power over his own behaviour other than the power that things have over his behaviour. But man subjects himself to the power of things over behaviour, makes them serve his own purposes and controls that power as he wants. He changes the environment with the external activity and in this way affects his own behaviour, subjecting it to his own authority. (Vygotsky, 1997: 212)

There are therefore moral imperatives to be found in an engaged version of social science. At the very least it refuses to be impervious to the potentially negative influences of the reflexivity of social research which were marked out by Giddens.

Chaiklin's practical solution is currently being worked through in his project on 'practice-developing research', which is driven by the question 'How can one investigate a practice in a way that creates better conditions for that practice to realise it aims?' (Chaiklin, 2009: 2). Here a central concept is that the development of understanding is realised in action which is in turn dependent on working conditions which allow such action. As a result, according to Chaiklin, the researcher, working alongside the participants, needs to focus on a dialectic that might give rise to such conditions. There is the potential for action research to take a similar focus (Elliott, 1993), but all too frequently the latter focuses primarily on individual development through attempts at improving practices without attention to systemic change.

Chaiklin's practice-developing research is quite clearly interventionist, addressing Giddens' concerns about research which spirals in and out of social life without recognising the consequences. It is not, however, alone in its intention within the field that comprises Vygotsky's legacy. Some Vygotsky-influenced educational research, because it is so close to practice as an 'engaged social science', often overtly positions itself as interventionist and, rather than ignoring the impact of its presence, it builds the spiralling into the design of the research (Edwards, Sebba, & Rickinson, 2007; Rickinson, Sebba, Edwards, in press). These intrusions into different practices are therefore not interventionist in the sense of quasi-experiments or randomised control trials. Rather they are part of the research process where practitioners and researchers work together in the co-production of knowledge about practice. Ellis's Vygotsky-framed enquiry with teachers of English is a nice example of this approach in teacher education (Ellis, 2010).

Lund, Rasmussen and Smørdal (2009) have described their involvement as social scientists in their study of wiki design in secondary schools as 'mutually beneficial infringement' (p. 225) and nicely exemplify this interventionist stance and the research-practice relationships that arise in this form of inquiry:

We have sought to demonstrate and reflect upon some activities of co-design for innovative practices that we have taken part in. It is a process that through technological as well as pedagogical development seeks to bridge supportive structures and meaning making. The research design involving discourse analysis as well as analysis of cyclical wiki design has enabled us to tap into the many layers of the process. We see how ideas are born from tensions or contradictions, picked up or shared by participants in the co-design team, and developed in interaction, design, and programming where ideas travel and take on aspects from research as well as schooling. In this way the improvable object emerges through a series of instantiations whether in talk, in teachers' expanded repertoire, or as material features of the wiki redesign. (Lund et al., 2009: 224)

The best known of approaches to interventionist research is perhaps Developmental Work Research (DWR) (Engeström, 2007), which is outlined in Chapter 3 (Section 3.5) and in Appendix A. The DWR interventionist methodology, which is founded on the Vygotskian principle of dual stimulation (Vygotsky, 1999), has been developed as a way of engaging participants in the resolution of the double binds or contradictions that constrain and hinder the development of practices. Working with carefully chosen presentations of data gathered from work settings, participants use the analytic tools of activity theory provided by researchers to model their own work situations and provide solutions to the contradictions that the methodology reveals.

DWR is particularly useful when examining the emergence of new ways of working, as the recorded transcripts and video data it produces can capture changing interpretations of the object and object motives of professional activities; how tools are developed for changing purposes; how divisions of labour shift in response to the new professional resources available; and how rules are bent or remade as systems are reconfigured. As I have already indicated, it was the central methodology in the LIW study (Edwards et al., 2009).

In addition, we saw one advantage of the methodology to be that our spiralling into the social world of the welfare professionals, while they were learning to work fluidly and responsively together, could also promote the development of these new ways of working. Echoing Holland's Vygotskian emphasis in Section 8.3 on how awareness builds agency, we argued that:

> ... by recognising that DWR would accelerate awareness of new forms of work, we were not obliged to hide the extent to which we were intervening in the worlds we were investigating. (Edwards et al., 2009: 175)

In interventionist research, the relational turn is therefore also a feature of researcher-practitioner interactions when developing the Mode 2 knowledge (Gibbons et al., 1994) discussed in Section 7.8. As such we too should become objects of study to be included in the unit of analysis. Engeström, Engeström and Kerosuo (2003) agree:

> ... in such studies, researcher interventionists make themselves contestable and fallible participants of the discourse, which means that their actions also become objects of data collection and critical analysis. (Engeström et al., 2003: 313)

8.6 The Challenges of Researching the Relational Turn

The three broad approaches to researching engaged agency in action over time, outlined in the previous sections, are not exhaustive. Also, although there are many more examples that could be included in each section, there is still methodological work to be done to develop designs which not only tackle Säljö's concern with how a unit of analysis captures changes in the object of enquiry, or how we maintain contact with Taylor's 'background' while focusing on the 'foreground', but also systematically reveal the dynamics and mutuality of responsively attuned object-oriented activity as objects of professional activity are pursued and worked on.

The relational turn in professional expertise is, as we have seen, not simply a matter of better communication, more robust information protocols or more well-defined work systems with clearer role allocation. Rather, as I have consistently argued, it is characterised by an additional capacity over and above the core expertise that distinguishes one professional practice from another. That capacity is the ability to work with others to create, together, the relational agency which enhances interpretations of, and responses to, complex problems.

Researching this ephemeral phenomenon, as practitioners take the lead and then withdraw while they co-construct their interpretations and responses, calls for attention to motives and values as well as to professional sensitivity to others and evidence of core expertise. I suggest, therefore, that one approach to researching the relational involves grasping the opportunities afforded by seeing research on practices as an engaged form of social science where researchers position themselves as legitimate participants in practices able to recognise the intentions and purposes of the orchestrations of interpretations and responses. At the same time, it is essential that they maintain their own core expertise as analysts to enable them to promote the conceptual awareness among practitioners that Vygotsky (1997) has argued is necessary for purposeful control of the resources available to us.

References

Barley, S., & Kunda, G. (2001). Bringing work back in. *Organization Science, 12*(1), 77–95.
Bruner, J. S. (2004). Life as narrative. *Social Research, 71*(3), 691–710.
Chaiklin, S. (1993). Understanding the social scientific practice of understanding practice. In S. Chaiklin & J. Lave (Eds.), *Understanding practice: Perspectives on activity and context* (pp. 377–401). Cambridge: Cambridge University Press.
Chaiklin, S. (2009). *Practice developing research*. Paper delivered to an OSAT seminar, University of Oxford.
Collins, H. (2004). Interactional expertise as a third kind of knowledge. *Phenomenology and the Cognitive Sciences, 3*, 125–143.
Donald, M. (2000). The central role of culture in cognitive evolution: A reflection on the myth of the "isolated mind.". In L. P. Nucci, G. B. Saxe, & E. Turiel (Eds.), *Culture, thought, and development* (pp. 19–38). Mahwah, NJ: Erlbaum.
Donald, M. (2001). *A mind so rare. The evolution of human consciousness*. New York, NY: Norton.
Dreier, O. (1999). Personal trajectories of participation across contexts of social practice. *Outlines, 1*, 5–32.
Dreier, O. (2000). Psychotherapy in clients' trajectories across contexts. In C. Mattingly & L. Garro (Eds.), *Narratives and the cultural construction of illness and healing* (pp. 237–258). Berkeley, CA: University of California Press.
Edwards, A. (2001). Researching pedagogy: A sociocultural agenda. *Pedagogy, Culture and Society, 9*(2), 161–186.
Edwards, A. (2002). Responsible research: Ways of being a researcher. *British Educational Research Journal, 28*(2), 157–168.

Edwards, A. (2005). Relational agency: Learning to be a resourceful practitioner. *International Journal of Educational Research*, *43*(3), 168–182.
Edwards, A. (2009a). Agency and activity theory: From the systemic to the relational. In A. Sannino, H. Daniels, & K. Guttierez (Eds.), *Learning and expanding with activity theory* (pp. 197–211). Cambridge: Cambridge University Press.
Edwards, A. (2009b). Relational agency in collaborations for the wellbeing of children and young people. *Journal of Children's Services*, *4*(1), 33–43.
Edwards, A., Daniels, H., Gallagher, T., Leadbetter, J., & Warmington, P. (2009). *Improving inter-professional collaborations:Multi-agency working for children's wellbeing*. London: Routledge.
Edwards, A., & Kinti, I. (2009). Working relationally at organisational boundaries: Negotiating expertise and identity. In H. Daniels, A. Edwards, Y. Engeström, & S. Ludvigsen (Eds.), *Activity theory in practice: Promoting learning across boundaries and agencies* (pp. 126–139). London: Routledge.
Edwards, A., & Mackenzie, L. (2005). Steps towards participation: The social support of learning trajectories. *International Journal of Lifelong Education*, *24*(4), 287–302.
Edwards, A., & Mackenzie, L. (2008). Identity shifts in informal learning trajectories. In B. van Oers, E. Elbers, R. van der Veer, & W. Wardekker (Eds.), *The transformation of learning: Advances in cultural-historical activity theory* (pp. 163–181). Cambridge: Cambridge University Press.
Edwards, A., Sebba, J., & Rickinson, M. (2007). Working with users: Some implications for educational research. *British Educational Research Journal*, *33*(5), 647–661.
Elliott, J. (1993). What have we learnt from action research in school-based evaluation? *Educational Action Research*, *1*(1), 175–186.
Ellis, V. (2010). Studying the process of change: The double stimulation strategy in teacher education research. In V. Ellis, A. Edwards, & P. Smagorinsky (Eds.), *Cultural-historical perspectives on teacher education and development* (pp. 95–114). London: Routledge.
Engeström, Y. (1999). Activity theory and individual and social transformation. In Y. Engeström, R. Miettinen, & R.-L. Punamäki (Eds.), *Perspectives on activity theory* (pp. 19–38). Cambridge: Cambridge University Press.
Engeström, Y. (2007). Putting Vygotsky to work: The change laboratory as an application of double stimulation. In H. Daniels, M. Cole, & J. V. Wertsch (Eds.), *The Cambridge companion to vygotsky* (pp. 363–382). New York, NY: Cambridge University Press.
Engeström, Y., Engeström, R., & Kerosuo, H. (2003). The discursive construction of collaborative care. *Applied Linguistics*, *24*(3), 286–315.
Evetts, J. (2009). New professionalism and new public management: Changes continuities and consequences. *Comparative Sociology*, *8*, 247–266.
Francis, R. (in press). *The decentring of the traditional university: The future of (self) education in virtually figured worlds*. London: Routledge.
Gee, J. P. (2003). *What video games have to teach us about learning and literacy*. New York, NY and Basingstoke: Palgrave Macmillan.
Gee, J. P. (2004). *Situated language and learning: A critique of traditional schooling*. New York, NY and London: Routledge.
Gibbons, M., Limoges, C., Nowotny, H., Schwartzman, S., Scott, P., & Trow, M. (1994). *The new production of knowledge*. London: Sage.
Giddens, A. (1990). *The consequences of modernity*. Cambridge: Polity Press.
Gorard, S., & Rees, G. (2002). *Creating a learning society*. Bristol: The Polity Press.
Hedegaard, M. (2009a). Children's development from a cultural-historical approach: Children's activity in everyday local settings as foundation for their development. *Mind, Culture and Activity*, *16*(1), 64–81.
Hedegaard, M. (2009b). A cultural-historical theory of children's development. In M. Hedegaard & M. Fleer (Eds.), *Studying children: A cultural-historical approach* (pp. 10–29). Buckingham: Open University Press.

References

Hedegaard, M., & Fleer, M.(Eds.) (2009). *Studying children: A cultural-historical approach.* Buckingham: Open University Press.

Hjorne, E., Larsson, P., & Säljö, R. (2010). Categorising children: Pupil health and the broadening of responsibilities for the teaching profession. In V. Ellis, A. Edwards, & P. Smagorinsky (Eds.), *Cultural-historical perspectives on teacher education and development* (pp. 78–91). London: Routledge.

Hjörne, E., & Säljö, R. (2004). "There is something about Julia": Symptoms, categories, and the process of invoking attention deficit hyperactivity disorder in the Swedish school: A case study. *Language identity and education, 3*(1), 1–24.

Holland, D., Lachicotte, W., Skinner, D., & Cain, C. (1998). *Identity and agency in cultural world.* Cambridge, MA: Harvard University Press.

Kozulin, A. (1998). *Psychological tools: A sociocultural approach to education.*. Cambridge, MA: Harvard University Press.

Lund, A., Rasmussen, I., & Smørdal, O. (2009). Joint designs for working in wikis. In H. Daniels, A. Edwards, Y. Engeström, & S. Ludvigsen (Eds.), *Activity theory in practice: Promoting learning across boundaries and agencies* (pp. 207–230). London: Routledge.

Makitälo, Å. (2003). Accounting practices as situated knowing: Dilemmas and dynamics in institutional categorization. *Discourse Studies, 5*(4), 465–519.

Makitälo, Å. (2006). Effort on display: Unemployment and interactional management of moral accountability. *Symbolic Interaction, 29*(4), 531–556.

Makitälo, Å., & Säljö, R. (2002). Invisible people: Institutional reasoning and reflexivity in the production of services and 'social facts' in public employment agencies. *Mind, Culture, and Activity, 9*(3), 160–178.

Mehan, H. (1993). Beneath the skin and between the ears: Case study in the politics of representation. In S. Chaiklin & J. Lave (Eds.), *Understanding Practice: perspectives on activity and context* (pp. 241–268). Cambridge: Cambridge University Press.

Mercer, N. (2004). Sociocultural discourse analysis: Analysing classroom talk as a social mode of thinking. *Journal of Applied Linguistics, 1*(2), 137–168.

Middleton, D. (1996). Talking work: Argument, common knowledge, and improvisation in teamwork. In Y. Engeström & D. Middleton (Eds.), *Cognition and Communication at Work* (pp. 233–256). Cambridge: Cambridge University Press.

Middleton, D. (2009). Identifying learning in inter-professional discourse: the development of an analytic protocol. In H. Daniels, A. Edwards, Y. Engeström, & S. Ludvigsen (Eds.), *Activity theory in practice: Promoting learning across boundaries and agencies* (pp. 90–104). London: Routledge.

Orlikowski, W. (2002). Knowing in practice: Enacting a collective capability in distributed organizing. *Organization Science, 13*(3), 249–273.

Orlikowski, W. (2006). Material knowing: The scaffolding of human knowledgeability. *European Journal of Information Systems, 15*, 460–466.

Rickinson, M., Sebba, J., & Edwards, A. (in press). *Improving user-engagement in educational research.* London: Routledge.

Ryave, A. (1978). On the achievement of a series of stories. In J. Schenkein (Ed.), *Studies in the Organization of Conversational Interaction.* New York, NY: Academic Press.

Säljö, R. (2007). *Studying learning and knowing in social practices. Units of analysis and tensions in theorizing.* Lecture on the occasion of the opening of the Oxford Centre for Sociocultural Activity Theory Research, Department of Education, University of Oxford. Retrieved March 14, 2007, from http://www.education.ox.ac.uk/research/resgroup/osat/osata.php

Sarangi, S., & Roberts, C. (1999). Introduction: Discursive hybridity in medical work. In S. Sarangi & C. Roberts (Eds.), *Talk, work and institutional order: Discourse in medical, mediation and management settings.*. Berlin: Mouton de Gruyter.

Taylor, C. (1995). *Philosophical arguments.* Cambridge, MA: Cambridge University Press.

Tsoukas, H. (2005). *Complex knowledge.* Oxford: Oxford University Press.

Valsiner, J. (2000). Data as representations: Contextualizing qualitative and quantitative research strategies. *Social Science Information, 39*(1), 99–113.

Vygotsky, L. S. (1997). Analysis of higher mental functions. In R. Rieber (Ed.), *The collected works of L.S. Vygotsky. Volume 4: The history of the development of higher mental functions*. New York, NY: Plenum Press.

Vygotsky, L. S. (1999). Tool and sign in the development of the child. In R. W. Rieber (Ed.), *The collected works of L.S. Vygotsky Volume 6: Scientific legacy*. . New York, NY: Plenum Press.

Wertsch, J. V. (1991). *Voices of the mind: A sociocultural approach to mediated action*. Cambridge, MA: Harvard University Press.

Wertsch, J. V. (1998). *Mind as action*. New York, NY: Oxford University Press.

Yanow, D., & Tsoukas, H. (2009). What is reflection-in-action? A phenomenological account. *Journal of Management Studies, 4*(8), 1339–1364.

Appendix A
Activity Theory

The studies of the prevention of social exclusion that are discussed in this book were all shaped by activity theory: in particular, the work developed at the University of Helsinki by Yrjö Engeström. This appendix outlines the development and key principles of activity theory; Engeström's (1987, 1999a) notion of expansive learning in professional work settings; and the use of developmental work research (DWR), Engeström's method of applying activity theory through interventionist research.

A.1 What Is Activity Theory?

Activity theory is rooted in the work of the Russian psychologist L.S. Vygotsky (1896–1934) and his collaborators and successors in the field, particularly Alexander Luria (1902–1977) and A.N. Leont'ev (1904–1979). Vygotsky's main concern was to study how relationships between human agents and their environments are mediated by cultural means, tools and signs. His work has therefore allowed us to understand that how we think is revealed in our actions, including our talk. The early development of activity theory, building on Vygotsky's groundbreaking work on mediation, examined human activity in terms of the dynamics between human actors (subjects) and the tools (both material and conceptual) that actors use in order to impact upon aspects the world around them (the object of their activities). For this reason, activity theory is often described as providing object-orientated analyses of human activity: that is, its starting point lies in understanding what it is that individuals (or collectives) are seeking to change, to shift or to act upon. Figure A.1 depicts this triadic conception of how we act in the world and captures Vygotsky's concern with mediation and Leont'ev's emphasis on object and object motive.

Leont'ev's contribution to the development of the theory was twofold. Firstly, he shifted attention from a focus primarily on mediation to a concern with the object of the activity (what was being worked on) and how interpretations of the object give rise to particular ways of acting. In other words, objects contain motives which give shape to how we respond to them. The idea of object motive is very important if we are looking at a value-laden object like a child's developmental trajectory out of risk

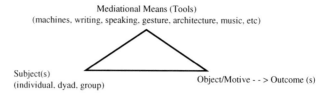

Fig. A.1 A representation of mediated action and object motive

of social exclusion, as it may be interpreted differently by different professionals who would then want to work on it in different ways. Secondly, Leont'ev introduced an emphasis on the division of labour, which he saw as shaping how we think, since he argued object-orientated activity is mediated by tools and is also performed in conditions of joint, collective activity.

For example, in the LIW project our analytical approach was object-orientated and concerned with forms of collective activity emerging in multi-agency children's services as they worked on children's trajectories to remove them from risk of social exclusion. We therefore asked practitioners to explain what it was that they were working on. When we asked this kind of question, we were not so much concerned with the broad outcomes they wanted to achieve, such as, improving referral systems; rather we wanted to encourage them to explain the focus of their work and so reveal the object motive and the conceptual and material tools they were using in their work. This question often took them to recognizing that they would need to change practices before they could work on the object they identified.

At that point the tools, rules of practice or division of labour would become the object of their work. For example, they might first say that they were working on children's pathways through the local systems of support. However, before being able to work on that with any degree of success, they would find that they needed a way of ensuring that a child and family only had to complete one assessment form, rather than a series of forms. In this case, the processing of assessment forms might be the new and temporary object of the activity; various children's services professional would be the subjects carrying out the activity; their tool would be the means by which they worked on improving assessment forms, this could be anything from a new electronic entry system to the appointment of a key worker/case coordinator to a new diary system.

A.2 Engeström and Activity Theory

Since the 1970s, Engeström has pioneered a form of cultural historical activity theory (CHAT) that builds upon the work of Vygostsky and Le'ontev. In order to develop activity theory, Engeström has expanded the original triangular representation of mediated activity (Fig. A.1) to enable an examination of activity at the level of the collective. This 'second generation' of activity theory represents the collective nature of activity through the addition of the analytic elements of community,

Fig. A.2 Second generation activity theory model

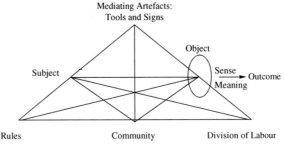

The structure of a human activity system Engestrom 1987 p. 78

rules and division of labour and an emphasis on their interactions with each other (Fig. A.2).

Engeström (2000) sees object-oriented joint practice as the unit of analysis for activity theory, not individual actions, and sees instability, internal tensions and contradictions as the drivers of change and development in professional and organizational practice. An important aspect of Engeström's version of activity theory is an understanding that object-oriented activity is always characterized by ambiguity, surprise, interpretation, sense-making and potential for change. In short, when we asked participants in the different studies what they are 'working on' the answers we received were complex, diverse and often contradictory.

Engeström (1999a) suggests that activity theory may be summarised with the help of five principles.

- The prime unit of analysis is a collective, artefact-mediated, object-oriented activity system seen in its network relations to other activity systems.
- An activity system is always a nexus of multiple points of view, traditions and interests. The division of labour in an activity creates different positions for the participants; the participants carry their own diverse histories and the activity system itself carries multiple layers and strands of history engraved in its artefacts, rules and conventions. This multi-voicedness increases exponentially in networks of interacting activity systems. It is a source of both tension and innovation, demanding actions of translation and negotiation.
- Activity systems take shape and are transformed over lengthy periods of time. Their problems and potentials can only be understood against their own history. History needs to be considered in terms local history of the activity and its objects but also as the history of the theoretical ideas and tools that have shaped professional activity. So, for instance, current developments in children's service provision to counter social exclusion need to be analysed against the history of local organizations and also against the more global history of the social service concepts, procedures and tools employed and accumulated in the local activity.
- Contradictions are historically accumulating structural tensions within and between activity systems, i.e. are not the same as problems or conflicts. Engeström's activity theory emphasises the importance of contradictions within activity systems as the driving force of change and development and sees them as

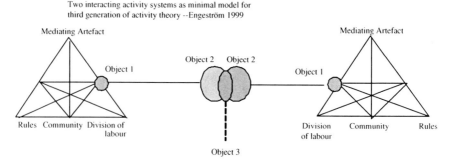

Fig. A.3 Third generation activity theory model

structural tensions that emerge over time in organizational practices. These contradictions may constrain professional practice at certain points, but they may also provide a source of change and development. For instance, in the LIW research we identified numerous instances in which the efforts of different professional groups (such as teachers, educational psychologists, health workers, social care staff) to work on a shared object (such as the trajectories of at-risk young people) revealed contradictions arising from having to work to different professional targets, referral thresholds and assessment procedures (that is, conflicting sets of rules and shifting divisions of labour). These were worked on so that understandings of the object of activity were expanded and, for example, rules were adjusted. This change process takes us to the final principle.

- Activity systems move through relatively long cycles of qualitative transformations. As the contradictions in or between activity systems are aggravated, some individual participants begin to question and to deviate from established norms. In some cases, this escalates into collaborative envisioning of the future and a deliberate collective change effort. An expansive transformation is accomplished when the object and motive of the activity are reconceptualised to embrace a wider horizon of possibilities than in the previous mode of the activity. A full cycle of expansive transformation may be understood as a collective journey through what activity theorists see as the zone of proximal development of the system.

A.3 Developmental Work Research

Much of Engeström's work involves developmental work research (DWR): a mode of research intervention based around series of sessions, which he terms 'change labs', in which researchers and practitioners jointly interrogate the structural tensions in and between the different dimensions of activity, such as the rules, tools and division of labour, that have emerged in collective work practices over time and which constrain the development of future activity. In brief, DWR is a methodology

Appendix A: Activity Theory

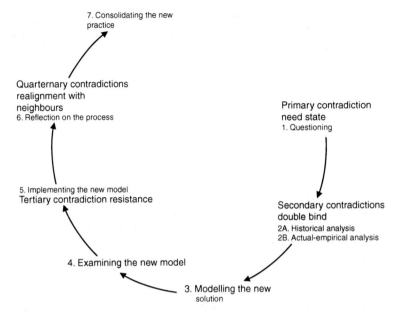

Fig. A.4 Cycle of expansive learning (Engeström, 1999b)

for applying activity theory in order to develop what Engeström (1987, 2001) terms expansive learning in workplace settings.

DWR sessions are designed to support cycles of expansive learning (Engeström, 1999b, 2007). Expansive learning cycles are predicated upon a progression from individuals questioning contradictions in current practice through to the modelling and implementation of new forms of practice (Fig. A.4). In DWR sessions the tools of activity theory are offered to participants in the sessions so that they might interrogate their practices and reveal the concepts in use as they accomplish their object-oriented activities.

The sessions move between interrogation of past present and future practices:

- *Past practice:* encouraging professionals to consider the historical development of their working practices;
- *Present practice:* identifying structural tensions (or 'contradictions') in current working practices;
- *Future practice:* working with professionals to suggest new forms of practice that might effectively support innovations in multi-agency working.

The aim of the DWR sessions is to address the challenges of, for example, interprofessional work by:

- encouraging the *recognition* of areas in which there is a need for change in working practices;

- suggesting possibilities for change through *re-conceptualising* the 'objects' that professionals are working on, the 'tools' that professionals use in their multi-agency work and the 'rules' in which professional practices are embedded.

A.4 Inside the DWR Sessions

In the LIW study, for example, six DWR sessions were conducted over a period of 12 months at intervals of around 2 months in each of the main case study sites. Each session ran for 2 hours and was conducted by a team of four or five researchers, though in other studies we worked with three researchers in each site. Sessions were organized around the presentation of 'mirror data': that is, everyday understandings of practices collected from individual interviews with staff and from previous DWR sessions. Another form of mirror we developed in the LIW study was to invite practitioners to present an anonymised overview of a case around which some form of inter-professional working had taken place. The purpose of these case presentations was for practitioners to discuss the objects (and related elements) of their professional activity. Joint analysis by professionals and researchers was supported though the use of a range of devices and procedures. These included templates or calendars (to summarise important events), maps (to depict the key parties involved) and agreements (summarising the division of labour amongst the parties).

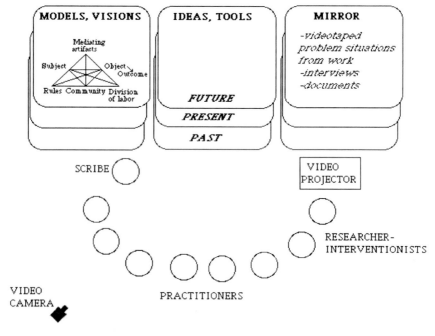

Fig. A.5 Plan of a DWR session (Engeström, 2007)

Professionals and researchers discussed the mirror data, using activity theory as an analytical framework with which to identify structural tensions in the practices of children's services providers and to move towards refining the concepts that were embedded in the practices. This refining led to a set of concepts or understandings which participants could work with and generalise from. The concepts identified across the cases in the LIW study are presented in Section 3.2 of the book.

Research team roles vary slightly at each meeting but can comprise a session leader who presents mirror data for discussion, a team member who summarises and presents discussion data on flipcharts, a team member who constructs a research note on the what ideas are being developed in the session, a team member who video records the session (video data are used both for subsequent data analysis by the team and to capture data for possible presentation at later session). We have found that the most viable arrangement, in relation to turn-taking and ease of data capture, was a composition of somewhere between eight and twelve practitioners in each session. Figure A.5 indicates the layout of a DWR session (Engeström, 2007).

A.5 Analysing the Data from the DWR Sessions

Analytic protocols were developed in order to analyse the talk in the DWR sessions in order to answer the research questions. The protocol developed for the LIW study is discussed in Appendix B.

References

Engeström, Y. (1987). *Learning by expanding: An activity-theoretical approach to developmental research*. Helsinki: Orienta-Konsultit.
Engeström, Y. (1999a). Activity theory and individual and social transformation. In Y. Engeström, R. Miettinen, & R.-L. Punamäki (Eds.), *Perspectives on activity theory*. Cambridge: Cambridge University Press.
Engeström, Y. (1999b). Innovative learning in work teams: Analysing cycles of knowledge creation in practice. In Y. Engeström, R. Miettinen, & R.-L. Punamäki (Eds.), *Perspectives on activity theory*. Cambridge: Cambridge University Press.
Engeström, Y. (2000). Making expansive decisions: An activity-theoretical study of practitioners building collaborative medical care for children. In K. M. Allwood & M. Selart (Eds.), *Creative decision making in the social world*. Amsterdam: Kluwer.
Engeström, Y. (2001). Expansive learning at work: Toward an activity theoretical reconceptualization. *Journal of Education and Work*, *14*(1), 133–156.
Engeström, Y. (2007). Putting activity theory to work: The change laboratory as an application of double stimulation. In H. Daniels, M. Cole, & J. V. Wertsch (Eds.), *The Cambridge companion to Vygotsky*. Cambridge: Cambridge University Press.

An Analytic Protocol for the Building of Common Knowledge: The D-Analysis

The particular focus of what became known as the 'D-analysis' grew out of a concern to examine the emergence of what we called in the LIW study 'what-it-is-to-learn' in settings as the developed their inter-professional work, across the three sites. In the terms used in the present book, we were examining the building of the common knowledge that mediated later responsive actions.

The analysis was developed by Dave Middleton to identify and code learning-related talk in the DWR sessions. Once sections of text had been coded, related sequences of communicative action on topics were identified and were grouped into strands of talk that wove their way through the progress of each series of sessions. These strands witnessed the progression of building shared knowledge based through and with talk in the sessions. A knowledge strand was defined as a narrative which focused on one and the same concept and was developmental in its nature, i.e. there was a movement from recognizing towards proposing an action.

These strands revealed the ideas in use as people developed, over time and across meetings, the common knowledge arising from their new ways of working. The main ideas that were identified have been described in Section 3.2. At the end of the project, participants were interviewed about what they gained from the experience and showed that the concepts captured by the D-analysis remained relevant for them. A more detailed description of the development and purpose of the analytic protocol can be found in Middleton (2009).

In brief, sections of talk were categorised using descriptors which captured how participants built the common knowledge that enables them to work together. The first step was to look for how a difference was noticed and worked with by the participants in their discussions in the DWR sessions. The protocol provided three categories which enabled these processes.

> *Deixis*: identify when there is some nomination or 'pointing' to a particular issue in terms of drawing attention to a distinction that is then worked up to make a difference in subsequent turns.
> *Definition and delineation*: look for how that issue is elaborated in the uptake of others in terms of how the following are warranted and made relevant through: (i) qualifications identifying further distinctions; (ii) orderabilities

in the organization and delivery of past, present and future practice; (iii) expansive elaborations of the problematics of practice.

Deliberation: identify how some working consensus on what is the case emerges in terms of evoking both particularities and generalities of marking distinctive features of past, present or future practice.

The analysis then turned to examining in what ways such sequences mattered. If we identified strands of deixis, definition/delineation and deliberation what were their contingent consequences for participants? Did they make visible distinctions that made the difference, so that participants could be identified as attending to what it was necessary in order to learn to do multi-agency working? In other words, did the talk lead to, or accomplish, some form of departure or development in claims about the practice of the participants? When this occurred we could assign one or both of the final two categories in the protocol:

Departure: identify shifts towards qualititatively different position in practices in terms of the formulation of emergent distinctions.
Development: identify when participants specify new ways of working that provide the basis for becoming part of, or have become part of, what they take to be and warrant as a significant reformulation of their practices.

This protocol allowed the DIW team to examine the sequential organization of session talk in terms of identifying distinctions that make the difference for participants in learning to do multi-agency work. It provided a basis for tracking the emergence of what-it-is-to-learn as an analytic focus of concern across sessions at each site. Its cyclical application enabled: reading, reviewing, interrogating, collating and comparing all the audio-visual evidence from the intervention sessions in order to identify the emergent strands of learning.

Reference

Middleton, D. (2009). Identifying learning in inter-professional discourse: The development of an analytic protocol. In H. Daniels, A. Edwards, Y. Engeström, & S. Ludvigsen (Eds), *Activity theory in practice: Promoting learning across boundaries and agencies* (pp. 90–104). London: Routledge.

Index

A

Accountability, 3, 46, 73, 118, 122, 132
Accountants, 70, 101, 118
Activity, object-orientated, 158
Activity theory, 5, 17, 35, 43, 51–52, 64–68, 71–72, 75, 102, 125, 139–140, 152, 157–163
Agency, *see* Relational agency
Analytic protocol in DWR, 103, 163
Apprenticeship, 61, 77, 106–107, 109
Artefacts, 27, 30, 48–49, 55–57, 65, 122, 125, 132, 159
Authenticity, 63, 67, 72
Autonomy, 3, 14, 36, 71, 82, 89, 94

B

Boundary/boundaries
  objects, 122, 130
  spaces, 45–48, 53–56, 61–62, 132
  work, 43–45, 54, 57, 145
Bourdieu's framework, 7
Bureaucracy, 3, 72–73

C

Care, meaning of, 2
Children's fund, 45–48, 54, 81, 83–84, 86–88, 119–120, 122–123, 126, 128, 131, 134
Client/clients, 1–5, 9, 11, 13–15, 30, 33, 44, 46, 52, 56, 64, 69, 71, 73, 77, 81–96, 99, 101, 108, 118, 131, 144
Co-configuration, 85–95, 124
Cognition, 12, 26–27, 74, 138
Collective competence, 34–36, 42, 74
Common knowledge, 10, 16, 28, 34–35, 42–45, 51–53, 55–57, 62, 65–66, 68–69, 75–77, 94–95, 118–119, 122, 125, 127–128, 132, 134, 138, 141, 143–145, 148, 164–165
Communities of practice, 13

Computer science/scientist, 75–76
Conceptual tools, 10, 101, 103, 113
Contradictions, 35, 44, 51–52, 55, 70–73, 102, 128, 140, 151–152, 159–161
Cultural Historical Activity Theory (CHAT), 5–7, 14, 17, 35, 48, 64–69, 71, 75, 84, 89, 102–103, 106, 111, 126, 158
Cultural historical analyses, 44, 110
Culture, 8–9, 16–17, 31, 34, 61, 65, 67, 76, 90, 101–102, 121, 141–142, 147

D

D-Analysis, 164–165
Developmental Work Research (DWR), 50–51, 152, 157
Disability, 86, 95
Discourse analysis, 143, 151
Discursive approaches to research, 144–146
Distributed agency, 16, 87
Distributed expertise, 16, 26–33, 36–37, 44, 74–75, 87, 106, 138
Distributed knowledge, 13, 15, 27, 30, 33, 36, 106
Doctor, 17, 42, 76, 103
Dual stimulation, 51, 152

E

Emotion, 5, 12, 24–25, 54, 70, 92, 101, 110
Engaged agency, 137, 142, 147, 152
Engrossment with knowledge, 9, 101
Epistemic objects, 9, 101–103, 112
Epistemic (or knowledge-oriented) practices, 7–12, 17, 130
Ethical commitment, 99
Expansive learning, 70, 157, 161
Expertise
  developing, 13, 25, 29, 75
  distributed, 16, 26–33, 36–37, 44, 74–75, 87, 106, 138

167

Expertise (*cont.*)
  prototype view of, 23
  psychological accounts of, 21–24
  as purposeful engagement, 36–37
  stretched across systems, 138
  task-orientated, 21
  See also Interactional expertise; Relational expertise
Expert teams, 22
Explicit mediation, 8, 56
Extended intelligence, 27, 74
Externalization, 6, 12, 67, 82, 84–85, 89–95, 113, 137

F

Field (Bourdieu), 6–7
Figured worlds, 24–26, 36–37, 70, 93–94, 126, 132, 134, 137, 139, 147

G

Generalization, 124–125
Germ cell in Vygotskian theory, 49
Goodwork project, 72

H

Habitus (Bourdieu), 6–7
Hard-to-reach clients, 82, 95
Harvard Business School, 85, 87
Hierarchies, 3, 45, 100, 103, 117–127, 129–131, 133–134
Hospital theatre work, 99

I

Identity, 1–2, 4, 10–12, 24–26, 31, 33, 36, 43, 52, 54–55, 63, 66, 75, 90, 92, 103–104, 119–120, 123, 125, 127–128, 130–131, 140, 147, 149
Implicit mediation, 8–10, 56, 132, 145
Innovation, 21, 26, 42–43, 45, 47, 124–125, 128, 159, 161
Intentionality, 35, 37, 41, 74, 137
Interactional expertise, 15–16
Internalization, 6, 12, 67, 82, 84, 137
Interpretation, 2, 6, 13–14, 16, 21, 24, 31, 33, 35, 41, 44, 48, 51, 53, 62, 64–69, 71, 102, 108, 117, 128, 138, 140, 142, 152–153, 157, 159
Inter spaces, 33, 43, 46, 57
Interventionist research, 143, 150–152, 157

K

Knotworking, 27, 62–63
Know-how-to-know-who, 30

Knowledge
  broker, 131
  champion, 131
  leaky, 117
  modes 1 and 2, 73, 92, 94
  moving upstream of, 117
  in practices, 7–10, 101, 103, 109–113
  representation of, 122
  sticky, 117, 130
  ties, 17, 31, 122

L

Lack, sense of, 12
Learning, 2, 4–6, 8, 10, 17, 27–29, 31, 41–42, 44–45, 48, 54, 57, 61, 63, 65, 67, 69–71, 75–76, 82–86, 89–92, 105, 107–109, 113, 117–123, 125–130, 132, 138, 141, 148, 152, 157, 161, 163–165
Learning in and for Interagency Working (LiW), 10, 29, 31, 35–36, 44, 48–56, 85, 87–88, 117, 120, 127, 148, 152, 160, 162–164
Local authorities, 29, 32, 45–46, 87, 119, 126, 133
Local strategic partnerships, 45
Long-term goals, 50, 57

M

Mass customization, 85–86, 88
Mass production, 85–86
Mediation, 7–10, 49, 56, 65–66, 102–103, 118, 129–132, 134, 145, 147, 157–158
Medical settings, 42–43
Meta-skills, 74
Methodology (research), 50–51, 142, 144, 152, 160–161
Mind, 6, 16, 22–23, 26, 33, 42, 47, 50, 55, 64–65, 67, 70, 89, 91, 133, 139, 142, 149, 153
Mirror data, 51–52, 162–163
Modernity, 33, 63, 73, 147, 150
Moral goals, 67
Motives, 4–5, 7, 10, 14–16, 25, 36–37, 51–53, 55, 57, 61, 64, 68–77, 95–96, 102, 110–111, 118–120, 122, 125, 127–128, 131–134, 137, 139–140, 152–153, 157–158, 160
Mutuality, 62–64, 153

N

Narratives, 49, 55–57, 69, 123–124, 126–127, 143, 146–150, 164
National Evaluation of the Children's Fund (NECF), 28, 46, 69, 84, 88, 119

Network, 4, 14, 22, 27–29, 31–34, 44, 62, 64, 74–75, 86–87, 91, 95, 103, 105, 108, 131, 134, 159
New Public Management (NPM), 3, 11, 43, 46, 49, 72, 82, 99, 103–104, 118, 121, 127
Nurses, 4, 12–13, 17, 31, 100–101, 107

O
Object of activity, 5–6, 14, 30–31, 35, 37, 64–66, 68–71, 75, 77, 87–88, 102–103, 108, 129, 140–141, 150, 160
Object of enquiry, 137–143, 148, 152–153
Objectivist research, 142
Object motives, 7, 68–69, 72, 76, 102, 152, 157–158
Object-orientated activity, 158
Occupational professionalism, 127
Organizational professionalism, 103–104, 112–113, 124, 127
Oxford Centre for Sociocultural and Activity Theory Research (OSAT), 17, 75

P
Parents, 15, 28, 42, 53–54, 71, 77, 88–89, 91, 93, 100–101, 106–107, 134, 150
Participation, 15, 52, 67–68, 74, 81–85, 87–88, 90, 93–94, 131, 149
Pedagogy/ Pedagogic stance, 42, 44–45, 56, 95–96, 103, 112, 120–121, 123, 134, 145, 150–151
Policy, 15–16, 28, 32–33, 83–85, 118, 121, 127, 132–134
 networks, 134
Practices
 constitutive order in, 26, 73
 figured worlds of, 24, 26, 36, 126, 137
 shaped by knowledge, 4
Practitioner knowledge, 112
Practitioners, 1–18, 21–22, 26–33, 36, 43–54, 57, 61–77, 82, 84–85, 87–89, 95, 100–102, 104–108, 112, 117–120, 125, 127–129, 131–134, 138, 143, 151–153, 158, 160, 162
Prevention (of social exclusion), 10, 14, 28–29, 32, 87, 106, 120, 157
Process enhancement, 85–86
Professional boundaries, 1, 4, 10–11, 16, 35, 111
Professional identity, 10–12
Professionalism, 1, 3, 37, 63, 100, 103–104, 112–113, 118, 124, 127
Professionalism as dehumanized work, 100
Professional multilingualism, 53
Professional standing, negotiation of, 96
Projective identity, 75, 147
ProLearn project, 4, 101
Psychology, 6, 9, 63–65, 67, 89, 139, 145, 150
Public sector reform, 6, 9, 63–65, 67, 89, 139, 145, 150

Q
Qualitative research analysis, 141
Quantitative research analysis, 141

R
Radiographer, 75
Relational agency, 2, 13–14, 16–17, 22, 27–28, 33, 36, 61–77, 81–82, 87, 89–96, 99, 101, 103–109, 140–141, 147–149, 153
Relational expertise, 13–16, 22–23, 31, 35, 44, 61, 75, 77, 99–100, 108, 118
Relational social work, 14, 95
Relational turn, 13, 15, 21–41, 58, 61, 73, 101, 111, 117, 137–138, 143–145, 150, 152–153
Research users, 132
Resilience, 44, 81, 84–85
Resourceful practitioner, 1–17
Resources, 1–17, 21, 25–27, 29, 31–33, 37, 41–44, 46–47, 49, 51, 54–55, 64–66, 74–77, 81, 91–94, 102–104, 106–107, 120, 125–126, 130, 137–138, 144, 148–150, 152–153
Responsiveness, 1, 3–5, 14, 26, 29, 34, 36, 44–45, 53, 56, 61–62, 71, 73, 75–76, 87, 99, 102, 107–108, 117, 120, 124–125, 132, 141, 152–153, 164
Risk taking, 44
Rule bending, 44, 68, 70, 104

S
Schools, 6, 8–9, 17, 29–30, 32, 42, 46, 50, 52, 54–56, 68, 83, 85, 87, 91, 93–95, 103–105, 109–111, 124–125, 140, 144–146, 151
Self-authoring, 147
Selfhood, 66
Sense making, 65, 90, 149, 159
Situated knowledge, 103, 112, 123
Social exclusion, 6, 10–11, 14, 16, 28–29, 32, 46, 48, 81–84, 87, 89, 96, 102, 106, 120–121, 157–159
Social inclusion, 15, 83–85
Social science, 77, 133, 141–142, 147, 150–151, 153

Social work, 6–8, 13–14, 25, 35–36, 41, 44, 50, 56, 65–66, 68–69, 95, 104–105, 108–109, 111, 118, 124, 127, 138, 144–146
Societal norms, 110
Socio-cultural psychology, 65
Soft Systems Methodology (SSM), 51–52
Staff development, 52, 107
Supervision of PhDs, 77
Systemic change, 17, 21, 51, 70–71, 141, 151
Systemic contradictions, 52, 140
Systemic learning from operational practices, 117–119

T
Tacit knowledge, 23, 53, 86, 111–112, 130
Teachers, 7–9, 13, 17, 23, 32, 44, 50, 52, 54–55, 62, 68–69, 93, 101, 105, 107–112, 118, 125, 140, 145–147, 151–152, 160
Teaching Assistants (TA), 32, 105
Teaching and Learning Research Programme (TLRP), 132–134
Temporalities, 124–125
Tools, 4, 6, 10, 17, 29–31, 35, 44–45, 48–49, 51, 65, 70, 85, 101–103, 112–113, 140–141, 152, 157–162
Trajectory/ies, 7, 14–15, 30–31, 35, 47, 54, 61, 65–66, 68–69, 84–85, 87–90, 92, 94, 96, 102, 106, 108, 125, 143, 146–150, 157–158, 160
Transfer, 42–43, 56–57, 66, 126

U
Unit of analysis (in research), 139
Upstream learning, 4, 121–122, 126–130
Upstream movement of knowledge, 123
User engagement, 132–133

V
Values, 1, 5–8, 10–11, 13, 21, 24–27, 29–33, 36–38, 44–46, 49, 51, 53–55, 57, 67–69, 72–73, 84, 86, 95, 100, 102, 104, 110–113, 122–125, 133, 137–138, 143, 146, 153, 157–158
Vygotsky's legacy, 5, 65, 67, 139, 142, 151

W
Welfare policy, 81, 84
Workforce remodelling, 32, 105

Z
Zone of Proximal Development (ZPD), 71, 160

Lightning Source UK Ltd.
Milton Keynes UK
UKOW040819050412

190189UK00008B/3/P